PRAISE FOR *WHERE THE WIND LEADS*

"Desperation. Overwhelming odds. Heroic rescue. This story has all the elements of great fiction. But it is not fiction; it is real life. The account of Dr. Chung and his family will inspire you to believe in second chances and miracles and the God who gives them both."

—MAX LUCADO
New York Times BESTSELLING AUTHOR

"I love true stories, and Dr. Chung's is the best I've read in a long time. It's packed full of family drama, plus really engaging recent world history, and it is woven from beginning to end with the consistent theme of God's sovereign mercy. This kind of real-life rescue story makes reality television pale by comparison!"

—LISA HARPER
AUTHOR AND WOMEN OF FAITH® SPEAKER

"*Where the Wind Leads* is an incredible adventure story of loss and survival, rescue and resilience. Once I started to read it, I simply could not put it down. It's a fascinating account of family life in warring Vietnam, but even more so it's an amazing tale of how God's grace can bring an individual, and a family, from certain death to flourishing life."

—LEIGHTON FORD
PRESIDENT, LEIGHTON FORD MINISTRIES

"*Where the Wind Leads* is a remarkable story of determination, dedication, resilience, and ultimate success. It is truly inspiring!"

—SANDY SANDERS
MAYOR, CITY OF FORT SMITH, ARKANSAS

"Vinh Chung's story reminded me to be grateful . . . to God for His faithfulness . . . and for the privilege of being an American. This book needs to be read by every person who has felt like a victim; the message of hope, endurance, and redemption will surely transform lives around the world."

—DEBORAH SMITH PEGUES
BESTSELLING AUTHOR, *30 Days to a Stronger, More Confident You*

"Powerful. Inspiring. *Where the Wind Leads* will touch your life forever, and that is why I gave a copy to all my family members and friends."

—PETER C. LEMON
MEDAL OF HONOR RECIPIENT AND AUTHOR, *Beyond the Medal*

"*Where the Wind Leads* takes us back to historical events many of us have conveniently forgotten. It is an amazing, vividly told true story. What happened to Vinh Chung and his family is an American miracle complete with painful rejection, enormous sacrifice, humble benefactors, terrific achievement, and deep love."

—GREG BRENNEMAN
CEO, PRESIDENT, AND CHAIRMAN, CCMP CAPITAL

"*Where the Wind Leads* will serve to remind all of us why America, at its core, is a country where freedom and opportunity can become reality for anyone, from every corner of the globe. It is a powerful, compelling story of discovery and overcoming challenges, ultimately leading to a life with meaning. I'm an off-the-boat American as well, and Vinh Chung's story is my story. I hope every American appreciates what we have here—where the winds led Vinh. This is a country that must continue to shine the light for all mankind."

—PETER GEORGESCU
CHAIRMAN EMERITUS, YOUNG & RUBICAM

"Dr. Vinh Chung's story is wrapped in a remarkable family, a miraculous rescue, a transplanted life, and achievement so clearly under God's gracious hand. I learned more about Asian culture from *Where the Wind Leads* than from my many trips to Asia. The impact of World Vision's ministry is magnified in this one life. I was personally challenged to see the potential of a single act of mercy and compassion and was captivated by this redemptive story."

—JERRY WHITE, PhD
INTERNATIONAL PRESIDENT EMERITUS, THE NAVIGATORS;
AND MAJ. GEN., US AIR FORCE (RET.)

"Dr. Vinh Chung's story is unbelievable. From the inside of Vietnam to the shores of Malaysia to the China Sea to a lost place called Arkansas, Dr. Chung brings a real life story of pain and redemption and suffering to victory. He shows how a family with everything can turn into a family with nothing. This nothing leads to forgiveness and true healing. Riveting and a definite page-turner. I encourage everyone to read *Where the Wind Leads*. It will change your life."

—SCOTTY SMILEY
PRESIDENT, HOPE UNSEEN LLC; AND AUTHOR, *Hope Unseen*

WHERE THE WIND LEADS

A Refugee Family's Miraculous Story of Loss, Rescue, and Redemption

VINH CHUNG

WITH TIM DOWNS

W Publishing Group

An Imprint of Thomas Nelson

Published in Nashville, Tennessee, by W Publishing Group, an imprint of Thomas Nelson.

Published in association with the literary agency of Alive Communications, Inc., 7680 Goddard Street, Suite 200, Colorado Springs, CO 80920. www.alivecommunications.com.

Thomas Nelson titles may be purchased in bulk for educational, business, fund-raising, or sales promotional use. For information, please e-mail SpecialMarkets@ThomasNelson.com.

Quotations in chapter 37 are reprinted with permission of the *American Legion Magazine*, © June 2013. www.legion.org.

The photograph of Clifford Pier is believed to have been taken in the early 1960s or late 1950s and is from Memories of Singapore, http://www.singas.co.uk.

Map Design: Kelsey Downs. All maps used are public domain.

Scripture quotations marked ESV are from the English Standard Version. © 2001 by Crossway Bibles, a division of Good News Publishers.

Scripture quotations marked NLT are from Holy Bible, New Living Translation. © 1996, 2004, 2007. Used by permission of Tyndale House Publishers, Inc., Wheaton, Illinois 60189. All rights reserved.

978-0-7180-3749-9 (TP)
978-0-529-10554-7 (IE)

Library of Congress Cataloging-in-Publication Data

Chung, Vinh, 1975—

 Where the wind leads : a refugee family's miraculous story of loss, rescue, and redemption / Vinh Chung with Tim Downs.

  pages cm

 ISBN 978-0-8499-4756-8 (hard cover)

1. Chung, Vinh, 1975—Family. 2. Chung family. 3. Chinese—United States. 4. Chinese Americans. 5. Chinese—Vietnam. I. Downs, Tim. II. Title.

 CT274.C496C58 2014

 920.0092951—dc23

                               2013039729

Printed in the United States of America
22 23 24 25 26 PC/LSCC 10

For my mother and father:
Thank you for your courage and sacrifice.

CONTENTS

Part Two

Part Three

FOREWORD

A FEW YEARS AGO A YOUNG DERMATOLOGIC SURGEON contacted me with something important to say. Over the phone that day, Vinh Chung told me one of the most amazing stories I had ever heard. This story is so precious to me because, as the president of World Vision US, I work to change the lives, literally, of millions of children every day. But I rarely hear the rest of the story thirty years later. The story of Vinh Chung is what I hope and pray for every vulnerable child.

The story you are about to read is the one I was told. It is the thrilling account of Vinh Chung and his family's harrowing journey from Vietnam to the South China Sea to the Deep South in Arkansas and eventually to the halls of Harvard. It is the story of a family who faced political persecution, who were forced to leave behind everything they had and take incredible risks to start a new life. Vinh's family, miraculously, began their new life from scratch, relying on their resilience and determination, learning a new language and starting new jobs. And then Vinh and his brothers and sisters achieved far more than most families ever dream for their children. You'll also see that Vinh and his family couldn't have made this journey alone. All along the way good people, and many good Christians, intervened with a helping hand.

In 1979, as the new communist regime in Vietnam consolidated its power, families fled by boat in search of a new home. Yet when the lives of hundreds of thousands of these "boat people" hung in the balance, most of the world decided to look away. Governments, politicians, and citizens wanted to forget the tragedy in the South China Sea.

But World Vision's president, Stan Mooneyham, believed he must do something. He believed that God hadn't turned His face from those who were suffering. So Mooneyham wouldn't allow the world to turn away. When he couldn't get others to help, he set out onto the open seas himself. Mooneyham believed that God didn't create any throwaway children—that we cannot look away when people are suffering.

As you read and when you've finished reading this book, I hope you'll reflect on the bigger picture. We live in a world where hundreds of millions of children like Vinh Chung have been driven from their homes in the last two decades.

Even now, at this moment, children are being driven from their homes in places like Syria, Central African Republic, and the Philippines. Today there are twenty million children living in refugee camps, tent cities, and other temporary shelters. And they are not throwaways either.

A few months ago I sat with refugee children from Syria. They had fled their country, forced to leave by the fighting in their cities. Their homes destroyed, their parents killed, they left simply for the chance to stay alive. Now their future hangs in the balance. Will they have the opportunity to grow up healthy and go to school and live ordinary lives?

Vinh's is the story of one—the incredible potential locked inside one refugee child. But it's also the story of every child in the world who is poor, forgotten, and abused, a refugee. It's a story that shows there is no such thing as a throwaway child.

Thirty years ago Stan Mooneyham did something outrageous because he believed that every child is precious and that God has created each of them with potential and gifts and talents. Among our staff at World Vision today, Mooneyham's resolve still resonates as an example of the lengths we must go to make good on our belief that every child is precious. What he did—to be frank—was reckless. Yet because Mooneyham wouldn't ignore these children, neither could the politicians who wanted to look the other way.

Mooneyham was only one link in a whole chain of actions that saved Vinh's life, the lives of his family, and hundreds, perhaps thousands, of others. It required a number of individuals, often strangers, who decided to do something, including the little Lutheran church in Arkansas that chose to adopt a large family of refugees from Vietnam.

Today, when we read in a newspaper about a famine or we watch as diplomats argue about how to resolve an international crisis, it is easy to think that such troubles are too difficult to fix. It is easy to feel helpless in the midst of a complex catastrophe. But the remarkable story told in this book is proof that we can turn the tide. We can shift the world's attention to those who are suffering. We may not be in charge of a global charity, but we can write letters to members of Congress; we can raise awareness online and in social media; we can donate to worthy causes.

Whatever you do on behalf of the world's forgotten, it can make a difference for generations. Today, because a few people did what they could, Vinh Chung is saving lives as a surgeon and as a World Vision donor. He is also now helping to lead our ministry after I invited him to become a board member. It's only fitting, after all, to have someone like Vinh, who can remind us that there truly are no throwaway children.

Don't ever underestimate the difference you can make in the life of one person. What if Nelson Mandela had died in a refugee camp, Mother Teresa had been forced into an early marriage, or Gandhi had died as a child for lack of clean water? One small act today can lead to another and another. Like a line of dominoes, where each one plays a minor but essential role, we can each play a part. It may only take one act to save one life that can change the course of history.

—Richard Stearns, Bellevue, Washington

Part One

The winds of heaven change suddenly;
so do human fortunes.
—Chinese proverb

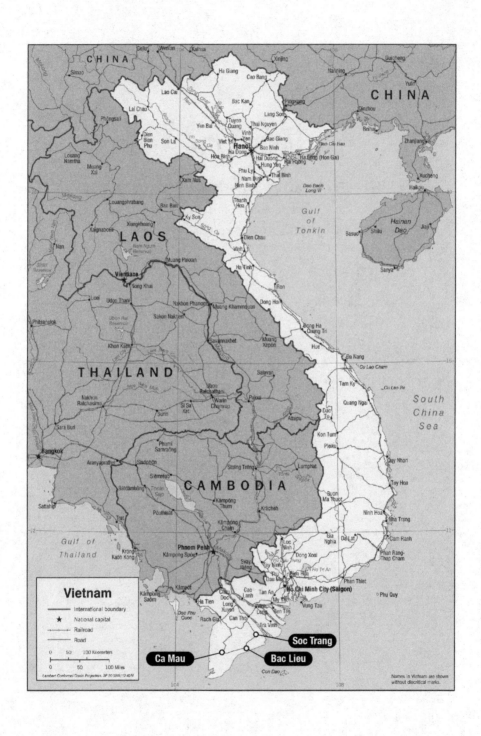

One

THE STORY BEGINS

T HIS IS A STORY TOO BIG FOR ONE PERSON TO TELL.
It's a story that spans two continents, ten decades, and eleven thousand miles. It's the story of a fortune lost and a treasure found, the story of two lost men and three extraordinary women who changed their lives.

My name is Vinh Chung. I was born in a country that no longer exists and grew up in a country I never knew existed.

I was born in South Vietnam just eight months after its fall to the communists in April 1975. But this is not a story about the Vietnam War—this is the story of what happened next, to more than a million people, including my family. For most Americans the final image of the Vietnam War was a grainy black-and-white photograph of an overloaded helicopter lifting off from the rooftop of the United States Embassy in Saigon. When that helicopter departed, my story began.

When I was three and a half years old, my family was forced to leave Vietnam and flee to a place we had never heard of, somewhere in the heartland of America, called Arkansas.

I am a refugee.

My family went to sleep in one world and woke up in another, and more than anyone in my family I was trapped between those worlds. I was born in Vietnam, but I was not Vietnamese; I was raised in America, but I was not an American. I grew up Asian in character but American in culture, a citizen but always a refugee. I had no lessons from the past to guide me, no right way to do things in the present, and no path to follow into the future.

Since I was so young when I left Vietnam, I never really had the chance to understand Asian culture or master the Vietnamese language. I grew up in America, where there was a new culture and a new language to learn, but there was no one to help me because no one in my family had been there before me. We were all lost and had to find our own way in America, and it was hard for each of us in a different way.

We are Chinese by ancestry, born in Vietnam, and raised in the jungles of America. We arrived in this country with nothing but the clothes on our backs and unable to speak a single word of English; my family now holds twenty-one university degrees, including five master's and five doctorates from institutions such as Harvard, Yale, Georgetown, Stanford, George Mason, Michigan, and Arkansas.

But in July 1979, my family lay half-dead from dehydration in a derelict fishing boat jammed with ninety-three refugees lost in the middle of the South China Sea.

How we got from there to here is quite a story.

Two

A WORLD ON THE EDGE

Within ten years of my father's birth, fifty million human beings died. He was born at a moment in history when the entire world was about to erupt in a frenzy of violence that left no one untouched.

My father's name is Thanh Chung; he was born in 1937 in the Mekong Delta of Vietnam. When my father was born, an emperor still ruled Vietnam, the nation was still a French colony, and communism was mostly an obscure political theory discussed by radical students in Paris.

It was a world that would soon cease to exist.

In 1937, Japan was already at war with China, Adolf Hitler was about to invade Poland, Britain and France were about to declare war on Germany, and the United States was desperately trying to maintain a fragile neutrality that was destined to fail. The earth's great powers were shifting like tectonic plates, and entire nations were about to be thrown off their feet by the resulting quake. Ancient loyalties were realigning; longtime friends became foes, and former enemies were forced to unite to survive. Chancellors and prime ministers spoke of thousand-year empires and mustered massive armies in pursuit of their dreams. Rapidly industrializing countries lusted for raw materials like oil and iron and rubber and overran neighboring nations to obtain them. All over the world soldiers and civilians alike began to perish in unimaginable numbers, and only a few fortunate nations managed to escape the violence and devastation.

Vietnam was not one of them.

One day, when my father was four years old, he heard the drone of an engine high above him and looked up into the sky to see a formation of cross-shaped silhouettes drifting overhead. They were the first airplanes he had ever seen, but these were no ordinary airplanes. They were Japanese long-range bombers being redeployed from China to air bases in southern Indochina, where they would be within easy striking distance of Malaya, the Philippines, and the Dutch East Indies. When America saw that Japan was extending its ambitions deeper into Southeast Asia, it immediately imposed an embargo that cut off Japan's supply of iron and oil—two resources vital to any industrialized nation. Japan was left with only two options: either withdraw its armies from Southeast Asia or eliminate America's ability to enforce its embargo. Japan chose the latter option by launching a sneak attack against a little-known American naval base, known as Pearl Harbor.

My father was witnessing the beginning of the Second World War.

The next forty years of his life would be a time of unceasing conflict as violently opposing powers battled to decide who would own Vietnam. The Japanese wanted to conquer it, the French wanted to keep it, and the communists wanted to overthrow it.

My father just wanted peace.

The Mekong Delta is a fifteen-thousand-square-mile river delta formed by the nine tributaries of the Mekong River, known to the Vietnamese as the "Nine Dragons." To Asians the dragon is a symbol of prosperity and good fortune, and the Mekong Delta has the very good fortune to possess nine of them. For thousands of years the waters of the Mekong have regularly flooded to deposit layer after layer of mineral-rich silt from as far away as the Tibetan plateau, creating some of the richest soil on earth. The fertile soil and tropical savanna climate make the region perfectly suited for agriculture, which, unfortunately for the region's inhabitants, has also made the Mekong Delta an object of desire for nations all over the world.

My father lived with his older brother and four sisters in the countryside near the provincial capital of Bac Lieu. His father—my grandfather—had two brothers, who also lived in Bac Lieu, and together the three Chung brothers ran a lucrative business. My grandfather was a seller of medicinal herbs and traditional Chinese remedies, while my grandmother sold fabrics imported from Saigon a hundred miles to the north. Business was good for my family in Bac Lieu; and for a family of merchants, when business is good, life is good.

By temperament my father was a kind and gentle boy who adored his father and mother and wanted nothing more than to live his life peacefully in the pastoral beauty of the delta. Unfortunately the peace he longed for was something he rarely experienced.

When he was five, he looked up from his chores one day to see a band of unfamiliar men walking toward him through the center of his village. The men were muttering to one another in voices too low to hear, and when one of them raised his arm to point to one of the houses, my father saw that the man was holding a long, silver-gray machete. The blade was stained red.

No—it was *dripping* red.

These were the men his mother and father called *Khmer*—the dark-skinned men who came from unknown villages somewhere to the northwest. My father had heard grown-ups whisper stories about the Khmer, but whenever he asked about them, he was told that he was too young to hear. But late at night his older brother used to tell him stories—stories about the vicious, dark-skinned men who hated the Vietnamese so much that they would use their machetes to hack off their arms and sever their heads and burn whole villages to the ground. My father had always thought his brother was lying, just making up ghost stories to watch his little brother's eyes widen with fear—but now he knew the men were real.

And they were looking directly at him.

He wanted to run, but his legs would not obey him. The men had the eyes of tigers—that mythical, paralyzing stare said to be able to hold a boy frozen in place until the beast devoured him. He couldn't move; there was nothing he could do but stand and wait to be torn apart.

The men gathered around my father and stared down at him. One of the men took a step closer and said something, but my father could not understand the man's words and said nothing in reply. The man cocked his head to one side and studied him for a moment, then raised his machete and pointed to my father's head. My father held his breath and wondered what it was going to feel like to have his head chopped off. *Will I still be able to see?* he wondered. *Will I feel it when my head drops to the ground like a coconut?*

The man made a comment to one of his companions, then pointed his machete at my father's left arm and drew an imaginary line from his shoulder to his hand. *Is he going to hack off my arm instead? Would it be better to lose my arm or my head? Which one hurts more?* He squeezed his eyes tight and waited for the stinging blow.

Then he heard the door to his house squeak open behind him, and when he turned, he saw his father hurry from the house and call out to the men in a frightened voice that didn't sound like his father at all. Then, to my father's amazement, my grandfather stepped aside and pointed to the door.

The men nodded and entered the house one by one, and as each one entered, he bent down and leaned his bloodstained machete against the wall.

My father entered last of all and watched as the men seated themselves around the small room. His older brother and sisters pressed themselves against the far wall and stared, wide-eyed, as my grandmother nervously ladled out bowls of rice and *pho* and passed them to her husband to distribute to the hungry men.

Half an hour later the meal was finished, and the men departed. As they left, each man retrieved his machete from the side of the house—except for one. One machete was left leaning against the wall, with its bloodstained tip glowing like a torch. My father was fascinated by the machete and reached down to pick it up, but when he did, my grandfather grabbed his arm and jerked him back.

"Never touch that machete," my grandfather said sternly. "Never touch the blade and never, *ever* move it from that spot."

My grandfather's solemn tone told my father that this was not a command to be questioned. As always, he obeyed, and the blood-tipped machete remained against the wall exactly where it had been left.

My father was too young to understand that his family had just served a sort of Passover meal. The Cambodian angels of death who dined at our house that day had just finished slaughtering a group of communist sympathizers and were passing through my family's village, searching for any others they might have missed.

For more than a thousand years, the Mekong Delta was ruled by the Chinese. For the previous hundred years the French had been in charge, laying claim to Vietnam as an official "colony of economic interests" and growing rich off the sale of its rice, rubber, coffee, and tea. When Japan invaded Vietnam at the beginning of the Second World War, communist leader Ho Chi Minh founded the League for the Independence of Vietnam, commonly known as the Viet Minh. Their initial purpose was to repel the Japanese, but their ultimate goal was to free Vietnam from all foreign oppressors, which led them to hate the French almost as much as they did the Japanese.

The Cambodians who dined at my father's house that day supported the colonialist French and despised the communist Viet Minh. My father's family had been spared a violent death because they were Chinese, and the Chinese were considered a neutral party to the conflict. Neutrality was a blessing, but it was also a difficult and dangerous balance to maintain. By feeding the Cambodians, my grandfather had won their favor—but an act of kindness to the Cambodians would have been viewed as an act of betrayal to the Viet Minh. The blood-tipped machete left leaning against their wall told other Cambodians that the family should be spared, but the Viet Minh would not have felt the same way. No matter what course of action my family took, someone could have been offended, and that meant their lives were in constant danger.

Random violence was a constant danger in Bac Lieu, and after my family's house had been burned to the ground twice, my grandmother decided she had had enough. After all, she was raising six children, and the rural delta was just too dangerous. She began to press her husband to relocate the family near the city of Soc Trang in Soc Trang province, about thirty miles north. They would be safer near a city, she insisted, and there would also be better education for the children there. My grandfather was reluctant to leave Bac Lieu because his business had prospered there, but eventually he relented and moved his family while his two brothers remained behind to protect the family property.

But the violence soon followed them.

After victory over the Japanese, nationalist sentiment was strong in Vietnam, and the communist Viet Minh were hurrying to attack the French before they had time to reconsolidate power. In Soc Trang the French were everywhere; there were French soldiers, French gendarmes, and French bureaucrats, and that made the region a target for Viet Minh attacks. Looting and assault became so common in Soc Trang that my grandfather found it almost impossible to conduct business there.

In the months that followed, things grew even worse for my family. Business slowed to a standstill, and the money they had saved from Bac Lieu was gone. Now the only way they could survive was by selling off their possessions, and the Viet Minh had already stolen the best of them.

Then on top of it all, my grandfather received the tragic news from Bac Lieu that one of his brothers had been killed in the recent uprising. His other brother had vanished without a trace and was presumed dead. This was the final straw in a lifetime of difficulties.

My grandfather fell into a deep depression fueled by alcohol. At times his gloom was so dark and overpowering that he became suicidal. In moments of deepest despondency he would sometimes race up to the rooftop to throw himself off, and my father and uncle would have to hold him back to keep him from jumping and ending his life. My grandfather's depression slowly descended into utter despair, and over the next three years the family could only watch as my grandfather withered like a drying leaf until he finally crumbled and died.

My father was only twelve when it happened.

At forty-one, my grandmother had been left to raise six children all by herself. Her children were poor and hungry, and all that had been left to her was the burned-out shell of a French colonial house. She had no money, no job, little education, and no one to help her. A forty-one-year-old woman with six children had virtually no prospect of remarriage; the only two options for a woman in her situation were servitude or prostitution, and she was too proud to do either. She faced an almost impossible challenge, the kind of Herculean task that would crush most men.

So Grandmother Chung rolled up her sleeves and went to work.

Three

A HANDFUL OF RICE

MY FATHER'S MOTHER WAS THE MOST FORMIDABLE woman I have ever known. It's almost impossible to describe Grandmother Chung in a way that is both accurate and believable. In my eyes the woman was taller than bamboo, tougher than a water buffalo, and shrewder than a mongoose.

An Kim Trinh was larger-than-life. At almost six feet in height, she towered half a foot over most Asian men and a full foot above most of their diminutive wives. She was broad shouldered and stocky in build and walked with such fearless confidence that people stepped off the sidewalk to let her pass. She could wield a machete like a Viet Cong regular and had a temper like a Laotian land mine, a woman whose angry glare could make my oldest brother wet his pants. You could love her, you could hate her, but no one could ever ignore her—she made sure of that. Grandmother Chung was the first of the three extraordinary women who would shape my life and alter my destiny. I loved her, I feared her, and I count myself fortunate that some part of her still lives in me.

Grandmother Chung was born just after the turn of the century to a Chinese family in the rural Mekong Delta. She married my grandfather in her early twenties, and together they set about building a business and raising a family. Unfortunately for them, they were doing it at a time when the Vietnamese, Cambodians, communists, French colonialists, and Japanese were warring all around them.

Three times my grandfather's business was completely destroyed, forcing him to begin again, and each crushing setback robbed a little more of his soul until, after his brothers died, he finally succumbed to alcohol and despair at age forty-eight. I have no way to comprehend the pressures my grandfather was forced to endure; what I do know is that the same pressure that can crush coal into dust can also turn carbon into diamond, and the same setbacks and disappointments that drove my grandfather to despair somehow only made my grandmother more determined. Tough times produce tough people, and my grandmother was the toughest of them all.

Grandmother Chung was widowed in the worst of times. The year was 1949. Vietnam, like most of Asia, was still struggling to recover from the ravages of a global war. In Vietnam entire industries had been destroyed, the few paved roads were left pockmarked by mortar shells and bomb craters, and rail lines were turned into little more than twisted knots of rusted steel. In the north almost two million Vietnamese died of starvation, when both the Japanese and the French made the monstrous decision to stockpile immense quantities of rice to burn in place of oil.

The economy of Vietnam was in ruins. No one trusted the currency because no one could be certain who would rule Vietnam next. Why trade in piastres if the French were about to depart? And why exchange piastres for the Vietnamese dong when the French might very well remain? And if the Viet Minh succeeded in their desire to throw everyone out—then what would happen? Commerce came to a standstill, food was scarce, and death was everywhere.

That was the world in which my grandmother found herself solely responsible for the safety and survival of six children ranging in age from seven to nineteen.

With all those hungry mouths to feed, her first priority was food, but she knew that scrounging for crumbs today would not provide tomorrow's dinner; what she needed was a business—something that could grow, something that could put food on the table today and provide for tomorrow as well. But what type of business was open to a woman like her? And how could she start a business without skills, equipment, or capital?

The answer was rice.

One thing the Mekong Delta has always had in abundance is rice, and rice is the staple diet of all Asian countries. Everyone needed rice, my grandmother knew, so she began to scavenge hand-fuls of raw rice wherever she could find them and mill them by hand. Hand-milling is an ancient process that is still employed in under-developed areas of the world; it involves pounding the rice in an improvised mortar and pestle until the inedible outer husk and bran are removed. The process is labor-intensive but free, which made it a perfect fit for the unskilled Chung family.

When the first few handfuls of rice were ready, the three oldest children sold them on the streets of Soc Trang. My grandmother used the money to buy more raw rice, set some of it aside, and sold the rest. She repeated this process again and again until she had finally collected enough raw rice to fill twenty sacks, a substantial enough quantity to allow her to approach a commercial rice mill and pay to have the rice milled by machine.

That was how the family business grew: handful by handful, sack by sack, year by year, until it became one of the largest businesses in the entire Mekong Delta—a rice-milling empire worth millions in today's dollars. It was a genuine rags-to-riches story, made even more impressive by the fact that it was accomplished by a woman with no financial resources and little formal schooling.

Education was never an option for my grandmother; in Vietnam girls rarely had the chance to attend school beyond an elementary level. Daughters were given a basic education and training in the domestic arts they would need to run a household one day. But build-ing a business empire required more than knowledge of domestic arts, and Grandmother Chung was left to accomplish the task with only her native intelligence and fearless determination. Fortunately for my family, she had plenty of both.

There was a darker reason to limit a girl's education in Vietnam—a timeworn Asian proverb that said, "A woman who cannot write is a woman of virtue." According to the proverb, a girl who was taught to write would become an unfaithful wife who wrote to other men while a woman who couldn't write would have no choice but to remain faithful and virtuous.

There was no tax-supported public school system in Vietnam, so education had to be funded privately. If you wanted your son to be educated, you essentially found yourself a teacher and hired him to teach. But in the Mekong Delta the uncertain economy and constant threat of violence made prosperity fleeting and education a stop-and-go process. Often a family could afford to send only one son to school at a time, in most cases the oldest first. When my family lived in Bac Lieu and my grandfather's business was still flourishing, my father's older brother started school. My uncle was an excellent student and was known for his beautiful penmanship, which to the Chinese is an indication of culture and intelligence. But when the family moved to Soc Trang and the business began to decline, my uncle's schooling ended. His education stopped at an elementary level, and he never had the chance to resume.

Because my uncle was the oldest and strongest, he was most needed to help with the growing family business, and that gave my father the chance to begin his own education. My father loved school and dreamed of becoming a doctor one day. He was especially adept at languages and became proficient at several, including Vietnamese, Cambodian, Cháo zhōu (pronounced chow-joe), and several other Chinese dialects.

The year 1954 was pivotal for my family and for Vietnam as a nation. That was the year the Viet Minh finally defeated the French, and Vietnam's hundred-year colonial era came to an end. It was also the year the United States first took an active interest in Vietnam. Fearing that all of Southeast Asia was about to turn communist, the United States backed a plan at a Geneva peace conference that split Vietnam into two separate nations, with a communist government in the north and a loosely democratic government in the south. No one could foresee it at the time, but that event made the Vietnam War inevitable.

When the nation split in two, an enormous migration took place in both directions at once. A million souls fled from north to south: Catholics, Buddhists, government workers, intellectuals—anyone who hated the communist land reforms or feared reprisals by the new government. About one hundred thousand Viet Minh activists migrated in the opposite direction to join their communist colleagues in the north, though many Viet Minh remained in their native villages in the south.

The migration put an end to open conflict and ushered in a brief era of peace and prosperity. That was the pivotal event for my family—a peaceful environment and stable economy that allowed my grandmother's rice-milling business to begin to grow exponentially. The business was given an official name: *Hoà Hiệp Lợi*.

Or in English: Peace, Unity, Profit.

For my father, the name could not have been more appropriate. For seventeen years he had loathed the constant violence and the poverty it spawned. He longed for peace and the unity of the many ethnic groups that shared the Mekong Delta—and five years of hunger and deprivation had given him a desire for profit too. At last he had the peaceful world he had always hoped for.

It didn't last.

Within two years the South Vietnamese government launched a campaign to root out and destroy the remaining Viet Minh in the south. To carry out that campaign, they needed soldiers, and in the war-weary south the only way to get them was to draft them. My father was at the perfect age for conscription, and the possibility of military service terrified him. He was a peaceful man who had always despised violence, and he was about to be forced to become part of it. And so, just a few years before American conscientious objectors began to head to Canada, my father fled to Cambodia.

It was my grandmother who gave the final order for my father to go. Her sons were the backbone of her growing business empire, and she was not about to let the political interests of the South

Vietnamese government take precedence over her corporate plans. For my father, dodging military service was a moral and ethical decision; for my grandmother, it was just good business.

My father spent the next two years in lonely exile in Cambodia; but by 1960, the family business was growing by leaps and bounds, and my grandmother sent for her son to return home. Peace, Unity, Profit was about to experience explosive growth and undreamt-of success under the iron rule of my grandmother and the tireless efforts of her two obedient sons. But two events that year would alter the course of my father's life forever. In the north Ho Chi Minh announced the establishment of the National Liberation Front with the expressed purpose of "liberating" the people of South Vietnam and reuniting the two countries. And in the south US advisers and journalists came up with a nasty pejorative to describe those remaining Viet Minh that the government just could not seem to eliminate.

Viet Cong.

Four

BUILDING AN EMPIRE

MY GRANDMOTHER'S FIRST TWENTY SACKS OF RICE quickly turned into a hundred, and a hundred had the potential to mushroom into thousands—but she knew it would be hard for the business to expand as long as she was forced to pay someone else to mill her rice. Rice mills were a monopoly in the Mekong Delta; every rice farmer had to have his rice milled before he could sell it, and unless he was willing to perform the laborious task of hand-milling, he was forced to do business with the local rice mill—and forced to pay whatever the mill demanded.

My grandmother didn't like that arrangement, so she built her own mill.

Our first rice mill was located in the Mỹ Xuyên (pronounced *Me Zoo-EEN*) district of Soc Trang, where my family lived. The site chosen for the mill was the banks of the Bay Sao River, a logical location since rivers were the only "roads" that could be trusted in the Mekong Delta. During the monsoon season, a truck often could be found mired to the axles in mud, but when the rivers rose, a boat just went faster. The mill was an enormous corrugated steel structure that rested on a concrete pad the size of several basketball courts side by side. Inside the building was a series of high-speed electric mills that could spit out a hundred-kilo sack of polished rice in minutes. There was ample floor space to allow for mountains of raw rice waiting processing, as well as hundreds of sacks of finished product ready for delivery.

From the western provinces of Phong Dinh and An Giang, boats came loaded with wet rice ready for milling. Some farmers were willing to unload their rice quickly and cheaply before it mildewed or spoiled, and that led to a second source of income for the business: the family began to buy rice wholesale and store it until a leaner season, when supply would be low and prices would be high. My family also bought large quantities of any commodity that happened to be cheap at the time—cement, sugar, fertilizer—and stored it in enormous mounds in the warehouse until prices were favorable for resale.

My family soon recognized that a second mill was needed, one farther to the south and west, and when that mill was completed in Tham Don, about five miles away, rice growers from all over the Ca Mau peninsula became potential customers. Some of the rice left the family mills by river barge, but to reach inland markets, trucks were needed, and a fleet was built. Some were bought and many more were leased, heavy delivery trucks capable of hauling twenty thousand pounds of rice at a time, allowing the business to expand as far as Saigon—and for those who lived in the Mekong Delta, Saigon was the edge of the known universe.

With an entire fleet of trucks, my family also saw an opportunity to enter the freight business. The big delivery trucks that off-loaded rice in Saigon were returning to the mills empty, so the company began leasing space on those trucks to other merchants in exchange for a fee. When no local merchant was in need of freight service, my family purchased goods and supplies in Saigon and trucked them back home to resell at a profit.

Rice milling, trucking, retail sales, commodities—the business kept rippling outward like a stone dropped into a rice paddy. At its peak the business employed several hundred workers in Peace, Unity, Profit mills and warehouses; it was by far the largest business in Mỹ Xuyên and one of the largest in the entire province of Soc Trang. It's impossible to calculate the company's actual net worth, but it was easily worth millions and growing fast.

It takes a lot of work to manage a business empire, and everyone in my family had to play a part. There was never any doubt as to who was in charge of the business or who controlled the purse strings. Firmly entrenched at the top of the food chain was Grandmother Chung, whose role might best be described as a combination of CEO, CFO, empress, and warlord. Her word was law, but she was no distant ruler handing down decisions from her mountaintop retreat; my grandmother was a hands-on chief executive who had literally helped build the business by hand. When the first rice mill was being constructed, my grandmother helped stack the bricks that formed the foundation walls, which was both admirable and dangerous. It was admirable because it proved to everyone that she was not afraid to get her hands dirty. It was dangerous because when my grandmother lost her temper, she had a habit of throwing anything she found within reach.

Everyone knew it was my grandmother's company and the money belonged to her. She gave her sons money as they needed it, and she did so generously, but it was clearly understood that the money was hers to give. Like most business owners in the Mekong Delta, she put little faith in the Vietnamese currency, so she made a practice of converting the company's profits into something a bit more secure: gold and diamonds. In Vietnam it was common practice to store wealth in the form of gold because gold was sure to retain its value and it was an international form of exchange. My grandmother kept lumps of gold hidden around the house because she didn't trust banks, and she kept her diamonds in a Café du Monde coffee can. It always seemed odd to me that she would choose to store the world's most precious commodity in the world's worst hiding place, but my grandmother liked to keep her wealth close at hand, and in her opinion a coffee can served just fine.

My father and uncle shared responsibility for the business's over-all operation, and they had no difficulty dividing up duties. Each simply gravitated to the role that suited his personality best, and their personalities could not have been more different. My uncle was the company's salesman, the one who lunched with potential clients and sipped iced coffee and jasmine tea while they haggled over prices and quantities. He was a successful businessman who worked for a wealthy company, and he wanted his clients to know it, so he wore expensive, Western-style suits with crisply starched shirts and always carried a briefcase—an unmistakable icon of achievement. No detail of his appearance was ever overlooked; he even brushed his toenails before he left the house each morning.

My uncle traveled by car—one of several he owned—and he had his own personal driver. Whenever he dropped by to visit one of the mills, every employee was careful to look busy. They knew there would be no friendly greetings or backslaps from the boss. My uncle was their employer, not their friend, and he expected to be treated with the respect and deference his position was due.

My father was just the opposite. While my uncle was out search-ing for new clients, my father was handling the day-to-day operation of the business. You might say my uncle drummed up business while my father figured out how to get it done. Even their childhood nick-names reflected the difference in their personalities: my uncle's nickname was Nam Sao, which means "southern stars," while my father's nickname was Nam Xuong, which means "southern mist." My uncle reached for the stars while my father stuck closer to the ground.

The term COO (chief operating officer) comes closest to defin-ing my father's job, though it fails to convey his style of leadership. My father's office was at one of the rice mills, and the employees were his friends. He worked with them, sweated with them, and some-times partied with them—even with the Cambodians, who were considered a lower class. He knew the employees by name, and he knew their families. He attended their weddings and funerals; he even napped with them. After lunch on an especially hot day, the mill workers would stretch out on the cool concrete pad and take a nap; and whenever they did, my father stretched out right along with them. My older brothers and sisters remember walking to the mill to see our father and having to pick their way through snoozing bodies to find him.

There was no need for my father to dress up to do his job. His standard outfit was a white V-neck T-shirt, cargo shorts, and sandals. And he didn't drive a car, though, like his brother, he owned more than one. My father preferred to speed along the dirt roads between the rice mills and home on a Suzuki motorcycle. When the business began to generate large amounts of cash, his motorcycle doubled as an armored delivery truck; it was his job to transport canvas sacks stuffed with cash to Grandmother Chung at home. That was a task he risked doing only during the day; in the daytime the roads were policed by the South Vietnamese authorities, but at night they were ruled by the Viet Cong.

Despite the family's growing affluence, my father was a kind, generous, and sympathetic employer, and everyone in the community knew it. His compassionate approach to business was not something he learned from his schooling in Soc Trang or his exile in Cambodia; it was the result of the poverty he had experienced as a boy. He knew how it felt to be poor and hungry, and he was quick to help those who were in need. Sometimes a poor rice farmer would need to borrow rice to feed his family until his own crop was ready for harvest. Loaning rice was a common form of business in the Mekong Delta, and the going rate was one-for-three; if you borrowed one sack, you were obligated to pay back three. My father's rate was always one-for-one; he never charged interest to the poor.

And he gave to anyone who asked—a habit that would later save his life. In the early 1960s, the South Vietnamese government began to require everyone to have written permission before they could have their rice milled, in an attempt to starve the Viet Cong into submission. But the Viet Cong were not foreign infiltrators; they were often ordinary Vietnamese villagers, and the government's strategy to starve the Viet Cong had the unintended consequence of starving ordinary villagers too. My father decided the most humane course of action was simply to ignore the law and mill all rice that was brought to him. To my father, they were all just human beings who needed to eat.

My grandmother was known as a kind and generous person too—a healer, in fact. She had learned a lot about traditional Chinese remedies from her late husband, and she maintained a large collection of medicinal herbs with exotic names like Creeping Lobelia, Chinese motherwort, Baikal Skullcap, and Devil's Trumpet, and she dispensed them to anyone in need. When ailing villagers from distant hamlets would float down the Bay Sao River and show up at my grandmother's door, she would treat them with whatever concoction she had on hand, and a week later she would find a chicken or duck on her doorstep as payment.

My father cared for the sick as well, but his treatment methods were more modern. He stockpiled antibiotics, such as tetracycline, and dispensed it to villagers of all ages to cure just about everything. Unfortunately when children take tetracycline, it has the unattractive side effect of turning their teeth an ugly yellow-brown—permanently. Luckily for my father, no one had heard of medical malpractice.

By the time my father was in his midtwenties, he was a very rich man. In just over a decade he had helped his family scratch their way up from abject poverty to wealth, power, and fame. They did it with their own hands and their own sweat, and they could honestly boast that they owed their success to no one. My family had done the impossible, and as a result my father felt confident that he could accomplish anything.

He stood almost six foot three—an unheard-of height among Asians—and had wavy black hair. He was young, tall, and handsome, and he had money. With that combination it wasn't hard to find a girlfriend, and he had plenty of those too. If you ask my father today what his life was like in those days, he will tell you, "I was a *playboy*"—a term that was just becoming popular in the '60s. Little did he know that his playboy days were about to end because he was about to cross paths with a woman who was almost as formidable as Grandmother Chung, though she stood barely five feet tall.

He was about to meet the second-most beautiful woman in all of Bac Lieu.

Five

THE PRINCE OF BAC LIEU

HOA TRUONG CRADLED HER LITTLE BROTHER ON HER hip while she worked at the stove. Though her family was wealthy and her house quite modern by Bac Lieu standards, the old stove was still heated by rice husks burning in the belly of the great black beast. Rice was one thing the Mekong Delta possessed in abundance, and no part of the rice plant ever went to waste. Cooking with rice husks was something of an art because the paperlike husks burned fast and hot, and the only way the cook could control the temperature was by manipulating a long, metal handle to shift piles of burning husks to just the right place at exactly the right time.

Hoa Truong is my mother. By the time she was seven years old, she already cooked, cleaned, and generally served as housekeeper and nanny to nine children ranging in age from the toddler on her hip to a twenty-two-year-old boy. Children had to grow up fast in rural Vietnam, and they were given major responsibilities at an early age. That made the days long and childhood short, and life could be hard for young girls like my mother—but her life was harder than most.

Her father was born in China in 1903, and immigrated to southern Vietnam as a young man. He settled in the town of Bac Lieu because it had a sizable Chinese population, and he opened a small business that quickly began to prosper and diversify. My grandfather soon became wealthy, and in Bac Lieu wealth commanded respect. The people of the town referred to him as the Bac Lieu Prince, and some even called him a living Buddha. A prince and an enlightened being too—not a bad résumé.

In 1925, my grandfather married, and that same year his eighteen-year-old bride bore their first child, a boy. Over the next several years their growing family kept pace with their expanding business, and by the time their fifth child was born, their exhausted mother decided she wanted domestic help. A family of seven was not unusual in Vietnam; lots of women single-handedly bore the burden of households larger than hers, but she was wealthy and could afford to hire help. After all, if her husband was a prince, didn't that make her a princess? What princess does her own cooking and cleaning?

The princess found a poor family in southern China who had a suitable teenage daughter, a girl sixteen years her junior. She was able to convince that family to allow their daughter to return with her to Bac Lieu to serve as au pair to the Truong family on a temporary basis. She traveled to China and personally escorted the teenage girl home.

That was when the trouble began.

The girl was not only capable and efficient; she was beautiful—a fact the princess could not have overlooked. The girl quickly caught the eye of the Bac Lieu Prince, and when the girl turned seventeen, he married her—with his first wife's full blessing.

At that time polygamy was common and accepted in Vietnam, but it's difficult to understand why a wife would not only allow her husband to marry another woman but actually encourage it. It may have reflected a rift in their marriage; after five pregnancies the princess might have been seeking someone to divert her husband's affections. Or it may have been a way of securing the young girl's services on a permanent basis. As an au pair the girl was free to return to China whenever she wanted, but as a wife she was bound to the Truong family forever.

Within the Truong family the girl was referred to as "little sister." Though she possessed the legal status of wife, the princess made it very clear who was in authority—and so did her children. The princess and her brood constantly reminded the girl that the servant-turned-wife would always be a servant to them.

But the prince found something different and special in this beautiful young girl, and it soon became clear to everyone in the family that even though the princess still held authority, the new wife held her husband's heart.

In 1941, at the age of eighteen, the girl began to bear children of her own. Her firstborn was a little girl she named Hoa—my mother. She was born prematurely and weighed less than four pounds at birth; given the state of medical care at the time, it's a minor miracle that she survived at all. In total my grandmother gave birth to eight children, only four of whom managed to survive childhood.

With the birth of each of my grandmother's children, the first wife's jealousy increased. The princess grew more and more hostile toward my grandmother, to the point where any display of affection at all between the prince and his favored second wife caused an angry and often violent outburst from the bitter princess and her supportive daughters. As wife number two, all my grandmother could do was bow and submit to their anger—and all my poor mother could do was watch.

One year before my mother was born, the Japanese had invaded Vietnam, and it was five years before the last of the Imperial Army finally withdrew. When they did, the Viet Minh immediately began to launch guerrilla raids against the French authorities and anyone else they deemed friendly toward them, which included much of the civilian population of the Mekong Delta. The result was that a sudden and violent confrontation by the Viet Minh could occur almost anywhere and at any time. The Viet Minh were dedicated and ambitious, but they were also hungry, poorly equipped, and underpaid. They were in constant need of money just to survive, and many of their "uprisings" were little more than raiding parties that pillaged successful businesses and the homes of the rich, in search of money. In Vietnam the rich were often the Chinese, and in Bac Lieu that included the prince.

One day, when my mother was seven, my grandfather traveled to Saigon on business. That night a Viet Minh raiding party gathered outside the Truong house and began to kick down the front door. Inside the house my grandmother saw the door coming loose from its hinges and grabbed the closest of her children—two-year-old Lam—and raced out of the house just as the door burst open.

My mother and one of her older half sisters were upstairs when they heard the intrusion, and when the men began to shout Vietnamese expletives, the girls crawled under one of the beds to hide; they screamed when two strong pairs of hands grabbed their ankles and dragged them out from under the bed.

"Where is the owner?" the men demanded. "Where is the safe? Where do you keep the money?"

The men soon found the safe, but the safe required a key to open it.

"Where is the key?" they shouted at the two girls.

My mother didn't know, and neither did her half sister, but the Viet Minh didn't believe them and threatened to kill them if they didn't tell. By then all of the children had been dragged from their hiding places, and they were marshaled outside and lined up along a ditch, facing away from their captors. The Viet Minh marched back and forth behind them, shouting and threatening to kill them all.

"Where is the owner?" they kept shouting. "Where is the key?"

My mother stared down at the empty ditch and wondered if the men were about to shoot her and throw her body into the ditch.

Then one of the Viet Minh heard a little child crying somewhere in the darkness, near the side of the house. He searched and found my grandmother and little Lam hiding in the outhouse, and they dragged my grandmother out and demanded the key to the safe. My grandmother took one look at her weeping children lined up for execution in front of the ditch and quickly relented, but by the time she could locate the key, it was too late; one of the Viet Minh had lost patience and fired several bullets into the safe in an attempt to open it. But the bullets not only failed to open it but jammed the mechanism, so the safe could never open again.

The frustrated Viet Minh shouted more threats, but there was nothing else they could do. They were forced to leave without money, but they did not leave empty-handed; as they departed, they stripped the house of everything they could carry.

At the peak of the communist uprising, it was no longer safe for my grandfather to even leave his house. The Prince of Bac Lieu would have been a prime target for kidnapping, blackmail, or even assassination as a member of the wealthy bourgeoisie. With my grandfather confined to home, the family business fell apart. To put food on the table, the two wives were forced to become merchants themselves, scavenging whatever items of value they could find and selling them in the town market.

With both wives out of the house, the children became my mother's complete responsibility. That was a full-time job, and it left no time for her to continue school. Her formal education hadn't even begun until she was nine years old, and because of her new responsibilities, it abruptly stopped when she was only thirteen. Whatever opportunities and challenges my mother would face in her life, she would have to face with only an elementary school education.

Despite all the domestic tensions within her family and the political conflicts that surrounded her, my mother still considered herself fortunate. She had a kind father and a remarkable mother, a woman who had been taken from her family in China as a teenager and forced to play second fiddle to a jealous and vindictive woman. Despite all that, my grandmother remained loving and kind. She was a woman who had known both poverty and wealth; a woman who had experienced the pain of losing a child; a woman who could manage a houseful of children and deal with communist cadres too. My grandmother was a strong woman, and she passed that strength on to her oldest daughter.

My mother was going to need it.

Six

ASSISTED MARRIAGE

THE TRADITIONAL RELIGION OF SOUTH VIETNAM WAS a strange brew. There were many committed Catholics and devoted Buddhists, but the religion of the average Vietnamese villager was a combination of beliefs and rituals borrowed from Confucianism, Taoism, and Buddhism. In Vietnam this was known as the *tam giáo*, or "triple religion." From Buddha they borrowed a pantheon of enlightened beings and an attitude toward suffering that seemed well suited to their experience in war-torn Vietnam; from the Tao they borrowed an ethical system that guided their relationships and daily behavior; and from Confucius they borrowed two practices that virtually define the traditional Asian family: filial piety and ancestor worship.

Filial piety simply means a child should have a pious and respectful attitude toward his mother and father, but in practice it means a lot more than that. It means a child should be faithfully devoted, unquestioningly obedient, and eternally bound to his parents. And not just his parents; in a traditional Asian family there is a strict hierarchy of authority and respect that is very easy to remember: the older has authority over the younger—forever.

My younger brothers are twins. Anh and Hon were born minutes apart—first Anh, then Hon. Because Anh is older, though by mere minutes, he enjoys the privilege of addressing his younger brother by his first name: "Hello, Hon." But Hon is required to address his older brother in a form that shows respect: "Hello, older brother Anh." Every casual exchange between them reminds them of their order within the family—and that hierarchy never ends. No matter how old they become, Anh will always be older than Hon, so Anh will always have authority, and Hon must always show respect.

For my father and uncle it meant that no matter how old they became they would always be Grandmother Chung's children. That gave her the right to discipline them—not only as children but even as grown men—and it was their duty to accept her discipline in complete submission. Which they did.

When things went wrong in the family business or a decision was made without Grandmother Chung's approval, the boys were required to kneel in front of her while she disciplined them with a bamboo rod—even when the "boys" were in their forties. It was their duty to quietly accept their discipline without objection or complaint even if the discipline raised welts or drew blood. To a Westerner that practice sounds unjust and even abusive, but to this very day my father and uncle think their mother was a saint. I have never heard them say a single bad thing about her, and if you ask about those disciplinary sessions, they are both quick to say, "We deserved it. She only did what was best for us."

If you can comprehend what I just described, then you're ready to understand ancestor worship. Ancestor worship is almost impossible for Westerners to understand, but once you fully grasp the concept of filial piety, you can see that one is just an extension of the other: you obey your parents when they are young, honor them when they are old, and worship them when they are dead. In the Mekong Delta every village and most large homes had a family shrine that held figurines of heavenly beings and framed images of ancestors long dead but never forgotten. It was the family's job to light incense and place bowls of fruit in the shrine to honor them and seek their blessing.

It was my father's duty to obey his mother regardless of his age—so it should come as no surprise when I tell you that when my father reached his early twenties, my grandmother informed him that he was going to get married.

She had two reasons for arriving at that decision, neither of which particularly appealed to my father. The first was that he was a playboy, which my father found very fulfilling but my grandmother considered immature and irresponsible. To her way of thinking, a grown man needed to settle down, and a wife was the best way to begin the process.

Her second reason was that she wanted grandchildren. Her son wasn't getting any younger, and neither was she. She wanted to hear the pitter-patter of little feet—or maybe the march of tiny minions. She wasn't just building a business empire; she was growing a family, and she decided it was time to expand. My uncle was already married by that time, and my grandmother decided that now it was my father's turn.

Of course, that left the problem of actually finding a wife for him. My father had met several young women who were interested in marriage, especially after he became rich and successful. There were even other business owners who approached my grandmother to suggest that a marriage between her son and their daughters might be beneficial to both of their businesses. But in each case Grandmother Chung considered them either a bad match or a bad merger and rejected all of their proposals.

My grandmother wanted her son to get married, but she knew he lacked the motivation to find himself a wife and probably lacked the wisdom to pick a good one—which meant one she approved of. The poor man needed help. My father thought he was happy and living the good life; how could you trust a man like that to make a decision for himself?

That was why my grandmother sent for a matchmaker.

Arranged marriage is a misleading term. It calls to mind secret alliances struck between mothers and fathers that bind their children from birth to marry someone they neither know nor love. I suppose that happens—at least in fairy tales—but that was not how it worked in Vietnam. My family practiced what might better be called *assisted marriage*, which is a respected tradition practiced all over the world. Assisted marriage is based on two basic but rarely recognized realities of life: very few young people know what kind of person would be best to marry, and even if they did, they probably couldn't find them.

That's where a matchmaker comes in. Some families in Vietnam employed the services of a professional matchmaker, an ancient and honorable profession that probably has a parallel in every culture of the world. Choosing a mate is not only a science but an art, and throughout history women have always handled the matchmaking. Women just seem to do matchmaking better, and it's a foolish man who is searching for a mate and turns to his brother for help.

The woman my family employed was not a matchmaker by profession; she actually was a caregiver who had once lived with my family. Matchmaking was only her hobby, but apparently she was good at it, and she kept her eyes open for potential clients all the time. One day the matchmaker was in Bac Lieu, the town where my father was born and lived until age nine. She struck up a conversation with a woman in the town marketplace, and the woman happened to mention that she had a single daughter—a daughter who would eventually become my mother.

When the matchmaker heard the word *single*, she was on it like a tiger. "Is your daughter promised yet?" the matchmaker asked. "Does she already have a family?"

"No," the woman said, "but she's a seamstress, and she makes very good clothes. Do you know someone who would make a good husband?"

"Yes, and he's from a good family. I lived with them once. I watched this young man, and I know him."

"Is he ready for marriage?"

"His mother says he is."

"What does he look like?"

Every good matchmaker carries a client portfolio, so the matchmaker showed the woman a photo of my father. The woman looked at the photo and saw that my father was very handsome and had thick, wavy hair—just the kind of son-in-law a woman would want.

The matchmaker immediately reported back to my family that she had found a possible match. My father's older sister thought the match had potential. She was particularly impressed when she heard that my mother had begun to take night classes to learn to be a seamstress when she was only eighteen and had become so skilled that she was able to set up a classroom in her house to teach other young women to sew. My aunt wanted to see this young woman for herself, and the fact that my mother was a seamstress gave my aunt the perfect excuse to meet her: she hired her to make an outfit for her. That gave my aunt the chance to spend time with her, and the more my aunt got to know the young seamstress, the better she liked her.

My aunt was sold, and my father's fate was sealed. From that point on it was just a matter of informing my father that a wife had been found for him and convincing him to accept his fate. My aunt met with my father and told him the good news, and she asked him to go to Bac Lieu and see this woman for himself.

But the matchmaker had not been working fast enough to suit Grandmother Chung, so she had been doing some shopping of her own. She, too, visited Bac Lieu—the place where she had found her own husband—and managed to find *two* women of marriageable age whom she thought might make a suitable match for her son. The two women were sisters, and they conveniently lived across the street from each other.

My father was not cooperating. The idea of marriage had been acceptable to him in theory, but when it came down to choosing an actual flesh-and-blood woman, he balked. My aunt couldn't convince him to travel all the way to Bac Lieu just to take a look at one woman—but when Grandmother Chung threw her two prospects into the ring, that made three, and at that point my father found it difficult to refuse. My grandmother added an extra incentive by threatening to beat him if he didn't go, and that's when a field trip was planned to look over the candidates.

He looked in on the two sisters first—literally. He figured there was no reason to waste time talking to them if they didn't even appeal to him physically, so he strolled up and down the street until he could get a good look at both of them.

The first sister wore way too much makeup; her face was so white that she looked like a Japanese geisha. That was a real turn-off to my father, so sister number one was eliminated in the first round.

The second sister seemed a bit odd. She walked around grinning all the time, and my father wondered if there might be something wrong with her. That was enough to eliminate sister number two.

That only left the seamstress.

My aunt felt confident that the seamstress was the one, but just to make sure my father didn't pass over her after a cursory glance, she personally escorted him to the seamstress's house and introduced him to her parents.

My father was sitting and chatting with my mother's parents when my mother came walking down the stairs, carrying a tray of tea to serve her guest. He looked up and saw her as she was descending the stairs; first he saw her legs, then her hips—and then he caught a glimpse of her left arm.

To this very day my father swears that when he saw my mother's left arm, he instantly fell in love with her. Her arm was so beautiful, so perfect, and her skin looked like velvety porcelain.

I would give my right arm to have seen that left arm. I try to imagine an arm so beautiful that it could make me fall in love before I even saw the rest of the woman that was attached to it. But that's the way it happened for my father; one glimpse of that perfect arm and his heart was gone forever.

My mother was a very beautiful woman. She was officially known as the second-most beautiful woman in Bac Lieu. There was never any pageant or contest to decide the issue, and no one seems to know exactly how that title was bestowed on her. In an Asian culture beauty involves much more than physical appearance; it also involves character, reputation, and achievement. My mother was considered not only physically attractive but an outstanding person—the second-most outstanding woman in the city. I don't know who number one was, but she must have been impressive.

A beautiful woman usually has options, and my father was not my mother's only suitor. More than a dozen hopeful young men had managed to make it past her parents' background check and land an actual interview. A potential husband's occupation was one of the most important considerations for a woman considering marriage, and my mother's suitors were referred to by their trades. There was Mr. Coal and Mr. Teacher. Her parents warned her not to marry Mr. Silk because the work would be too exhausting. Mr. Ice Cream did sound tempting, but none of her suitors made as good a first impression as did my father, so she decided to go with Mr. Rice.

Since the first interview went well, it was time for their first date. In that culture a date meant a lot more than it does in the West; by appearing together in public, they were announcing that they were considering each other for marriage. The date itself was not a candlelight dinner for just the two of them; it was a public event. They decided to go to a movie, and everyone in both families went with them. As the crowd walked to the movie theater, people came out of their houses to watch.

The young couple sat side by side in the movie theater with their families packed around them. Popcorn was not served in Vietnamese theaters in those days, so my mother sat beside her suitor and held out a handful of pumpkin seeds while my father picked them from her hand and ate. My mother doesn't remember what the movie was, but my father does.

My parents still had a few obstacles to overcome before they could marry. A fortune-teller, hired in Saigon, first had to evaluate their compatibility based on the years of their births. In the Chinese zodiac each year is represented by an animal. There are twelve of them in all, and not all animals get along. A rat should never marry a goat, for example, and a tiger with a monkey is a recipe for disaster. Fortunately my mother was a horse, and my father was an ox, so the stars were in their favor.

Another obstacle came from people who wanted to prevent the marriage. My father was a wealthy man, and other families still had hopes of marrying one of their daughters to Mr. Rice. Some of them dropped by my mother's house and tried to plant seeds of doubt about my father: "Have you noticed his dark skin? I've heard he was adopted. They say he's really half-Cambodian."

Others visited my father to tempt him with other options: "Did I mention I have a single daughter? I just happen to have a picture." Then they would pull out photographs of their daughters—in bikinis.

But none of the obstacles were insurmountable, and my parents went ahead with their marriage. They met for the first time in January, and four months later they were married. My father returned home to Soc Trang after their first date while my mother remained in Bac Lieu. They met only twice more before the wedding: when my father stopped by to present a formal request to marry and again for an engagement ceremony. During the presentation of the formal agreement, their relationship took a giant leap forward—they were actually allowed to talk without a chaperone.

One date, two meetings, then marriage.

I've asked my mother many times, "Did you love Dad when you agreed to marry him?"

My father likes to answer the question for her: "Of course she did!"

But my mother answers a different way: "My father said he was the right choice."

"I know, Mom, but did you *love* him?"

"My father said . . ."

Same answer every time. Even love bows to filial piety.

My parents' marriage was not arranged, but it was thoroughly assisted by their extended families and communities. Without my grandmother's assistance my father would have probably remained a playboy. Without my aunt's assistance he never would have met my mother, and she might have spent her life as Mrs. Silk, slaving in a garment factory, or as Mrs. Ice Cream, trying to lose weight.

In the West, where individualism is all but worshiped, this kind of assistance might be called intrusion. We prefer to choose our own partners, thank you, and we are convinced we know how to do it best.

I wonder.

My parents' approach to marriage seems almost laughable in today's world, but there is nothing laughable about the fact that they have been married for almost fifty years or that their marriage has survived unimaginable hardship and challenge. Modern marriages might be more romantic, but they are rarely as enduring.

And few of us will ever have to face what they were about to.

Seven

THE DRAGON LADY

H OA CHUNG LOOKED AT HER NEW HOME, A TWO-
story building in French colonial style with masonry walls
and a tile roof verdant with moss and mildew. It looked
like a row house, narrow but deep, with two units occupied by her
husband's family. The house was large, but not as large as the house
she had come from in Bac Lieu. It was definitely larger than most of
the homes in Soc Trang, many of which were little more than single-
story huts with thatched roofs. Only the wealthy could afford a house
with multiple levels, and the second story of the Chung house was a
clear statement that the house belonged to someone with status and
power—specifically, Grandmother Chung.

There had been no discussion of where the newly married
Chungs would take up residence. By Chinese custom it was expected
that they would move in with my father's extended family, regardless
of how large or unpleasant that family might be. The issue wasn't
space or compatibility; it was simply a matter of tradition, a force so
influential in Asian cultures that it is impossible to overestimate and
sometimes difficult to understand.

The tradition of a new bride coming to live with her husband's
family helps explain why sons have been preferred to daughters in

most cultures throughout history. When a son marries, he *takes* a wife and brings her into the household, thereby increasing the size and influence of the family. But when a daughter marries, her father *gives* her away, and the family decreases in size. It's simply a matter of *give* and *take*. Sons add, but daughters subtract.

There are even preferential forms of address for the father's side of the family. We always referred to Grandmother Chung as *Lai Ma*, a term that literally means "inside grandmother." But my maternal grandmother was always referred to as *Woa Ma*, which means "outside grandmother." There are similar rules of address for uncles, aunts, and older and younger siblings. In a Chinese family there are no generic forms of address; every time someone addresses you, you are reminded of your position and status within the family.

My mother was about to become an "insider," but she wasn't just moving into a new house; she was about to begin living under the same roof as Grandmother Chung.

The honeymoon was over.

When her husband died in 1949, Grandmother Chung, though destitute, continued to live in her house with my father, Thanh, and his five siblings—an older sister, an older brother, and three younger sisters. By the time my father brought home his new bride in April 1966, three of the sisters had already married and moved away, and only the youngest sister remained. That left Grandmother Chung, my uncle and his wife, my father, and my unmarried aunt.

My mother made six—but it was about to get a lot more crowded. In the first month of her marriage, my mother became pregnant with my sister Jenny. Jenny was born in January 1967, and an almost uninterrupted string of pregnancies and births followed: Bruce in '68, sister Yen in '70, sister Nikki in '72, and brother Thai in '73. That made five more additions to the household, and my uncle and his wife had children too—four in all. Every new addition to the household contributed to the chaos and added to my mother's growing list of responsibilities.

My mother was now an official resident of the Chung house, but there was no mistaking whose house it was. Though my father and his older brother were grown men of twenty-nine and thirty-two, everyone knew Grandmother Chung was the dowager empress. Her word was law—and if you somehow forgot, she was sure to remind you. There were two reasons for Grandmother Chung's long and uncontested reign. The first was tradition—she was the senior member of the Chung family and by tradition deserved respect and unquestioned obedience. The second reason was more apparent: Grandmother Chung was a formidable woman with an unpredictable temper, and her cane could raise a sizable welt. Only a fool messed with Grandma—and my mother was no fool.

Grandmother Chung had very clear ideas about how her household should run. Every morning she would rise by five o'clock, and it was the job of her two daughters-in-law to be up before her and already downstairs, building a fire to cook breakfast. There was no electricity or running water in the early years; everything had to be done just as it had been done in Vietnam for centuries—and most of it had to be done by my mother.

The upstairs of the house was divided into rooms by corrugated metal walls that were easy to reposition as the family expanded. Regardless of how late my mother had been up the night before, she always kept one ear glued to the wall of Grandmother Chung's room. The instant she heard movement on the other side of that wall, she was out of bed and headed down the back staircase to beat her mother-in-law to the kitchen and get that fire going.

To fail in her duty was to incur her mother-in-law's wrath, and that was something she did not want to do. Grandmother Chung's temper tantrums could last for days—shouting, throwing things, swinging her cane at anything within reach. When she ran out of steam at the end of the day, she would nod off, then wake up the next morning refreshed and ready to pick up right where she left off.

My mother faced a language barrier with Grandmother Chung that made conversation frustrating, and frustration could quickly turn to anger. My mother spoke Cháo zhōu while Grandmother Chung spoke mostly Vietnamese; her Chinese, though similar to my mother's, had a different accent that made it difficult for my mother to understand. It was hard enough for my mother to meet all of Grandmother Chung's demands; it was even harder when she couldn't understand what they were.

When breakfast was finished, my father and his older brother headed off to work at the rice mill while my mother headed for the town market. Since there was no refrigeration, the day's food had to be purchased every morning, 365 days per year. There was no such thing as a leftover, so by nine every morning my mother was headed for the market with a basket woven from rice reeds and her money wrapped in a small handkerchief.

The marketplace in a Vietnamese village was always located near the center of town and usually near a river because the river allowed even the poorest farmers to transport their goods to market. In my mother's hometown of Bac Lieu, the market had been situated just a hundred yards from her front door, but in Soc Trang it was a longer walk, so it was important for my mother to buy everything she needed on the first pass. Her ability to do so was considered a test of her household skill; an efficient homemaker needed to go to the market only once. There were no late-night runs to the grocery store to pick up a few forgotten items; either you bought them in the morning or you were out of luck.

The marketplace itself was a square concrete pad about half an acre in size. In the center of the square was a tall, roofed pavilion where wealthier merchants paid for space to showcase their goods and stay out of the rain—something that happened a lot in Vietnam. The majority of the vendors sat cross-legged around the perimeter of the square, each with his own wares displayed on a mat or plastic tarp in front of him. The vendors grouped themselves by product, much like the shelves in an American supermarket. Fishermen displayed a dozen varieties of fish and eels in metal buckets, most of them caught in the smaller local rivers but some from the mighty Mekong or even from the South China Sea just a few miles to the east.

Next were the poultry vendors selling chickens and ducks, all still alive but without much of a future. The chickens lay clucking and ruffling their feathers with their legs tied together to prevent escape. My mother's job was to pick a good one—a lost skill in the Western world. The feathers told her how old the bird was, and if the chicken looked back at her with drowsy eyes, that was an indication that the bird was sick. Then she would lift the bird and feel under its breast, which should feel plump and firm; if she could feel bone, she moved on. When she found the chicken she wanted, the vendor would tuck its wings back and cross them so they formed a kind of handle, and my mother could carry it home like a little feathered basket.

The meat section was next. In Vietnam pork was the preferred meat, displayed in the form of an entire pig hanging from its haunches, with its head removed. The pig had probably just been slaughtered at three or four o'clock that morning, then beheaded, gutted, and drained of blood. No part of the pig went to waste; every part of its body could be used to prepare some Vietnamese dish, and all the parts were neatly displayed on a table in front of their former owner. The heart, the kidneys, the liver—even the intestines could be cleaned and used to pack sausages, and the head was always kept intact because a pig's head was considered a delicacy. My mother would simply point to the cut of meat she wanted—the flank, the shoulder, the loin—and the vendor would slice it off and hand it to her wrapped in banana or coconut leaves. There were no bags or butcher's paper; leaves were used to wrap just about everything.

The vegetables came next, and there were dozens of varieties. Then came the spices—dozens of those too—and baked goods, including both native breads and airier pastries adopted from the French. The more entrepreneurial vendors even set up a few stools in front of their offerings, creating a sort of sidewalk café where buyers could stop and eat—but it was generally considered unsophisticated to eat in the market, and the Chung children were never allowed to do so.

By ten o'clock my mother was finished with her daily shopping and headed back home. There the food was put away and the still-breathing chicken was set aside to reflect on its fate. In America we think a fresh chicken is one sold before the expiration date stamped on the plastic package; in Vietnam a fresh chicken was one that still had a head five minutes before it was thrown into the pot.

My mother's next chore was the laundry. Though technically she was only responsible for her own husband and children, she always did Grandmother Chung's laundry and the unmarried aunt's laundry too. It was supposed to be the maid's job to do their laundry, but Grandmother Chung thought my mother did it better, so she was given the job. The maid was supposed to mop the floor, too, but once again my mother did it better—so every night before bedtime my mother was on her knees, scrubbing the wooden floor. They apparently had a very unskilled maid, but it seems to me that what the woman lacked in talent she made up for in intelligence.

Laundry had to be done by hand with an old-fashioned washboard and tub. Soap had to be cut from a solid block; it was a few years before my mother had the luxury of buying imported American laundry detergent. She made her own starch, a concoction made by soaking rice in water, then using a homemade venturi device—basically a narrow pipe with a piece of rubber tubing attached—to blow the starch onto the laundry. My mother was always in a rush to get the laundry done because it had to be line-dried, and that required as much daylight as possible.

Next came the ironing, which was accomplished with a hand iron heated by hot coals from the stove. It was difficult to keep the iron at just the right temperature, and there was always the danger of burning the shirt or blackening it with coal dust—then back in the washtub it would have to go.

By the time the laundry was finished, it was time to start dinner, which took hours to prepare. Vegetables had to be sliced and diced, sauces had to be prepared, soup had to begin simmering, and then it was finally time for the chicken to walk the Green Mile. My mother performed the task with surgical skill; she would grab it by the head, pluck a few feathers from the neck, and then with one quick flick of a knife, it was done. Next she drained the blood, dunked the carcass in boiling water to make the feathers easy to remove, then plucked it, and cooked it any way she wished.

After dinner it was time to do dishes, and after the dishes it was time to bathe the kids and put them to bed—and there were eventually five of us. There were dozens of miscellaneous chores to do as well, like refilling the fifteen kerosene lamps that lit the house and cleaning the oily soot from all the glass chimneys.

When all the daily chores were finally finished, my mom still had one last task to do: she was required to go into Grandmother Chung's bedroom and give her a massage. That was supposed to be the maid's job, too, but as usual my mother did it better. I've often wondered if during one of those nightly massages my mother ever looked at Grandmother Chung's neck and thought about grabbing her by the head, plucking a few feathers . . .

One time my mother and her sister-in-law failed to finish the dinner dishes and left some soaking in a tub overnight. The reason for their gross dereliction of duty was they had both been distracted all evening by a houseful of crying infants, and they were so exhausted that they left a few dishes to finish the next day. But Grandmother Chung beat them down to the kitchen the next morning, and when she saw those unfinished dishes, she grabbed the entire washtub and threw it across the kitchen floor. Dishes shattered, water went everywhere, and the tub clattered across the floor. My mother and her sister-in-law had to clean up the mess, then go shopping to replace every one of those broken dishes. Grandmother Chung never said a word to them about the incident, but they got the message anyway; there's nothing like a visual aid to help get a point across.

To my grandmother's credit, she could be very tender. At night, when the pace of life slowed down and she had mellowed a bit—at least on her good days—she spoke very kindly and appreciatively to my mother. "You've been working hard," she would say, or "You're a good daughter-in-law." The problem was that Grandmother Chung had a mercurial temper, and living with her was like camping in a minefield; you just never knew when something would set her off.

My mother's day would end about midnight—even later if any of us was sick or needy. It was my mother's unspoken responsibility to be the last one in bed at night; to go to bed earlier might suggest laziness or, even worse, that she did not have enough to do. The last one in bed and the first one up every morning—that was daily life for my mother, and she completed her backbreaking list of chores every day from May 1966 until our family left Vietnam in June 1979.

Thirteen years.

You might wonder if my mother ever complained. She did from time to time—but no one listened. When she complained to my father about her workload or the way Grandmother Chung treated her, my father would simply tell her, "It's okay because I love you." Sometimes my mother tried complaining to my uncle, but whenever she did, she was simply told that it was her role in the family to be a good wife and to fulfill her mother-in-law's wishes.

You might be tempted to think of my mother as overly submissive or even self-destructive. But to understand my mother's thirteen years of sacrificial service, you have to view it in the context of a traditional Asian culture. My mother's desire was to be a good wife to her husband and a good daughter-in-law to my grandmother—but it was a lot more than that. To fail as a wife and daughter-in-law would have been to shame herself and her whole family as well. To the Chinese, the family as a whole supersedes any individual within it. Family comes first—the family's reputation, the family's honor, the family's wishes. If you view my mother through Western eyes, you'll see her as a mistreated individual who should have stood up for her rights; but if you view her the way she saw herself, you'll understand that she made an enormous contribution to an affluent and prosperous family, and to Asian eyes, that is the very definition of success.

Thirteen years of selfless service—and as each additional child was born, it became a greater challenge for my mother, not only on the domestic front but in her marriage. My father worked hard, and my mother worked harder, and their exhausting workloads left little time for a relationship. The same pattern repeats itself in marriages across all cultures: busyness produces fatigue, fatigue leads to isolation, and isolation ends in loneliness.

When Jenny was born, my father began to seem a little distant; when Bruce was born, my mother began to suspect that something was wrong; by the time she bore her third child, Yen, that's when she knew for sure.

My father had taken a mistress.

Eight

DECEPTION

I N February 1965, the United States began strategic bombing in Vietnam, and the Vietnam War was in full swing. When my parents married a year later, a quarter of a million US combat troops were already on the ground, and by the time the war reached its peak, that number would more than double.

Americans sometimes have the impression that during the Vietnam War, every square inch of Southeast Asia was embroiled in bloody conflict, but that was not the case. Some parts of South Vietnam were left relatively untouched by the war, and the Mekong Delta was one of them. True, a riverine war was fought between the Viet Cong and US swift boats on the larger distributaries of the Mekong River, but in more remote areas, such as the district of Mỹ Xuyên, life went on as usual.

For my family, war was even good for business. They weren't purposely trying to profit from the war; it was just a mathematical reality that with more mouths to feed more rice was needed, and it all had to pass through rice mills like the ones that belonged to Peace, Unity, Profit. Lucrative government contracts now filled the big river barges that transported tons of rice from our mills down the Bay Sao and up the coast to Saigon. Employment was up, too, because there were plenty of young Vietnamese men who fled south to avoid military service. Because of my father's two-year exile in Cambodia, he sympathized with their plight, and he offered jobs to many of them at our mills.

Business was good for my family, and that meant life was good for my father. Though he was married now, his lifestyle had not changed all that much. He still left for his office every morning and returned at night. He still did what he wanted, bought what he wanted, and generally lived the same life he always had—only now he had a wife waiting for him at home. My father was well known in the community and highly respected. People knew him, liked him, and wanted to be with him—including women.

There was a young woman in Soc Trang who was ten years younger than my father and very attractive. She liked my father very much, and she wanted to get closer to him, but there were two problems: she was from a poor family with no status, and my father was married. The first problem would be difficult for her to overcome, but the second problem didn't bother her at all. She knew her family's low status would never allow her to cross paths with my father in a social setting, so instead she took a job at his rice mill, which allowed her to be around him every day.

There was nothing personal about their relationship at first. She was just a kind and considerate employee who paid special attention to my father and spent time with him every chance she got. Her family lived not far from the rice mill, and sometimes at the end of a long and tiring day, she would invite him to stop off at her house to rest and wind down before he headed home. Everything she did was innocent and acceptable—and carefully planned.

My mother's becoming pregnant in the first month of her marriage made for a quick transition to family life—so much for the honeymoon. But she came from a large family and knew she wanted one of her own. She carefully counted the days, and one week before her due date, she left Soc Trang and traveled to Bac Lieu, where her mother could be with her to help with the delivery and recovery. My mother was more than happy to go because it was the only excuse she had to escape the endless household duties and her mother-in-law's iron rule. Maybe that's why she had five of us in six years.

My father did not go with her to Bac Lieu. After all, he was responsible for running the family business, and business didn't stop just because his wife was having a baby. My mother was left to travel to Bac Lieu alone, but the moment she went into labor, word was sent to my father that his wife was about to give birth. As soon as that message arrived, he dropped everything, hurried to her side, and stayed with her for a day or two before returning to the mills.

My mother remained in Bac Lieu for another month, and there was a reason for her extended stay: the child mortality rate was high in Vietnam, and the first month of a baby's life was a crucial time. If the baby managed to survive that long, it was likely to live; if not, it was a comfort to have your mother nearby.

My mother returned to Soc Trang with a healthy baby girl, my sister Jenny, in tow. Life soon returned to normal, which for my mother meant her usual exhausting daily routine of shopping, cooking, cleaning, and massaging, only this time with an infant to care for. Grandmother Chung wasn't particularly sympathetic since she had managed to raise six children in abject poverty all by herself. I imagine my mother heard that story more than once.

And Jenny was not the only baby in the house. My uncle and his wife had already added to the chaos with a baby of their own. Each time a baby was born, a local twelve- or thirteen-year-old girl was hired to help with the newborn or care for the older children while the mother nursed the baby. So every new birth added two more bodies to the household, the infant and a teenage nanny, and each additional body meant extra cooking and cleaning for my mother.

One year later she was pregnant again.

It was during this pregnancy that my mother first began to suspect that something was wrong. My father seemed increasingly cold and distant. There was nothing specific my mother could point to or put her finger on—just a vague intuition that something was different. When she asked my father about it, he denied that anything was wrong and told her it was just her imagination.

In late August 1968, my mother traveled to Bac Lieu to be with her mother for her second delivery. A week later my brother Bruce was born, and once again my father went to visit when news of the birth arrived. He came a little later this time and didn't stay quite as long, but my mother didn't expect him to because he was a busy man.

Busier than she knew.

The year 1968 was a very rough one for everyone in South Vietnam. It was the deadliest year of the Vietnam War. In May alone more than two thousand American soldiers were killed, and by the end of the year, three hundred more were dying every week.

Every evening fifty million Americans were tuning in to their nightly news, and 90 percent of every broadcast was devoted to images of napalmed children and bleeding American boys being dragged to waiting helicopters. As a result the American people's attitude toward involvement in the war radically changed. Just three years earlier, 80 percent of Americans had supported the war, but that number now had been cut in half. A new president, named Richard Nixon, was elected in the fall, and he had campaigned on the promise that he would withdraw American troops from Vietnam. That may have been a welcome promise for the war-weary people of America, but it was a sobering thought for the people of South Vietnam. Even with all their military might, the Americans had failed to root out the Viet Cong and halt the advancing army of North Vietnam. How would the South Vietnamese army manage all by itself? As the rumor spread that the Americans might leave, a sense of dread began to grow.

It was also a rough year for my mother. The return to Soc Trang after her second delivery was much harder. My uncle and his wife had just contributed a second child and another nanny to the Chung household, and my mother's return with baby Bruce added two more. Her responsibilities were growing exponentially, and as the physical and emotional demands on her increased, she began to feel depressed. Take one part physical exhaustion, two parts emotional disconnection, add a dash of postpartum depression, and you have a recipe for a nervous breakdown.

Or a suicide.

One day my mother's depression finally overwhelmed her, and she ran from the house with two-year-old Jenny in her arms. Our house was situated near a bridge that spanned the Bay Sao River, and her plan—if that word can be used to describe an act of spontaneous desperation—was to throw herself off the bridge with Jenny in her arms. She couldn't swim a stroke, and the river was deep, and she knew she would sink to the bottom like a rock.

It isn't clear why she intended to take Jenny with her. It may have been that she didn't want her daughter to be left to grow up in that environment, or it may have been that Jenny was her most precious possession and she didn't want to be separated from her, even in death. Or it may have been that she was not thinking at all—she simply happened to be holding her toddler when she was overcome by depression and ran.

But as she ran toward the bridge, baby Bruce began to cry in the house behind her, and when she heard his cry, she stopped. She knew she couldn't abandon him even if it meant she would have to go on living. She turned, walked slowly back to the house, set Jenny down, and picked up a broom.

I believe there is a profound lesson to be learned from my mother's actions. There is no greater love than to give one's life for a friend, but giving one's life does not always mean dying—sometimes it means living. Living can be a sacrifice, too, and a noble one, especially when it's done to benefit someone else. Dying might require more love, but living takes a lot more endurance. To me, my mother's sacrificial act of continuing to live for the sake of others is more than an inspiring story—it's the reason I am alive today.

Nine months after Bruce was born, my mother was pregnant for the third time. It was during this pregnancy that my mother heard a shocking report: a young woman who worked at my father's rice mill was also pregnant—and she was unmarried. It was scandalous news. The young woman's pregnancy meant that she had lost her virtue, and that was a loss no single woman could afford. Who would ever marry her now?

But to my mother the report was more than juicy gossip. She suspected that my father was responsible, and once again she confronted him, and once again he denied it. This time she took her suspicions to Grandmother Chung, but my grandmother rebuked her for making scandalous accusations about the family.

"Besides," she said, "aren't you his wife? Aren't you the one he comes home to every night?"

My uncle had a similar response. In fact, everyone with whom she shared her suspicions told her the same thing: "It couldn't be true. He loves you. It must be your imagination."

My mother's suspicions were not confirmed until it was time for her to deliver her third child—my sister Yen. This time, when the message was sent to my father that his wife was once again in labor, he didn't come at all. Though she remained in Bac Lieu for her usual month, her husband didn't come to visit her even once.

That's when she knew—and she decided to do something about it.

My mother was sick and tired of confronting her husband only to have him deny the accusation, and the rest of his family would probably just remind her that she was lucky to have a husband who came home to her every night. She knew she would get nowhere by going to his family, so she decided to confront the other woman herself.

My mother's half brother, who lived in Bac Lieu, owned a big Suzuki motorcycle just like my father's. She ordered him to teach her how to operate it, and after one quick lesson my five-foot-two mother hopped on that three-hundred-pound motorcycle and went wobbling off down the road toward the mistress's house.

After only one lesson she had learned to work the throttle but had no idea how to switch gears, and she wasn't really clear about how to work the hand brake. She knew how to get started but wasn't quite sure how to stop, so when she came to the mistress's house, she had to keep circling until she figured out the best way to get off the motorcycle with most of her skin intact. She dropped the bike on its side with the wheels still spinning and charged into the house, wielding two long pieces of sugarcane like a ninja warrior—a disciplinary technique she learned from Grandmother Chung. The mistress was there, and so was my father—he had stopped by to take a nap during a break from his work. My mother was breathing fire and had every intention of using the sugarcane to teach the mistress a well-deserved lesson, but when she saw her, she couldn't do it—the young woman was cradling an infant in her arms no older than my mother's own. My mother may have been furious, but she was still a mother, so instead she turned her fury on a table that was set with cups and saucers and smashed everything on it.

When the young woman's mother heard the crash of dishes, she came running from the back room, and when she realized what was happening, she tried to attack my mother. But at that point my father stepped in and defended his wife. I wish I could make his actions sound more heroic, but considering the situation, I don't believe it's possible. My father's decision to take a mistress and his family's willingness to turn a blind eye seem despicable in today's world, but polygamy was common in Vietnam, and so was the practice of taking a mistress. A mistress was viewed much like a luxury car; if you could afford one, you could get one. My father could afford one easily, and when my mother complained to anyone about her husband's infidelity, she was always told, "It's his money. He earned it. He can spend it however he wants."

What seems even more incomprehensible is that the mistress's parents not only knew about their daughter's behavior but encouraged it. They were a poor family whose daughter had managed to hook up with a wealthy man, and now that she had borne his child, he was responsible for her. The mistress understood the culture's rules: she knew she was just like a luxury car, and she knew that when a man buys one, he is responsible for taking care of it. My father was her meal ticket, and in the eyes of her parents, any meal ticket was better than none. They believed it was better for their daughter to be a rich man's mistress than a poor man's wife.

But just because a practice is culturally acceptable does not make it right, and my father's infidelity was breaking my mother's heart. What did she care that she possessed more status than the mistress or that she was allowed to use the lofty title of wife? Her husband was sleeping with another woman—a woman five years her junior. It was not fair, and it was not right, and her heartbreak once again was turning into depression.

A few months after my mother's confrontation with the mistress, she tried to take her life again. When my father was away at work one day, she tried to overdose by downing an entire bottle of one of my grandmother's alcohol-based herbal remedies. It was not enough to kill her, but it was enough to make her very sick and very drunk. When my father came home, he found his wife lying unconscious while baby Yen nuzzled her body, trying to breast-feed.

My father panicked. He had to revive his wife before Grandmother Chung came home or large objects would begin flying through the air—most of them in his direction. In Vietnam a common treatment for general ailments was *coining*, a practice that involved rubbing a hard object, such as a coin or a spoon, over the patient's back until the skin turned black-and-blue with bruises. The theory was that the bruises brought blood to the surface of the skin, and when the blood released its heat, the malady would be cured. The treatment worked but not because it cooled my mother's blood; the coining just gave her time to sober up.

My father never really explained or defended his actions to my mother. Whenever she complained about his mistress, he simply responded by assuring her that she was the only woman he really loved and the one he came home to every night.

His relationship with his mistress continued, and over the next few years the mistress matched my mother baby-for-baby. When my mother got pregnant, the mistress got pregnant; when my mother had a baby, the mistress had one too. By the time my mother had borne eight children, the mistress had delivered four of her own.

I wish I could tell you that my father had a change of heart and gave up his mistress out of love for my mother, but he didn't. He lived in a world of wealth and privilege, and in that world a mistress was just one of the perks.

And I wish I could tell you that the reason my mother remained married to my father was her boundless love and devotion, but it wasn't. She simply had no other option. In Vietnam a woman with eight children had nowhere else to go.

What I can tell you is that my father eventually did give up his mistress. He experienced a radical change of heart, and that caused him to leave his faithless past behind and become a devoted father and a committed husband.

All it took was for his entire world to collapse.

Nine

A NATION FALLS

THE TWO-STORY HOUSE IN SOC TRANG HAD A FLAT roof that my family could access and use as a balcony to look down on the surrounding neighborhood. My sister Yen remembers staring down from the rooftop at the neighborhood children, who always seemed to be having so much fun despite their shabby clothes and relative poverty. Yen envied them. She wished she could play with them, but other children were afraid to play with her because they were from poorer families and they feared what might happen to their parents if they ever dared to get into a fight with one of the privileged Chung children.

Family wealth permitted the purchase of luxury items no one else in town could afford. My grandmother bought the family a refrigerator, but because electricity was unreliable, she never plugged it in, and it sat in the corner like a chrome-trimmed storage cabinet. But it was a storage cabinet that impressed all the neighbors, and for Grandmother Chung that was its chief purpose. My family also owned a television, and though there were very few programs to watch in rural Vietnam, the neighbors still pressed their faces against the windows to try to catch a glimpse. My brothers and sisters had their own little luxuries; Nikki had a special cabinet that she kept under lock and key and filled with cookies and candies that Grandmother Truong used to bring to her on her visits from Bac Lieu. We even had grapes to eat, and grapes were a luxury almost unheard of in Vietnam.

By the end of 1973, there were five children in my family: Jenny, Bruce, and Yen, followed by my sister Nikki and brother Thai. Grandmother Chung was in command of a growing army, and times were good for my family. Jenny and Bruce were old enough to begin their education, and they attended a private school my family helped fund, which meant, for all practical purposes, my family owned the school. A teacher once made the mistake of speaking harshly to one of my cousins, which caused my cousin to throw a tantrum; the following day my cousin attended school as usual but the teacher was absent. Unlike most of the students, the Chung children didn't walk to school; they were driven in a Mercedes, and my sisters were always dressed in crisp blue or white skirts with white socks and shoes to match.

While my family was enjoying all the benefits of wealth, there was a brutal war raging in the north, and it was growing closer every day. By March 1973, the last of a half million American soldiers had departed from South Vietnam, and fewer than ten thousand military personnel remained behind, mostly to help maintain the vast array of military equipment the United States had turned over to the South Vietnamese government. In retrospect the fall of South Vietnam to the communists was inevitable, but at the time no one was certain what would happen after the Americans left. The American departure strategy was called "Vietnamization," which basically meant the Americans planned to go home and let the South Vietnamese fight their own war—with the promise of continued funding and more weapons from the United States. But it didn't turn out that way.

Vietnam had been an extremely divisive event for the American people, and when the last of their boys returned home safely, they wanted nothing more to do with a distant Asian war. The United States Congress drastically reduced funding to South Vietnam, leaving the South Vietnamese military with an impressive collection of weaponry they could no longer afford to maintain and forcing them to fight what one historian called "a rich man's war on a pauper's budget."

When the last of the US troops had departed, the North Vietnamese army began to cautiously advance southward, fearing that their move might trigger an American reentry into the war in defense of her former ally. That didn't happen, and the moment the North Vietnamese army realized the Americans were gone for good, they began to rush south like a devouring fire.

The Ho Chi Minh Trail—the legendary communist supply line that for the previous ten years had been little more than a broken string of bombed-out dirt roads and jungle trails—was now widened and paved to allow six-ton Soviet trucks to rapidly reinforce the North Vietnamese army as it raced south. Cities began to fall one after another, then entire provinces, and by April 1975, two-thirds of South Vietnam was under communist control. Within two weeks nine divisions of communist forces had converged on the South Vietnamese capital of Saigon while the opposing South Vietnamese army crumbled in front of them. South Vietnamese soldiers were deserting at a rate of twenty-four thousand per month while officers with better connections and larger bank accounts began fleeing the country on anything that moved.

South Vietnam was doomed, and everyone knew it. It was no longer a matter of months or years; it was only a matter of days.

My family did almost nothing to prepare for the fall of their nation. They were aware of the war, of course, and they were surrounded by constant reminders. At night they could hear the sound of distant gunfire and occasionally caught a glimpse of a passing helicopter silhouetted against a glowing red horizon; in 1968, the corrugated roof of one of their rice mills had even been ripped apart by shrapnel. They knew that when the last of the American forces had withdrawn from the south, the North Vietnamese army had begun to advance on Saigon; but for Peace, Unity, Profit, business went on as usual—right up to the very day the first Soviet tank crashed through the gates of the presidential palace in Saigon.

You may wonder why my family didn't follow the example of so many army officers and government officials, who stuffed a few belongings into a duffel bag and fled before the communist advance. The chief reason my family didn't leave is that they had a lot more to leave behind. It was one thing to give up a government position or a military assignment, but it was something else entirely to abandon an empire—especially one that you scratched from the dirt with your own sweat and blood.

But why didn't my family at least shut down the rice mills, send the employees home, and take off on a timely vacation? As the Vietnamese wisely point out, "It is no disgrace to move out of the way of the elephant." Why would they keep doing business as though nothing was going to happen?

The reason is they weren't sure anything *was* going to happen. My family had been caught in the middle of political upheaval all their lives. First it was the Vietnamese, then the French, then the Japanese, then the Vietnamese again. This time it was the communists—so what? At first their country was a kingdom, then a colony, then a vassal state, then a democracy. This time it would become a socialist republic—did it really matter? For decades my family had been bending with the prevailing wind, and they had no reason to believe that the current wind would be any more powerful or permanent.

This time they were greatly mistaken.

Saigon fell to the communists on April 30, 1975. In Soc Trang word spread that communist forces could arrive en masse at any moment, and everyone scrambled to display any scrap of red cloth and yellow star they could find to proclaim their loyalty to the new regime—and hopefully avoid destruction.

But the North Vietnamese army never came. A week later one lone personnel carrier with a handful of uniformed troops and a megaphone mounted on top rolled into town to announce the new government. That was it—there were no mortar blasts, no rumbling tanks, no battalions of vengeful soldiers breaking into homes and dragging weeping people into the streets. The residents of Soc Trang had braced themselves for attack by an invading army, but the army never showed up.

They didn't need to.

There were two enemies that had been working for decades to overthrow the government of South Vietnam—an enemy from without and an enemy within. The enemy from without was the People's Army of Vietnam that marched on Saigon from the faraway north, but the enemy within did not have to march south because they already lived there—they were the Viet Cong.

When word reached Soc Trang of the fall of Saigon, the Viet Cong began to come out of the woodwork like cockroaches. My family was astonished to discover how many neighbors had been Viet Cong sympathizers all along. Poor farmers who had brought their rice to the mills; one of the teachers from the private school; even rice mill employees, people with whom my father had associated for years—they were all Viet Cong.

And they were now in charge.

It was predicted that when the communists came to power, the changeover to a socialist system would be immediate, but in areas like the Mekong Delta the new way of doing things was introduced gradually to reduce resistance. First, a series of town meetings was held to reassure the residents they had nothing to fear from their new government and little would change in their daily routines. Everyone would go to work as usual and do what they had always done; only now they would be working for the government. The government would take its share, the residents were told, but it would only take what was fair, and it promised not to abuse its authority. "If there are ten roads," one of the new administrators announced, "the government will take only nine and leave one for you to walk." That sounded reassuring at the time.

It was also announced that the new Vietnamese government had no intention of interfering with the ethnic Chinese who lived in Vietnam—the government even promised to punish anyone who made a threat against the Chinese. That came as a huge relief, and it served to reinforce my family's belief that the changeover to the new regime would probably prove to be a temporary nuisance but otherwise have little effect.

Over the next five months, however, things began to change. Government administrators began to visit my family's rice mills to take "inventories" of the assets. They took a similar inventory of the house, though at the time it wasn't made clear why the government would need a list of personal possessions. Each inventory became more and more invasive until it finally became obvious that the government's intention was much more than inventory—it was seizure. After repeated inventories of the house, the family began to find potted plants dug up and ceramic tiles pried from the floor in search of any hidden wealth.

At the rice mills it was becoming more and more difficult for my father to do business. The business still generated lots of cash, but now the government claimed it and hauled it all away. Then the government claimed the exclusive right to sell gasoline and oil, and strict limitations were enforced. But milling machines need gas and oil to run, and with dwindling fuel supplies, the family rice mills began to process less and less rice.

The Chung family empire was in a graveyard spiral.

In September the new socialist government made its ultimate intentions clear: there would be no more inventories. Instead, my family was informed its rice mills were being permanently "borrowed" by the government and the government's own employees would be brought in to work them. My family was left with no alternative but to walk away and leave behind everything they had worked for.

Now it was Grandmother Chung's turn for despair. She had spent the last twenty-five years of her life building a successful business, and it was all being taken from her—without excuse, without apology, and without remuneration. It was the same devastating loss that had helped drive her husband to an early grave. When her husband had succumbed to despair twenty-five years earlier, she had remained strong, but now she was sixty-seven, and the thought of starting over was almost more than she could bear. She even talked about throwing herself off the bridge near our house and drowning her grief in the deep water of the Bay Sao River—but it was only talk. My grandmother was a woman who opened Pepsi bottles with her teeth, and she still had a lot of fight left in her.

My grandmother and uncle began to skim off large amounts of cash from the rice mills before the government could take it away. Past profits that had been converted to gold bars were carefully hidden to avoid possible inventory, and my grandmother quickly removed her coffee can of diamonds from the house. The communists who conducted the household inventories were sometimes neighbors or former employees, and it was no secret to them that the Chung family possessed wealth. My grandmother knew they would eventually tear the house apart in their search for hidden treasure, and that meant there was only one safe place to conceal her diamonds.

The bottom floor of the house was the throne room from which my grandmother ruled her kingdom. The front entrance was covered by a pair of wooden doors that hung side by side like the doors of a barn. Every morning those doors were rolled apart to open for business, and whenever the doors opened, my grandmother would be found seated in the center of the doorway on her throne—a tall, round-backed rattan chair that framed her like a shield. Her thick arms rested on the wicker armchair, and her large hands dangled loosely, with her long fingernails pointing at the ground like daggers. The house had no need of a security system because anyone wishing to enter had to make it past Grandmother Chung.

When the communists arrived for their final inventory of the house, they found my grandmother seated as always on her throne. To the right of her throne was a table that held a tray and a small knife, and on the floor to her left sat a brass spittoon. My grandmother had the delicate habit of chewing betel nut, an ancient Asian habit that remains especially popular among truck drivers and construction workers in Taiwan. The green-husked areca nut, known to the Vietnamese as *cau*, is chopped into small pieces and wrapped in a betel leaf along with a pink calcium powder and spices like clove and cardamom for flavoring. The concoction is chewed like tobacco and has a similar stimulating effect, and the pink lime has the attractive side effect of turning the teeth bloodred. Empress Chung's glare alone was enough to start fires and make strong men cower; imagine the added effect when she bared her red teeth and ejected a spurt of blood into her spittoon. My brother Bruce assures me that at least one of those men lost bladder control.

My grandmother could not prevent the men from entering our house, but she could stare each one down as he passed. The men did what they came to do, but each time they passed through that doorway, they gave my grandmother a wide berth. Their inventory included carrying off most of our possessions, but no matter how hard they searched, they were never able to find the diamonds. My grandmother had hidden them in the one place she knew none of them would ever dare to look.

She was sitting on them.

The communists eventually confiscated my family's house to use as a civic building for the new local government. The eviction notice allowed the family only a few hours to gather what they could and leave, but by that time there was very little left to take anyway. Everyone packed a few personal belongings and household items and literally walked away. Walking was the only option because all the cars had been confiscated.

The loss of the business and home was devastating, but it could have been worse. When the war ended, more than a million South Vietnamese government officials and military officers were sent to reeducation camps to be taught the error of their capitalist ways and punished for their participation in the war. Some were sentenced for years, and many never returned.

New Economic Zones were also created to help stimulate the economy and increase food production. These were areas of previously uncultivated land, some of which were located in remote and densely wooded areas. Those sentenced to New Economic Zones were handed primitive hand tools and left to survive off the land, though many of them were highly educated and skilled professionals who had no previous farming experience. The zones did nothing to help the economy, but they did an excellent job of punishing the formerly rich and powerful.

In the Mekong Delta the local communist committee decided who would be sent to a reeducation camp or New Economic Zone and who would be allowed to remain. The authorities who decided my family's fate were local rice farmers and former employees, many of whom had been helped by the kindness and generosity of my family. It was a classic example of "cast your bread upon the waters." Though wealthy, my family had given generously to the poor; though powerful, the Chungs had shown compassion to those in need. Now that bread was returning.

My family's kindness may have saved everyone's lives, but it did not provide for the future. The house was gone, the source of income was gone, and my mother and father had five hungry children to feed.

And my mother was once again pregnant—this time with me.

Ten

THE FARM

THE COMMUNISTS CONFISCATED EVERYTHING MY family owned: the business, the house, the cars and motorcycles, the television, even the slightly used refrigerator that had never been plugged in. But there was one asset that the Chungs managed to retain, and the only reason my family didn't lose that, too, was that the communists knew nothing about it.

It was a farm.

At least everyone called it a farm, though a more accurate description might be *orchard* or *garden*. It was a ten-acre tract of land in the Mỹ Xuyên district on the opposite side of the Bay Sao River; about a mile away was the house from which my family had just been evicted. When the family business had been at its peak, my grandmother was searching for places to invest money, and one venue she decided to try was real estate. She bought the farm and planted it with fruit trees and a garden with the intention of making it a sort of weekend getaway or private retreat. She never expected to have to live there.

In fact, she never did. There were eighteen in the extended family at the time they were evicted from their home, and it was impossible to find a new house large enough for all of them to live in together. The problem wasn't money, because my family had managed to stash gold, diamonds, and a fortune in currency before the communists could take it away. The problem was no one could risk spending any of it. The new government had required all assets to be declared, and my family was expected to be poor now. If my father or uncle had started doling out cash for a large house, my family would have found themselves headed for a New Economic Zone. To avoid suspicion, it was decided that my grandmother and my uncle, with his wife and children, would search for an inauspicious house in Soc Trang while my family would move to the farm.

The farm was an L-shaped parcel that backed up to the Bay Sao River. Facing the river was a house, if you could call it that; in reality it was more like a hut. The front wall of the house was made of brick, but the other three walls were a patchwork of palm and coconut thatch combined with the occasional sheet of plywood. The roof was made of corrugated tin, which my father would later cannibalize to extend the front of the house as the family grew larger. The house itself was shaped like a square, and in the center there was a tall wooden pole that supported the sagging roof. The beds consisted of two wooden platforms covered with rice mats. My father and the boys slept on one of them, and my mother and the girls slept on the other; each bed had one thin blanket that had to stretch to cover everyone.

The house had no running water. Water for drinking had to come from captured rain while water for bathing and cleaning had to be carried from the river and stored in cisterns outside the house. The Bay Sao was part of a river system that emptied into the South China Sea, and every night the rising tide forced salt water into the river and made it undrinkable. The next morning, when the tide went out again, the brackish water retreated to the sea and fresh water from upstream filled the river again. It was easy to remember: when the river was low, it was safe to drink; and when it was high, it wasn't.

There was no outhouse on the property. The younger children used a ceramic chamber pot that had to be taken to the river and cleaned out after each use. For the older children and adults, the toilet consisted of a trowel and any patch of dirt they cared to use.

They simply dug themselves a hole, squatted, then covered the hole again—all the time hoping that they were the first one to dig there.

There was no electricity either. Light had to come from oil lamps, and the stove was an old cast-iron unit that burned rice husks, coconut branches, and wood when we were able to find it. My mother set up the kitchen with the few household items she had been able to bring, and Jenny helped with the cooking, which was no easy task for a tiny nine-year-old. The stove burned fast and hot, and the opening where the wood had to be inserted was almost level with Jenny's face. It was like working in front of a blast furnace for her, but as always she did it without complaint.

There were five children in the family when my parents first arrived at the farm, but before they left, there would be three more—me and my twin brothers Anh and Hon. The biggest challenge was finding enough for a family of ten to eat, and that was where living on a farm came in handy. The farm was part orchard and part garden, and they ate everything the land would produce. There were papayas, bananas, coconuts, guavas, mangos, and figs; my family grew corn, sugarcane, watermelon, several kinds of potatoes, and yams. They even grew lemongrass to keep the mosquitoes away.

Nothing on the farm was ever wasted. My mother had an almost supernatural ability to multiply loaves and fishes and to turn inedible objects into dinner. Rice was a staple, but there was never enough to go around, so my mother made it go further by cooking a thin porridge. Cassava root could be soaked in water until it fell apart, then dried and ground into flour that could be used to bake bread and muffins. There was an irrigation ditch that ran from the river to the garden, and when the river rose at night, water would fill the ditch and bring the occasional fish with it. There were also small frogs that came up from the river, and when my brothers and sisters could catch enough of them, my mother served them for dinner.

Behind the house there was a chicken coop, where the family raised chickens and ducks for their eggs and geese because they were believed to kill snakes—a comforting thought in a land that had serpents such as the banded krait. American soldiers used to call it the "two-step snake"—one bite, two steps, and you're dead. That was an exaggeration, but the story kept American soldiers on their toes and made my family take very good care of the geese. Whenever my mother killed a chicken, it was a feast, and a single chicken had to feed the entire family. My father always got to eat the best parts, which were the head and butt, where most of the fat is found.

My family also kept dogs but never fed them. In Vietnam there was no such thing as dog food, and giving human food to a dog was unthinkable. The dogs ate whatever they could find, just like everyone else, and they seemed to do just fine.

Whatever my family didn't eat was sold to earn a little bit of money. Yam and potato leaves, for example, were sold for food. My father would bundle them and take them into town on a bicycle to sell. Sometimes his entire load earned just enough to buy two loaves of bread or a can of condensed milk. The most profitable item was coconut branches, which were commonly used for fuel. A wooden pull cart was used to haul them into town; the cart was nothing more than a flat wooden platform with a wheel on each side and two long poles protruding from the front. My mother took hold of one pole; Bruce would take the other; and together they would drag the cart through town until they found a buyer; and after the sale they were expected to haul the cart to the buyer's house to off-load and stack his purchase.

The family made and sold anything they could think of: small arrangements of fruit, a slaw made from our vegetables, rice wrapped in banana leaves folded into the shape of little boxes—Jenny even sold lotus flowers that grew in the garden. There was too much competition in the town market to sell merchandise there, so my father or Bruce or Jenny would just sit on a street corner with a tray displaying our wares until someone stopped to ask, "How much?" Ironically, most of the buyers were communist officials; in the new regime they were the only ones who had money.

My family raised pigs, too, because it was the only way to get pork. In the market only communists could buy pork—only those with rank could afford to buy meat at all. Though the family had hundreds of thousands in currency hidden away, my mother was afraid to buy pork in the market; revealing the fact that she had any money at all would have raised eyebrows and started inquiries.

When North and South Vietnam were reunited, one of the first things the new government did was establish a new currency. The old Vietnamese dong was replaced by a currency of the same name, but the value changed radically. One new "liberation dong" was worth five hundred of the old dong, which meant the money my family had managed to hide away was worth only a fraction of its original value. By revaluing the currency, the new government made sure the formerly rich remained *formerly* rich. Citizens were allowed to exchange their old currency for the new, but they were allowed to exchange only a limited amount. My family had mounds of the old currency, but only a fraction of it could be converted, and the rest was worthless.

For a while the family held on to the cash in hopes the Americans might return and the money would regain its original value. But after a couple of years, it became apparent the Americans were not coming back, so the Chung family resigned themselves to the fact that they no longer had stacks of money—they had reams of paper.

But paper at least burns, and pigs need to be fed, so my parents began to burn the money to cook pig food. They didn't dare burn the money in the daytime because the community had become a network of spies and informers, and there were always prying eyes. The family wasn't supposed to have any money, so it wasn't a good idea to let anyone know they had money to burn. Burning money at night was risky, too, because the ink on the old currency burned a distinct color of green, and even from a distance it would be obvious what they were doing. So they were forced to burn the money a little at a time—a stack here to cook the pigs' food, a stack there to cook their own.

Another challenge on the farm was keeping everyone alive and well. Because doctors were highly educated, many of them had been shipped off to reeducation camps or New Economic Zones, and there were very few left, so medical care was left up to the family. Maladies that would send any sensible American rushing to an emergency room were things they either had to cure on their own or simply learn to live with. As an infant I suffered from what my sisters called a "rotten ear." It was a persistent infection that caused one of my ears to swell shut and constantly seep. Traditional Chinese cures did nothing to help, and the condition persisted for months. I cried for hours at a time, and Jenny still remembers having to hold me with one arm while she played jump rope with the other.

But for the most part my family was healthy during our stay on the farm. There was never enough to eat, but what we did eat was always simple and farm-fresh: fruits, vegetables, rice, and the occasional chicken or fish. We could have eaten more, but in terms of nutrition and health benefits, we couldn't have eaten better.

You would think the transition from a spacious two-story French colonial to a run-down shack without electricity or running water would have been overwhelming for my mother, but she had no problem making the adjustment. That's one of the many things I admire about my mother: she is a remarkably flexible and adaptable person, which, I suppose, is the result of growing up in an environment that was constantly unpredictable. My mother believed it was a waste of time and energy to long for the past or grumble about new circumstances; the only thing to do was just keep moving forward. That perspective might sound a bit callous, but as I would learn later on, it has tremendous practical value.

My mother had no illusions about the reality of life on a small farm. She knew it would require backbreaking physical labor, and it didn't help that she was pregnant with me at the time. But pregnancy was not a new experience for her; out of the ten years she had been married, she had been pregnant five of them. For my mother, being pregnant was like having a cold; sometimes she felt miserable, but she still had to go to work. She thought there were even benefits to being pregnant on the farm. One time the pig got out of its enclosure, and when she tried to stop it, the pig bowled her over, and she had to chase it down. She said chasing the pig was her exercise program, and staying in shape was the reason her deliveries went so well.

She knew it would be an enormous challenge to raise her family on the farm, but then again, for the first time in her married life, she had only one family to raise. Leaving the house in Soc Trang cut the size of the Chung family in half, and that reduced her household duties considerably. Best of all, leaving the house meant leaving Grandmother Chung; that meant no more broken dishes, no more nightly back rubs, and no more temper tantrums with dangerous objects flying through the air. My mother was finally free—or so she thought.

As it turned out, my grandmother visited the farm almost every single morning, which my mother found extremely irritating. Grandmother Chung lived in town with my uncle and his family— why couldn't she stay there and mind her own business? But to my grandmother the farm *was* her business. The way she looked at it, our family had not left the rice-milling business; we had just switched to the farming business, and that still made her CEO. The farm belonged to her, along with any profit it produced, and so did any money she had hidden away there—that made her CFO too. Each day she dropped by the farm to bring us a little money from her secret stash—just enough to buy a few groceries for the day, but not enough to make tomorrow's visit unnecessary. My grandmother liked to be needed, and she knew that of all the ties that bind, purse strings do it best.

She also took a daily accounting of exactly what the farm had produced, and she kept a record down to the individual piece of fruit. That made it difficult for us children because when we got hungry, we were always tempted to climb a tree and pluck a papaya or mango. But we knew that if we did, the next day my grandmother would give us one of her smoldering glares and say, "We're missing a papaya," and that tended to keep our feet on the ground. My grandmother could be a very kind and gentle woman, but my brothers and sisters knew not to mess with her; during her visits she used to trim the coconut and banana trees, and I'm told it left quite an impression when you saw her walking down a row, swinging a machete like a Kabuki chef while branches rained down around her.

Since my grandmother had intended the farm to be a private retreat, she made sure the property included all the accoutrements of home—including a family shrine. The shrine was constructed entirely of palm and coconut fronds and rested on a square concrete base. Inside the shrine was the usual assembly of deities and honored ancestors, and in the back there were a hammock and a coffin. The hammock was for my grandmother to rest in when she visited the shrine, and the coffin was for her to rest in when she died. Grandmother Chung liked to plan ahead, and it gave her a sense of security to know that she had a final resting place waiting for her. She was also used to approving all decisions, and the only way she could approve the choice of her coffin was by making the choice herself.

The coffin may have given my grandmother a sense of security, but it had a different effect on my brother Bruce. It was supposed to be my father's job to visit the family shrine each evening to light incense and place the traditional bowls of fruit, but when my father was too tired to carry out his duties, he sent Bruce to do the job instead. At night the shrine was dark and damp, and Bruce remembers seeing geckos clinging to the walls and abandoned snake skins draping from the roof like strips of gauze. Near the back of the shrine, there was a statue of a lesser deity. To place incense in front of it, Bruce had to stand beside the coffin, and the instant his duties were completed, he took off like a rifle shot and didn't stop running until he reached the house.

For my brothers and sisters, the hardest adjustments were outside the farm. When the communists first came to power, school simply stopped, and when classes finally resumed, everything had changed. There was no more Mercedes to deliver Jenny, Bruce, and Yen to the front door; they had to walk to school now, and the school was two or three miles away. When it rained, the half-mile dirt path that led from the farm to the main road could get knee-deep in mud, and my father had to carry one of them on his shoulders and one under each arm as he trudged his way through. Even on dry days it was hard to stay clean, so Jenny, Bruce, and Yen used to stop at a friend's house halfway to school, where they could wash the dust off their shoes before they went on.

Jenny had been a star pupil before the communist takeover. She especially loved math and writing but excelled at everything she tried; she even dreamed of becoming an engineer, a lofty goal for a young girl in Vietnam in those days. When the end-of-year exam was given, Jenny always finished first in her class, which granted her the right to sit in the honored position of front row, first seat on the right. When the teacher entered the room at the start of each day, it was Jenny's privilege to be the first to snap to her feet and call out, "Good morning, teacher," and when she did, the rest of the class was required to follow her lead.

But when the communists came to power, there were no more crisp school uniforms and far fewer of the math and writing lessons that Jenny loved; much of the school day was now spent learning songs of praise to Ho Chi Minh—"Uncle Ho," they were told to call him. Translated into English, one of the popular songs went something like this:

Last night I dreamed of Uncle Ho.
His beard is long, his hair is so white.
I'm so glad, I kissed his cheek.
Uncle Ho smiled and told me I'm a good kid.

But some clever student composed a parody that became even more popular:

Last night I dreamed of a money bag.
In the money bag, there were four thousand dollars.
I was so glad, I told Uncle Ho.
Uncle Ho smiled at me, "Give all the money to me."

Only two hours per day were devoted to learning, and the rest was spent planting trees, picking up trash, and collecting dung on the streets of Soc Trang. Jenny became frustrated; she just couldn't understand how singing communist songs and collecting dung would help her become an engineer.

The entire atmosphere of the school had changed. There were no more friends, and there was no more talking. Even children understood that the wrong accusation—even a false one—could land a family in prison. In the old school everyone had known that the Chung children came from a wealthy family, and we were proud of it, but in the new school we prayed that no one would remember. My parents even gave Jenny, Bruce, and Yen false names to disguise their true identities. Instead of Chung, they were told to use the name Diep and later Nguyen. My sister Yen didn't even know her real last name until we came to America.

When I listen to the stories my older brothers and sisters tell about life on the farm, it sounds as if it was a grand adventure, and in a way, for the children, it was. The farm was our little oasis in a world that had changed overnight, a world that none of us understood anymore. But life on the farm was simple: work hard, find enough to eat, go to bed, then get up and do it again. There was hard work, but there was play too. There were trees to climb, frogs to catch, ducks to chase, and geese to run from.

For my parents the experience was different. My father, once the COO of a multimillion-dollar business empire, had been reduced to a common street peddler. My mother, who used to carry home baskets of food from the market each morning, now struggled to scrape together enough for her children to eat.

And they knew their new life wasn't temporary. The communists may have spared our lives, but they would also see to it that my family would never again have money, position, or power. My parents knew the farm wasn't just their new home; it would be their entire world for the rest of their lives.

Hardest of all was the realization that the farm would also be their children's world. We would spend the rest of our lives scraping to get by each day, and we would never be allowed the opportunity to change our fate. If times were good and the rains came at the right time, we would live; if not, we would starve—my mother and father were not willing to take that chance.

That was when they knew we had to leave Vietnam.

"Anything would be better than this," they said.

But they had no idea.

Eleven

GATHERING STORM

I**T ISN'T CLEAR WHO FIRST DECIDED THAT MY FAMILY** should leave Vietnam. It may have been Grandmother Chung, when she realized that her "farming empire" was never going to amount to more than ten acres or when she recognized that her hidden gold and diamonds would have no value in the new Vietnam. As long as the communists prevented her from spending them, they were worthless.

It may have been my uncle who first decided we should leave because he didn't even have ten acres where he could stretch his legs. He was confined to a small house with his wife and six kids and no business enterprise to give him an excuse to leave each morning. Even worse, he was trapped in a small house with my grandmother, and at close range flying objects seldom miss.

Or it might have been my mother. By the end of 1977, she had borne eight children, including newborn twin boys. She breast-fed each of us as long as she possibly could—a necessity on a small farm with barely enough food to go around—but her own restricted diet made it difficult for her to produce enough milk to feed two hungry boys. The possibility of starvation was beginning to loom large, not just for her babies but for all of us. Almost as terrible to her was the stark realization that her children had no future in Vietnam. Our education would be severely limited, and she knew from her own hard experience that limited education meant limited opportunity. Her greatest fear was that her children would be forced to accept what she considered the lowest of all jobs: herders of water buffalo. To my mother that was the worst possible fate, and she was determined that her children would do better.

It definitely was not my father who decided to leave, and it wasn't because he disagreed with his wife or didn't care about us. My father grew up in an unpredictable environment where circumstances and even life itself could change overnight. That kind of unstable environment can affect different people in different ways; the effect it had on my father was to cause him to fear change—any change, even if it brought the possibility of improving his lot in life. There is an old Chinese proverb that says, "Better the devil you know than the devil you don't," and that captures perfectly my father's fearful mind-set. It wasn't that he wanted to stay in Vietnam; he just didn't want to leave.

In a sense, the decision to leave Vietnam was made for us. My ancestors were part of more than a million Chinese who migrated to Vietnam from the southern provinces of China in the late nineteenth century. The Chinese are a very cohesive people, which is why in cities all over the world there are large communities of Chinese living and working together. In New York and San Francisco, they are called Chinatown; in Saigon it's known as Cholon. The Chinese place a high value on discipline and hard work and as a result tend to be very successful in business. The Chinese who chose to settle in North Vietnam became farmers, fishermen, coal miners, and small merchants; but in South Vietnam they were more ambitious and quickly came to control the rice trade, transportation, banking, and insurance. My family was extremely successful in business, but among the Chinese we were not the exception.

When the communists took over South Vietnam, their anger was directed at everyone who had been rich or powerful in the former regime, regardless of ethnic group. Vietnamese, Chinese, Cambodian, Thai—it didn't matter. If you were rich, you were part of the property-owning bourgeoisie, who had been oppressing the poor working class, and you were about to feel the wrath of the proletariat.

In the late 1970s, my parents began to sense that the government's attitude toward the Chinese was changing. Vietnam shares a northern border with China, and there was a growing conflict between the two nations that became so hostile they briefly went to war. As hostility increased with China, Vietnam grew more and more suspicious of its own Chinese citizens because they feared the Chinese might be more loyal to their ancestral homeland than they were to Vietnam. Fear began to erupt into violence, and in Cholon, Saigon's Chinatown, houses were searched, money and property seized, and businesses shut down. The Chinese living in northern Vietnam sensed the growing hostility, and so many of them began to flee into China that the government was forced to close its borders to its own people.

Because my parents had been exiled to a small farm, they were more or less insulated from the growing hostility, but we could see the handwriting on the wall. We had been spared the wrath of the proletariat, but we understood our sentence was more of a parole than a pardon. When we began to sense that public sentiment was about to turn against us, we decided to leave before it happened. There was a saying among the Chinese in those days: "If streetlamps had legs, they would have tried to escape as well."

And the government was willing to let us go—for a price. Since the fall of South Vietnam, more than 130,000 refugees had fled to other countries, which made the refugee business extremely profitable for the government. With so many people wanting to flee the country, the government realized they had only two options: they could try to prevent everyone from leaving, which would have been a violent and expensive business, or they could allow them to leave but administrate the process—and bureaucracy is something communists do very well.

When the Chung family first gathered to discuss the idea of leaving Vietnam, my uncle suggested the most practical option would be for some of us to leave while some remained behind; a smaller party would make planning easier and reduce the overall cost. His suggestion might sound a bit cold and calculating, but splitting up was a common practice among Vietnamese refugees since leaving the country was extremely expensive and always dangerous. Instead of an entire family leaving together, someone, usually a father or an oldest son, would leave first and find a job; when he had earned enough money, he would send for the rest of his family to join him. That was the theory anyway, but it often didn't work that way. Many families were often separated for years, and because of the dangers involved, many of those fathers and sons were never heard from again.

Since my immediate family was the largest, it was suggested we should be the ones to split up, leaving the younger children behind—especially the twins. The journey might be too rough for them, it was suggested, and a pair of eighteen-month-old boys would be too much of an annoyance and possibly even a danger to the rest of the group. When that suggestion was made, my mother put her foot down. She made it very clear to everyone involved that there were two non-negotiables: our whole family was going to stay together, and our whole family was going to leave Vietnam—end of discussion.

Once it was understood that everyone in our family would be leaving, planning could begin in earnest. My uncle, along with another man, named Mr. Hong, spearheaded the effort. It was a role that suited my uncle well because his prior job as director of sales for Peace, Unity, Profit had made him very good at making connections and negotiating deals.

There were two basic ways my family could leave the country—by land or by sea—and each had its benefits and risks. At first glance a land route seemed easier and safer because no one in my family had ever been on a boat or had even seen the ocean. But the northern border into China was closed, and land routes to the west would force us to pass through the killing fields of Cambodia or the minefields of Laos. Even if a safe land route could be found, the distance we would have had to travel would have been staggering, and most of it would have had to be done on foot—not a pleasant prospect for a family with eight children under the age of twelve.

It was quickly decided our best option was to leave by sea, but that meant we would have to obtain a boat, and in Vietnam boats were in short supply because almost every seaworthy vessel in the south had already been taken by earlier refugees. It would have been much too expensive and time-consuming to construct a boat, so an existing boat would have to be found that could be patched up and made seaworthy.

My uncle and Mr. Hong made contact with the Public Security Bureau, a department of the Ministry of the Interior that was responsible for overseeing all would-be refugees. The two men quickly discovered that the process of leaving Vietnam was going to be complicated and extremely expensive; and like many things run by the government, it was also corrupt. Even to begin the process there was a "registration fee" of two taels of gold per person, the equivalent of about $2,700 per person in today's dollars. (The *tael* is an Asian unit of measure equivalent to about 1.2 ounces.) The total fee would amount to eight taels of gold per adult, four per child between the ages of five and fifteen, and children under five traveled free—what a bargain. The government even controlled the sale of all boats and gasoline; at every step of the departure process, the government had figured a way to take a cut.

My uncle did the math and realized that the cost for my extended family to legally leave Vietnam would be almost a quarter of a million dollars. Half the money would go directly to the government, 40 percent would cover the cost of the boat and fuel, and the remaining 10 percent traditionally went to a professional organizer or to pay bribes—and everyone had a hand out.

The government had a final requirement: at the time of departure, all refugees had to sign a document turning over all their property and possessions to the government, waiving any future claim. That made leaving an irreversible decision; it meant my family would not be able to rent out the farm, just in case we had second thoughts or if the voyage turned out to be too difficult. When we left Vietnam, we would be leaving for good, and if we changed our minds, there would be nothing to return to.

My uncle decided that if we included more people in our party, we would be able to afford a larger boat. That was more than a financial decision; a larger boat would be safer because a small boat had a much greater chance of being capsized or swallowed by rough seas. He began to search for other refugees who might be willing to join us by making discreet inquiries through trusted family connections like distant cousins, family acquaintances, and friends of friends. By the time he was finished, our little family outing had expanded to an exodus of 290 people and included sixteen different families.

At any point in the departure process, some government official could ask for a bribe, and if he did, we would have no recourse but to pay him whatever he demanded. Professional organizers were notoriously corrupt. Every additional refugee meant more profit, so at the last moment before a boat's departure, an organizer often showed up on the dock with several additional passengers, and the current passengers would have no choice but to take them aboard, even when additional passengers overloaded the boat and made it dangerous for travel. The refugee was never in control of his fate, and potential dangers were at every step of the journey. Old and unreliable boat engines could break down at any moment, inexperienced captains had never steered anything larger than a river barge, and incompetent navigators had nothing but a compass to navigate by.

Finding a salvageable boat, repairing it, and making all the other necessary arrangements should have required at least six to eight months to complete, but two events occurred that shifted the project into high gear: in the middle of 1978, devastating storms and floods made the struggling Vietnamese economy even worse than it already was, and in February 1979, Vietnam went to war with China. When that happened, Vietnam's Chinese citizens became Vietnam's enemies, and the government began an organized campaign to eject as many ethnic Chinese from the country as possible. That was when my family knew it was *really* time to go.

The soonest we could be ready to leave was June, and we didn't dare leave later. June marked the beginning of the typhoon season in the South China Sea, and even the big commercial ships didn't risk crossing in a typhoon. A departure date was chosen—June 12—and we hurried to make all the final arrangements.

It was around that time my mother had a dream.

In the West we're too sophisticated to pay much attention to dreams anymore; psychiatrists are about the only people left who seriously entertain the idea that a dream could have a deeper meaning. But in the rest of the world it's different: people take dreams very seriously, and they are willing to consider the possibility that sometimes a dream could be more than a dream—it might be a message.

One night my mother dreamed she was in the marketplace in Soc Trang along with our entire family. Grandmother Chung wasn't there—it was a dream, not a nightmare—nor was my uncle or his family. It was just the ten of us: my mother, my father, and the eight children. The market was noisy and crowded with people from all over town, talking, haggling with vendors, calling to one another across the square.

Suddenly everyone fell over dead.

My father and all eight of us children—we were dead too. Even my mother was dead; though in the manner of dreams, she was still conscious, and her eyes were open. At the far corner of the market, she saw a solitary standing figure: a man dressed in a white robe, with long brown hair and a beard to match. As my mother watched, unable to move a muscle, the man began to make his way across the market toward her, stopping from time to time to point down at one of the reclining bodies—and whoever he pointed to, that person came back to life and stood up.

My mother began to fervently pray that the man would point to her, too, and sure enough, when the man finally stood over her, he pointed to her, and my mother rose to her feet. She was ecstatic—until she remembered that her husband and children were still lying dead. She didn't dare speak to the man, but she began to pray again, this time that he would extend the same kindness to her entire family and bring them back to life too.

And he did. As he pointed to each of us, we rose to our feet until our whole family stood alive and well again.

Then the dream ended.

But my mother wanted to know what the dream meant. For some reason this dream seemed different to her—so vivid, so powerful, so suggestive of some deeper meaning. She began to ask her friends to help her understand the dream, and they offered different interpretations.

"That was the Buddha," one of them said. "He was appearing to you, trying to tell you something."

"The Buddha is bald and fat," my mother replied. "This man looked nothing like that."

"It was one of your ancestors trying to communicate with you," another friend suggested.

But my mother shook her head. "None of my ancestors ever looked like that."

And that was where it ended. No one was able to interpret her dream, so my mother simply filed it away as one of those unexplained mysteries of life.

Besides, she had more important things to worry about.

Leaving the land of their birth was no longer just an intriguing idea that our family discussed in whispers behind closed doors—it would soon be a reality. We were actually leaving Vietnam, and there would be no turning back. My mother remembered that dark day of despair, when she almost threw herself into the Bay Sao River with Jenny in her arms; now she was about to cast her entire family into an ocean, and the prospect terrified her. She had heard the radio broadcasts from the Voice of America, Voice of Australia, and the BBC warning potential refugees about the extreme peril; she had heard the stories about the refugees who didn't make it, the ones who died of thirst or sank into the sea or just disappeared without a trace. Would her family be among them? Was it really better to die than to live in communist Vietnam? Would her family have enough food, enough water for the voyage? And if they survived the voyage, where in the world would they live?

Little did my mother know, half a world away, someone else was asking the very same questions.

Twelve

WHY ME?

S TAN MOONEYHAM RELAXED IN A COMFORTABLE CHAIR in the pastor's study at Mt. Zion Missionary Baptist Church in South Central Los Angeles. Across the desk from him sat the pastor himself, Dr. Ed Hill, who had invited Stan to speak at Mt. Zion that Sunday evening in early December 1977. The two men couldn't have been more different. Stan was white and lean with a full head of snow-white hair; Ed was black and stout and had no hair at all. Stan lived in the suburbs of the San Gabriel Valley; Ed lived in one of the worst parts of Los Angeles. Stan's organization was fewer than twenty-five years old; Ed's church had been around for more than a century.

Despite their differences, they shared a common background and passion that made them friends, and their meeting that night was like the crossing of two live wires.

Ed tossed a recent edition of the *Los Angeles Times* across the desk to Stan and pointed to a photo on the front page. "What are you going to do about that?" he asked.

Stan looked at the photo, then at his friend. He had no idea what to say.

Walter Stanley Mooneyham was born in a small farming town

thirty miles south of Tupelo, Mississippi, just three years before the Great Depression began. He was the seventh son of a poor cotton sharecropper, and when the bottom dropped out of the cotton market during the Depression, he experienced the effects of poverty and hunger firsthand. Like many young men of his generation, Stan couldn't wait to escape the dreariness of farm life and see the world, and when he came of age in 1944, he joined the navy and served the remainder of the Second World War in the South Pacific, where he added death and destruction to his list of life experiences.

Stan had a strong desire to tell others about those experiences, so after the war he studied journalism at Oklahoma Baptist University on the G.I. Bill. When he graduated, he took a job writing obituaries with the Shawnee, Oklahoma, *News-Star*, but he wasn't satisfied writing about the dead; he wanted to write about the plight of the living and the suffering of the poor, and before long he realized he wanted to do more than just write about those things—he wanted to help. His vision for assisting the poor and suffering kept expanding, from his city to his nation to the world. He first took a job as pastor of a small local church, then put his journalism training to work as a media liaison and advance planner for a large international ministry, where he saw up close what he later described as "the awesome human needs." He was working in Singapore in 1969, when he was asked to become the second president of a fledgling relief organization called World Vision.

World Vision was started in the early 1950s, to provide food, clothing, and medical supplies to orphans in the wake of the Korean War. They began their relief work by soliciting clothing and supplies from corporations to meet emergency needs, and they developed an innovative child sponsorship program to assist on an ongoing basis. By the 1960s, the organization was global in scope; and by the 1970s, they were expanding their relief efforts to include agricultural and vocational training for families to create self-sustainable relief from poverty and hunger.

The organization was a perfect match for Stan, and he dove into the job of president with all the passion and energy he had—and he had plenty. When Stan came in as president, World Vision had an annual budget of $7 million; by the time he left, the organization had an annual budget of $158 million and a worldwide staff of eleven thousand. He constantly challenged others to "Come walk the world," and he practiced what he preached. He spent three-quarters of his time traveling the globe and made connections in capitals all over the world.

Stan pioneered the use of direct mail and telethons to raise awareness of the needs of the poor and to solicit donations, which he did with great passion. He was sometimes criticized for his emotional financial appeals, but he was a passionate man and he refused to treat poverty and hunger as academic topics. "We are accused of emotionalism," he once said, "but hunger is emotional, death is emotional, and poverty is emotional. Those who wish to make it all seem neat, clinical, and bureaucratic are the ones falsifying the picture, not us."

Ed Hill grew up during the Great Depression too. He was one of five children raised by a single mother in rural Texas, where men like Ed usually dropped out of school by the tenth grade and spent the rest of their lives doing manual labor for $2 a day. But Ed managed to finish high school—in a log cabin, no less—and even enrolled in college at Prairie View A&M, though he had no money to pay for it. He got off the bus in Prairie View, Texas, with a suit, a couple of pairs of jeans, a few shirts, and $1.83 in his pocket. But Ed received an unexpected four-year scholarship that paid his tuition, room and board, and $35 each month that he could spend any way he wished. That was more money than he had ever seen in his entire life.

"I didn't really know I was poor," Ed said. "Poverty was a matter of spirit, and we were always rich in spirit. The fact that I lived in a log cabin was not embarrassing to me. The fact that my shoes had holes in them wasn't embarrassing to me because everybody else's did. But we all said, 'It won't be that way forever.'"

That spirit led Ed to become a pastor and to get involved in the early civil rights movement, where he became a confidant of Martin Luther King Jr. Ed worked tirelessly and passionately to meet the needs of the poor in his community, and he pushed for social and economic reform at a national level. In Houston Ed became known as "the Hellraiser," which was an odd title for a pastor, but it accurately described his passion and determination.

In 1960, he came to Mt. Zion Missionary Baptist Church and he brought his zeal to help the poor with him. Mt. Zion was located in one of the poorest sections of Los Angeles, which gave him plenty of opportunities to help. "The average income is between Skid Row and welfare," Ed used to say, and he knew that his community was struggling with not only poverty but with all the social problems that came with it.

Ed made the struggles of the poor and underprivileged the focus of his preaching, and he was known for preaching with tremendous passion—and endurance. "I can only guarantee here what time we get started," he said. "I'm not in charge of the close." But he didn't just preach about the problems; he got busy doing something about them. Under Ed's leadership Mt. Zion started the Lord's Kitchen on Fifty-Ninth and Main, which eventually served between two thousand and five thousand meals every week free of charge, and they set up a clothing store that distributed hundreds of thousands of articles of clothing at no cost.

South Central Los Angeles was the focus of many studies on the problem of poverty in America, but Ed had little patience with people who only wanted to study a problem without getting involved. Ed believed in getting things done, and he knew from long experience that people can accomplish great things if they will only try—especially when they work together. J. Edgar Hoover once called in Ed and two hundred other leaders to discuss the problem of violence that was being caused by the Black Panthers in New York City. The Panthers were about to ruin New York, Hoover said. Stores were forced to close at four o'clock, and every day four million people jammed the bridges, trying to make it safely into suburbia before dark.

Ed raised his hand. "How many Black Panthers are there?" he asked.

"Eighty-one," Hoover replied.

Ed shook his head. "If eighty-one Black Panthers could plan

the disruption of New York, could not eighty-one people plan the construction of New York?" That was Ed's philosophy: even a small number of dedicated individuals can produce radical results.

Ed got involved in community relief work at all levels, and he didn't hesitate to get involved in politics when it served the interests of the poor. At different times he served as chairman of the Los Angeles City Housing Authority, chairman of Economic Development, chairman of the Los Angeles City Fire Commission, and vice chairman of the Los Angeles Department of City Planning and Zoning. He was happy to work with anyone who shared his burden for the underprivileged, and he was willing to cross traditional lines to get things done—politically, ethnically, and even religiously. "I'm a born-again Christian," he once said, "but I'm willing to cross religious lines for the good of the whole of the community." That was an unusually flexible attitude at the time, and it earned him a lot of criticism from some circles.

It was also an attitude he shared with Stan Mooneyham. Stan was a Christian, too, and a former pastor. Stan's goal was to provide relief for the poor and hungry all over the world, and just like Ed, he understood that to accomplish his goal he would have to work across political, ethnic, and religious lines. World Vision was a Christian organization, but many Christians at the time placed a greater emphasis on meeting spiritual needs than physical needs. Stan wanted to combine them. In order to work across political lines, he refused to be identified as either a conservative or a liberal, and in the politically polarized Vietnam era, that approach earned him criticism from both sides of the aisle.

Both men were products of the Great Depression, both had experienced poverty and suffering, both possessed boundless passion and zeal, both were deeply committed followers of Jesus, and both were determined to express their faith by helping the poor and suffering wherever they found them and in any way they could. Though they couldn't have looked more different, Stan Mooneyham and Ed Hill could not have been more alike.

So when Ed tossed the *Los Angeles Times* across the desk, Stan picked up the paper and looked at the photo. It was a picture of a terrified Vietnamese woman and her unconscious daughter cowering under a canvas in the bow of a small boat. The article said they were refugees who had risked their lives to flee Vietnam, and though their boat had managed to make it safely to Thailand, the authorities there would not allow them to land, and they were waiting to be pushed back to sea, where they would most likely die. "Boat people," the article called them, and it said there were thousands more like them, and the number was increasing every month.

Stan was stunned by the photograph. "The agony on the woman's face wrenched my heart," he said later, and he was dismayed that though he was president of an international relief organization, he had never even heard of the boat people. Stan had spent most of that year in Africa, where World Vision was expanding its work. Somehow he had failed to hear about this tragic development in Southeast Asia.

Now he knew—but he had no idea what he was supposed to do about it.

He looked up at Ed. "Why me?" he asked.

"Why not you?" Ed replied with a shrug.

"It's not my responsibility," Stan countered, but he had heard that excuse from others so often that he couldn't believe he just used it himself.

Ed just looked at him. He had heard that excuse a thousand times, too, and it carried no weight with him.

"It's too big for us," Stan went on. "World Vision is a young organization. We don't have the budget or the manpower for something like this—it could cost millions."

Ed said nothing, so Stan kept going.

"We're an army, not a navy—we have no experience with operations like this. Besides, it's too political. We've got projects going on all over Asia, and if we put our foot in the middle of something like this, we could be risking everything."

Ed still said nothing, and it was making Stan angry. Ed wasn't known to be a man of few words, and when he said nothing, he was trying to make a point. Stan knew that Ed didn't have to argue with him because Stan was arguing with himself. His reasons for not getting involved with the boat people were good reasons, logical reasons, practical reasons—but somehow none of them could stand up to that poor woman's photo.

"I'll look into it," Stan mumbled, "and I'll pray about it."

That was all Stan agreed to do, but Ed smiled and nodded, and Stan knew why. The two men could not have been more alike, and that sly old fox knew that in his heart, Stan Mooneyham was already committed.

Thirteen

NO TURNING BACK

THE DAY OF OUR DEPARTURE WAS THE FIRST TIME MY family had ever seen the boat on which we were to sail across the world's third-largest sea. None of us knew who supervised the boat's repair or whether he knew what he was doing; no one knew for sure whether the boat would spring a leak and sink the first time everyone climbed aboard.

But it was no river barge. The boat looked enormous, bigger than any of us had expected, but in reality it was only about seventy feet long and thirteen feet wide, just barely large enough to hold all 290 of us and without an inch to spare. The boat was constructed entirely of wood and painted in a color so innocuous that no one in my family can remember what it was. It was flat in the back and came to a point in the front and curved up a little, in the style of Asian fishing boats, with the number 0726 painted across the bow. There were two decks, an upper and a lower, and a hatch and ladder allowed passengers to move between them. There was a small captain's cabin near the boat's stern, and near the bow was a covered section that looked like a carport, where the women, children, and anyone else who needed shelter from the sun could sit. In front of the covered section, there were two large tube-shaped vents intended to allow plenty of fresh air to circulate to the coach-class passengers down below.

The boat was moored at a wooden dock in the city of Ca Mau, an inland port in the southern Mekong Delta near the juncture of the Ganh Hao and Bay Hap rivers. Just a few miles south of Ca Mau the two rivers diverge, with the Ganh Hao turning east toward the South China Sea while the Bay Hap snakes its way west to the Gulf of Thailand. Easy access to both great bodies of water is what made Ca Mau an important shipping center and a logical point of departure for my family.

Transporting our whole family to Ca Mau had involved an intricate ruse. Though we had official permission to leave Vietnam, it was still crucial that no one suspected we were going. Refugees had become not only a big business for the government but an easy target for anyone wanting to make a quick buck. A refugee lived in a kind of limbo; he was no longer a citizen of his home country but not yet a citizen of any other. The government had taken almost all of his life savings, and the moment he stepped out his front door for the last time, he no longer owned a house or property. He owned nothing, he belonged nowhere, and no one liked him—they were either angry that he would leave his native country or jealous that they could not go with him. Worst of all, everything the refugee had left in the world, he was carrying with him—and everyone knew it.

There was an even more important reason to leave secretly: if something went terribly wrong on our voyage, we would need a home to return to, and "terribly wrong" was a definite possibility.

For months prior to our departure, we did everything we could to make our daily routine look as normal as possible. The younger children—Yen, Nikki, Thai, and me—had been told that we were going on a trip, but nothing more. We were excited because our family was going on a sea voyage; what could be more fun than that? A child who had never seen the ocean had very little idea what a sea voyage entailed, but we didn't care. We knew that Mom and Dad would be with us, so what could possibly go wrong?

But Jenny and Bruce were old enough to understand the risks

involved. They had overheard our aunts trading dark stories about refugees who had gone insane from thirst or become so hungry that they turned into cannibals and ate their children. For some reason, Jenny and Bruce didn't seem quite as excited about the trip as the rest of us were.

In the weeks before our departure, my mother gathered rice cakes, dried fruit, and other nonperishable food for the journey, and she made a mixture of powdered lemon and sugar that we could mix with water to drink. We packed clothing but left almost everything else behind, and just before we departed, my mother invited my father's mistress to come to the farm and take anything she wanted. Considering the nature of their relationship, I find that a remarkable act of kindness; many women in my mother's position would have burned everything first.

Jenny and Bruce continued to go to school right up until the day of our departure, not for the sake of their education but to avoid raising suspicion. Every night at dinner my mother and father sternly warned them to say nothing about our plans in school. One careless comment to a friend might be repeated to a parent, and before long everyone in town would be asking questions my family didn't want to answer.

We left the farm in small groups because we knew that a family of ten, all leaving at the same time, would look about as inconspicuous as a wandering herd of water buffalo. Grandmother Truong took the older children, my aunts took the ones in the middle, my mother kept the twins, and my father traveled alone because women traveling with children raised fewer eyebrows. Ca Mau was a well-known port, and everyone knew it was a common point of departure for refugees; so to conceal our destination, we divided our trip there into three legs. First we traveled from the farm to Bac Lieu, which we hoped would look like nothing more than a regular visit to my mother's family home. From Bac Lieu we traveled by bus in the direction of Ca Mau, but we took the precaution of stopping halfway there in case anyone on the bus recognized us; we even spent the night in a temple instead of staying with friends to avoid starting any rumors about our plans. The drive from Soc Trang to Ca Mau takes less than two hours, but my family was so cautious that the trip took us three days to complete.

We arrived in Ca Mau late in the morning of June 12, 1979. The temperature was already approaching ninety degrees and the humidity was over 80 percent and rising. The air was barely moving, and our fellow passengers were dripping with sweat as they stacked their precious possessions in teetering columns all over the crowded dock. Either no one got the memo about baggage restrictions or they chose to ignore it. People seemed to have brought everything they owned: steamer trunks, bedding, pots and pans, rice cookers—even furniture. It was hard to blame them since they were leaving Vietnam for good and knew that anything they left behind would become the government's property. Everyone knew they should bring less, but apparently everyone thought they would be the only ones to bring more.

The families who arrived first began to board the vessel, dragging all their worldly goods behind them; but it quickly became apparent that not everything would fit, and angry arguments began to break out over who had brought too much and what should be left behind. The boarding process ground to a halt, and it looked as if the issue might take days to resolve, but we didn't have days; we had only a few hours to get everyone aboard so that we could depart at night while the river level would be high enough to allow our heavily laden boat to reach the sea without running aground on a sandbar. Under the cover of darkness our boat could slip away without being noticed, and avoiding attention was still important; it was never too late for some local bureaucrat to foul things up.

One of my cousins decided to take charge of the baggage dilemma and devised a simple solution that solved the problem but at the same time made him the most hated man on the boat: he simply walked around the dock, grabbing random suitcases and slinging them into the river. He didn't bother to ask each family which precious heirloom they would prefer to part with; he just grabbed and heaved, and before long the boat was surrounded with suitcases bobbing in the water like pieces of pork in a stew.

My mother was furious that our own cousin had thrown some of our most valuable belongings into the river. Almost everyone lost something precious in the baggage-reduction process—that is, with the exception of Grandmother Chung. Anyone who tried to throw her luggage into the river was likely to find himself treading water beside it. Grandmother Chung even managed to bring her wicker throne along, and she set it beside the captain on the top deck and planted herself on it for the entire voyage.

The dock was crowded with local merchants and vendors who had built their businesses around refugees. It was a shrewd business strategy, since refugees often brought the last of their Vietnamese currency with them and this would be their last opportunity to spend it. While the boat was still loading, my parents handed stacks of money to Jenny, Bruce, and Yen and let them go ashore to buy anything they wanted. Our family had been dirt-poor for the last four years, and none of my brothers and sisters was experienced in handling money, a fact the vendors quickly recognized and took full advantage of. Jenny, Bruce, and Yen were overcharged and shortchanged for everything they bought, but it didn't really matter; if the vendors didn't take the money, it would soon be useless anyway.

Yen found a vendor selling pineapples. He held one out to her and quoted a price.

"How much for all of them?" Yen asked, and she handed the man a stack of money. She lugged an entire box of pineapples back to the boat, and one of our aunts sliced them up and passed them around.

Jenny felt dusty and sticky from our journey to Ca Mau, and she found an entrepreneurial vendor who had constructed a makeshift shower with a wooden stall and a water barrel and hose hanging over it. Jenny asked the price and the vendor told her, "Five thousand dong," so she handed over a stack of money and took the most expensive shower of her life.

Bruce was always hungry, so he bought corn, sugarcane, and anything else that was edible and brought it back to the boat to share with the rest of us. We all stuffed ourselves until our mother warned us that if any of us got diarrhea, we would not be allowed to go on the trip. We didn't believe that threat, but the thought of getting diarrhea was sobering enough to make us stop eating. Our boat was originally designed to carry cargo, not passengers, so a few niceties had been left off—like bathrooms. Several days at sea, 290 passengers, and no bathrooms; I'm not a naval architect, but I think that was a bit of an oversight.

An agent from the Public Security Bureau met us on the dock to take a final head count to make sure the government wasn't being cheated out of any money. We had paid all the required fees and appropriate bribes, but there was also a law that allowed each refugee to take no more than two taels of gold with him when he left the country; any amount he possessed beyond that was required to be turned over to the government. When the PSB agent reminded our group about that law and also reminded us of the severe penalty for disobeying it, some of the passengers began to surrender money they had hidden away.

But when the communists first came to power, each citizen had been required to declare every one of his assets, and those of us who had refused to report them then were not about to hand them over now. My uncle had instructed the people who repaired our boat to hollow out a section in one of the beams below deck, where we could hide things that we didn't want the government to see—like gold. My uncle's intent wasn't simply to defy the government; he just wanted to take enough money along to allow our family a fresh start in a new country; and after losing our house, our furniture and possessions, two rice mills, cars, and our school, my uncle thought the government already had taken enough.

My mother agreed. A seamstress by training, she put those skills to work by sewing jewelry into hidden pockets in our clothing and the hems of our caps. She even sewed American hundred-dollar bills into the lining of my father's pants without telling him. My mother knew Grandmother Chung had raised him to obey authority without question, and if her husband was ever ordered to surrender all of his money, he was likely to do it. My father was a kind and generous man whose kindness could border on compliance, and compliance is not a quality that a smuggler needs. My mother knew the only way to protect the money was for my father to carry it without knowing it was there. My father was a mule—but then, everyone in our family was a mule in one way or another. Even the twins were carrying hidden bits of jewelry or gems; a full diaper makes a terrific hiding place.

It was evening by the time everyone was on board and ready to depart. There were no seats or benches on the boat, so we all sat cross-legged on the rough wooden decks and squeezed in as tightly as possible to make room for everyone. The lucky ones had something to lean against, and the rest just took turns leaning against each other.

Before the boat even left the dock, the passengers below deck had already begun complaining. They were packed together like cattle and forced to share what little space they had with the baggage, food, and fuel. The twin air ducts that were supposed to funnel fresh air to them had no fans; they were nothing more than gaping ducts that were useless until the boat started moving, and even then the antiquated engine would not push the boat faster than seven knots. What the poor souls below deck needed was a brisk sea breeze, and unfortunately for them we were still a long way from the sea.

Because my family was considered the boat's owners, we were allowed to sit on the upper deck. Jenny, Yen, and Nikki sat with our mother and aunts under the covered section while Bruce and my father wandered free. I was only three and a half years old, and I snuggled beside my mother while she held one of the twins in each of her arms.

Just before our departure two local men managed to slip by the PSB agent and sneak aboard our boat. Anyone could have called out and turned the men in, but no one did. We were all refugees, and many of the families on board had paid their very last dong for the chance to escape. Everyone knew these were poor men who had no way to pay the government's exorbitant fees, and we knew they were risking years of imprisonment by attempting to escape. Everyone understood their desperation and pitied their plight, so we allowed them to stay despite the fact that we didn't have an inch of extra space.

It was late at night when our boat finally cast off ropes and slowly pulled away from the dock. The boat's engine made a tinny, rattling sound, not the deep, throaty rumble everyone expected to hear. But at least the boat was finally under way, and that meant air was moving, which was a great relief to everyone below deck. The night was sultry and still, and the only sounds besides the rattling strain of the engine were the rolling chorus of insects from the mangroves and the dull flutter of fruit bats as they dipped low to snatch invisible mosquitoes from the air.

After months of careful planning and fearful secrecy, our final departure should have been a time of loud celebration, but no one spoke a word. Maybe it was the ominous effect of the shadowy mangroves that reached toward us over the black water, or maybe it was just the sobering realization that we were really leaving Vietnam— leaving home, leaving families, leaving ancestors in graves we would never visit again.

It would take all night for our boat to crawl slowly down the narrow Ganh Hao River from Ca Mau to the South China Sea, but by morning the river would widen and the mangroves would grow smaller. Black water would empty into blue, darkness would give way to light, and we would leave everything familiar behind us as we sailed off the map into the unknown.

Part Two

Do not believe that you will reach your
destination without leaving the shore.
—CHINESE PROVERB

	Our first boat from Ca Mau with 292 passengers
	Our fishing boat towed to sea along with three others and set adrift
	Course of the three other fishing boats
	Seasweep's course from Singapore
☆	Point of rescue

Fourteen

FIRST DAYS AT SEA

O UR FIRST DAY AT SEA WAS RELATIVELY SMOOTH, which was a very good thing, considering that few of us had ever been on a boat before, and almost no one had experienced the sea. The black waters of the Ganh Hao River had been as smooth as glass the night before, and some were expecting the sea to be the same.

They were disappointed.

A Vietnamese navy patrol boat had followed us until dawn, when our boat cleared the sandbars at the mouth of the Ganh Hao and entered the South China Sea. No one was sure why the patrol boat was bothering to escort us. Our fear was that they planned to stop us and demand one last bribe, illegally collecting money from people who illegally possessed it, and if they had decided to do so, we would have had no choice but to pay whatever they asked. But one of the sailors just shouted up to us, "You're on your own now," and everyone heaved a sigh of relief when the patrol boat veered off and sped back toward shore.

The weather was good that first day, but the gentle rolling of the sea was enough to give our boat a slight rock; that motion was enough to make even some of us on the top deck queasy, but it was far worse for those down below, who had no horizon line to focus on to steady their lurching stomachs. Those who became violently seasick had no chance of making it to the top deck to lean over a railing, so they just vomited into cups and plastic bags and passed them up to the top deck to be dumped over the side of the boat in a disgusting bucket brigade. Some in our party had been told that eating raw sweet potatoes would prevent seasickness, and they had been faithfully consuming them ever since our voyage began. As it turned out, sweet potatoes had no effect on seasickness, but they did add a lovely orange hue to all those cups and plastic bags. A nauseating odor began to creep over the ship, which caused seasickness to spread like a virus and filled the lower deck with moaning and grumbling.

The moment our boat entered the South China Sea, we turned south, which was about as far as our travel plans went. We had no definite destination in mind because we knew that virtually every country in Southeast Asia had already been overrun with refugees and the welcome mats had been taken in a long time ago. To the north lay China, our ancestral home, but the journey up the coast to mainland China would have been more than a thousand miles, and China was not accepting refugees anyway. We could have headed east toward the Philippines, but that would have meant a voyage of more than nine hundred miles across open sea with no comforting coastline in sight. We had only enough food and diesel fuel for a few days' journey, and every day we spent at sea increased our chances of running into bad weather. That was a risk no one wanted to take— especially those below deck.

It was decided that our best bet was to head south toward Malaysia, fewer than three hundred miles away. We knew Malaysia was not accepting refugees either, but it was a chance we had to take. "Any port in a storm," as the saying goes, and we needed to find a port—any port—before we ran out of fuel and found ourselves at the mercy of a summer typhoon. The one direction we did not consider was west toward Thailand, and it wasn't because of Thailand's official policy toward refugees.

It was the pirates.

The southern half of Thailand is shaped like the letter C, curling around from Cambodia in the north to Malaysia in the south and surrounding the Gulf of Thailand. That long, curling shape gives southern Thailand more than two thousand miles of coastland and has made fishing the dominant industry there for thousands of years. Commercial fishing in the Gulf of Thailand has always been a dangerous and labor-intensive trade, and only large exporters grow rich while the average Thai fisherman barely scrapes by.

There have been pirates in the Gulf of Thailand for centuries. Most of them have just been common fishermen trying to make ends meet, and most piracy has been little more than one fisherman stealing another's catch because stealing fish is easier than fishing. But piracy started to change when the first Vietnamese refugees began to cross the Gulf of Thailand in search of a new home.

At first Thai fishermen were kind to refugees and often stopped to lend free assistance to stranded boats, but when the fishermen realized the refugees could afford to pay for their assistance, they began to charge, then overcharge, then steal. That was when Thai fishermen turned into Thai pirates, and that was when the real horrors began.

Refugees were fleeing with gold and jewelry, not their former country's worthless currency, and that made refugees a perfect target for pirates. Large amounts of foreign currency would have been difficult for fishermen to exchange and hard to explain to Thai authorities, but gold didn't have those problems. Vietnam allowed its refugees to leave the country with two taels of gold per person, which made some boats floating bank vaults. Our boat was probably carrying more than half a million dollars in today's money, and that wasn't counting the gold and jewels that had been smuggled aboard.

Refugees were usually civilians, not soldiers, so they were unarmed and unprotected. There was no country to protect them either; a nation's territorial waters extended only twelve miles from its shores, which meant that in the Gulf of Thailand and the South China Sea there were hundreds of thousands of square miles of unpatrolled and unprotected waters. There was no law at sea, a brutal fact refugees soon discovered for themselves.

Two kinds of pirates prowled the waters of the Gulf of Thailand and the South China Sea: amateurs and professionals. The amateurs were just ordinary Thai fishermen who heard about the floating gold mines and occasionally decided to get in on the action. They could be violent and cruel at times, but they were nothing like the professionals. Professional pirates used large ships powered by three hundred–horsepower engines that no refugee boat could outrun. They were equipped with radar and modern Soviet and American weaponry: fifty-caliber machine guns, M79 grenade launchers, and even antitank weapons. They hunted in wolf packs like German submarines did during World War II: seven or eight boats would form a ring five to ten miles in diameter and wait for a refugee boat to enter; then one of the boats would circle in for the kill. Sometimes the pirate ship would rake the refugee boat with machine-gun fire as the pirates approached, to let everyone know the seriousness of their intentions. At other times they would ram the refugee boat until the hull cracked and the boat began to take on water because there was nothing like a sinking ship to make people cooperative. The usual approach was for the pirate ship to cast its anchors onto the refugee boat and then reel it in until it was close enough to board.

What happened next would be anyone's guess. The pirates' supposed intention was theft, but with no law to restrain them and no concerns about trivial issues like human life and dignity, the atrocities became worse and worse.

Eight months before my family sailed into the South China Sea, a thirty-foot refugee boat called the *KG 0729* left Vietnam with thirty passengers aboard. When their engine died, a Thai pirate ship pulled up alongside and forced all the refugees to board the Thai ship, where the men were searched and robbed and a few were thrown into the sea to drown. The rest were taken below and locked in a refrigerated hold. When one man was unable to remove his wedding ring fast enough, his ring finger was chopped off, and he was beaten to death and thrown into the sea while his horrified wife looked on. The younger women were repeatedly raped over a period of three hours, and when the half-frozen men were brought up from the hold, some were thrown overboard with their hands still tied behind their backs. The survivors were returned to their boat and released—but not before the pirate ship rammed the boat twice in an attempt to sink it.

There were often brave and capable men aboard refugee boats, and many of them had the strength and courage to fight the pirates—but they were often accompanied by wives and children, and they feared what might happen to them if they resisted the pirates and failed. When one refugee boat was attacked by eight Thai pirates, the refugees fought back and prevented them from boarding. In response the pirates called in a second boat that rammed the refugee boat so hard that it split in half and threw everyone into the water. The pirates then began to fish the refugees out of the water one by one, decapitate them, and throw their bodies back into the sea. Out of seventy-six refugees, only sixteen managed to survive.

Such violent and extreme cases sound as though they must have been exceptions, but the truth is they were common events. There was no way to stop the Thai pirates. Though the Royal Thai Navy ordered all of its ships to prevent piracy at sea, almost nothing was done. There was too much water and not enough ships, and the crews on ships the navy did possess weren't particularly motivated to risk their lives in defense of a few worthless refugees.

Piracy was clearly illegal in Thailand, and Thai authorities made the penalties severe, but those penalties only served to make things worse for the refugees because they forced the pirates to make sure there would be no survivors who could testify against them. When one pirate ring was finally arrested, the ringleader turned out to be a respected local merchant who owned a grocery store and sold sup-plies to local fishermen. He was well-known and easily recognized, which made it especially important for him to leave no survivors behind. The pirates became a floating mafia; they were so efficient at eliminating witnesses that to this day no one knows how many refu-gees actually perished at sea, but according to some estimates only one out of two boat people survived. So many refugees were dying at the hands of pirates that legitimate Thai fishermen were forced to abandon entire fishing areas because their nets were dredging up too many human bodies. As one fisherman put it, "The jungle has its tigers and the sea has its pirates. It's something we live with."

The earliest refugees were just robbed and set free, but the pirates' desire for greater profit led them to greater atrocities. Refugees were held for ransom; women were kidnapped and made the objects of repeated assault; young girls were abducted and sold into the sex trade. Piracy was so common that it became expected. A survey was done of a hundred refugee boats that had arrived safely in Indonesia over a four-month period: ninety-six of the boats had been attacked by pirates, an average of four times each. One boat had actually been attacked twenty-three times and somehow managed to survive. Accounts of the atrocities committed against boat people became so regular that relief workers conducting survivor interviews in refugee camps grew tired of repeatedly writing out the words *rape*, *murder*, and *pillage* and replaced them with a three-letter acronym: RMP.

My parents had heard all these stories and more, and still they risked everything by sailing an unarmed ship carrying half a million dollars in gold into a sea that pirates virtually owned. My parents knew they were risking their lives—and ours, too, because children were not exempt from pirate brutality—but still they thought it better to risk drowning at the hands of pirates than to face slow suffocation under communist rule.

On the second day of our voyage, the weather was fair again. Jenny was old enough to be allowed to wander the boat, and she loved to hang over the bow to feel the salt spray on her face and watch the silver flashes of fish leaping alongside the boat. Below deck there were still a few problems; there was supposed to be enough food for everyone, but the unsweetened rice cakes and dehydrated food made everyone thirsty and didn't fill anyone's stomach. The boat had only one cookstove, located near the stern, and it was intended to serve the entire boat, but some hungry passengers grew impatient waiting for their daily allowance of rice porridge and set up their own small stove below deck—which promptly tipped over and caused everyone to panic and scramble.

We were tired and cramped and hungry, but we had a lot to be thankful for. We had safely escaped from Vietnam, our family was all together, and Grandmother Chung was seated on her rightful throne, glaring like a lighthouse to guide our way to our new home. Blue skies, calm seas, leaping fish—it was a beautiful day at sea.

Until noon—that was when my mother looked at the horizon and spotted the ominous silhouette of a ship growing larger by the minute and heading in our direction.

For the first time in her life, my mother wished she wasn't the second-most beautiful woman in Bac Lieu.

Fifteen

PIRATES

SOME OF THE MEN ON OUR BOAT ACTUALLY TRIED TO wave the ship down because at that distance there was no way to tell what kind of ship it was. Pirates were not the only ones operating in the South China Sea; the ship might have been a commercial vessel that could replenish our dwindling water supply or point us in the direction of a refugee camp.

But as the ship came closer, the men stopped waving. It was a fishing trawler, easily twice the size of our boat, with a wooden hull that was black from years spent at sea. The ship had a forward deckhouse and an aft working deck, where twin wooden outriggers projected from the mast like a pair of antennae. A knotted gray trawl net draped from each of them, and cables crisscrossed everywhere like the strands of a spider's web.

The ship approached from the east at high speed, apparently hoping to overtake us before we could speed away, but if they had known how old and feeble our engine was, they could have taken their time. My father stood and watched as the ship drew closer, and he caught a glimpse of a name on the ship's bow. He couldn't read the name, but his familiarity with Asian languages told him it was written in Thai.

Everyone on our boat held their breath as the ship approached; there was no way to be sure of the ship's intentions. The fact that it was a Thai fishing boat meant nothing. There were honest Thai fishermen, too, and everyone prayed this would turn out to be a crew of good Samaritans stopping to offer a helping hand.

But their intentions became clear when the trawler did not slow down.

It rammed us amidships with a tremendous thump and rocked our boat hard to starboard. The loudest screams came from below deck because the coach-class passengers didn't see the ship approaching and had no way to anticipate the impact. They were completely blindsided, and their screams grew even louder when a spray of water began to shoot through a crack in the hull.

As the stern swung around and the ship came alongside ours, we saw men lined up along the gunnels, clinging to the steel rigging with one hand and holding knives in the other. Some were dressed like ordinary fishermen, in fish-stained shorts and tattered T-shirts, while others were shirtless, their dark-skinned shoulders and chests emblazoned with tattoos that looked like scrolling veins. Some of them wore bandanas pulled back tight, and many had painted their faces with bright zigzags and symbols to make them look as frightening as possible. They waved their knives in the air and shouted, and when their ship drew close enough, they began to pour onto our boat like rats.

Fifteen pirates boarded our boat, and when they did, everyone began to scream and cry. Some of the women were wearing gold necklaces, and they quickly slipped them off and tucked them under their legs to hide them while others removed their own earrings and held them out in cupped hands to keep the pirates from ripping them off their ears and taking flesh with them.

My mother was worried about more important things than gold.

Jenny was twelve, and Yen was only nine, but pirates had been known to assault girls even younger, and my mother knew both of them were in danger. The women on our boat had all heard about the tricks that other refugee women had tried to avoid being singled out and raped. Some had tried smearing their faces with diesel oil, to make themselves look dirty and unappealing, while others tried basting themselves with a repugnant fish sauce, called *nuoc mam*. But pirates knew those tricks, too, and all they did was demand that the woman bathe first.

My mother pulled Yen in close and shoved her down to make her look smaller, and she covered Jenny's head with a towel to try to disguise her as an old woman in a shawl. Some of the single women grabbed for other women's children and held them in their laps, hoping that a mother might be shown more compassion—but pirates were not known for compassion. Other women pretended to be seasick or ill or anything else they could think of that might make a pirate pass them by. Women who had spent their entire lives making themselves as attractive as possible were now frantically trying everything they could think of to make themselves unappealing.

The pirates waved their weapons and shouted demands, but no one on our boat spoke Thai or could understand a word they were saying. But the pirates didn't wait for someone to translate; they just charged around the top deck, jerking the jewelry from women's necks and ears and demanding rings and watches from the men. One of the pirates ducked under the covered section, where my family was huddled together. When my mother saw him coming, she quickly pulled off her earrings and dropped them into her bra, but it was too late—the pirate saw what she had done and grabbed at her shirt to get the earrings back. But retrieving my mother's earrings was apparently more trouble than they were worth, and when the pirate noticed that Yen, sitting beside her, was wearing earrings, too, he shoved my mother aside and pointed a knife at Yen's throat instead. When my aunt saw what was about to happen, she pulled one of the earrings from Yen's ear and handed it to the pirate, who then ripped off the other earring himself.

The pirates worked quickly, almost frantically, screaming and shouting as they rushed around the deck, grabbing any shiny thing that caught their eye. They searched my father and ripped his pants in the process, but for the most part the pirates took only what was easily accessible. When they found books or paper, they ripped them apart and threw them on the deck, acting as if they planned to start a fire and torch our boat before they left. That was the most terrifying thought of all because our boat was more than a means of transportation for us—it was life itself. While we were at sea, our boat was our country and our home. If it stayed afloat, we lived, and if not, we died. The thought of being trapped in a flaming tomb started a panic, and the women began to beg for mercy and plead with the pirates to take whatever they wanted and go.

Grandmother Chung shouted at the men to leave everyone alone, but they ignored her. She was clutching a framed image of Quan Âm, a Chinese goddess of compassion, mercy, and kindness. When the pirates snatched it out of her hands and threw it on the deck, it broke apart, revealing jewels my grandmother had hidden inside.

Oddly enough, the pirates never bothered to go below deck, though half of our passengers were down there, and the pirates could have doubled their take by doing so. But that was more than a simple oversight on their part. There was a reason they worked so quickly: they were afraid too.

These pirates were young. Most of them looked to be in their twenties, and some were even teenagers. They were doing their best to puff themselves up to look and sound as terrifying as possible, but they were too young and too skinny to be physically intimidating. Some of them carried knives, but they were small boning knives that fishermen used, not the infamous long knives that Thai pirates used to mutilate their victims. Some of the pirates weren't wielding knives at all—they were carrying screwdrivers. These pirates were not only young and skinny but underequipped, and with limitations like that, the only way they could terrify and intimidate was to bluster and bluff.

My father noticed that one of the pirates looked different from the others and seemed to be their leader. The man did not look Thai; he looked Chinese, and he was the only one who had not painted his face. When the man noticed my father staring at him, he turned and said under his breath, "Don't be afraid. It'll be okay." My father began to realize we were being threatened with only hand tools and the pirates who wielded them were almost as frightened as we were.

There were only 15 of them and more than 290 of us, and our party included some strong young men. My father and uncle and the other men began to whisper back and forth about the possibility of fighting back and throwing the pirates off our boat. Looking back, my father thinks they could have done it; they could have overwhelmed the pirates with numbers, disarmed them, recovered all the stolen jewelry and gold, and probably could have stolen their ship.

But no one did a thing because it was not the pirates they feared—it was the stories.

They had heard so many stories about confrontations between pirates and refugees that ended in horrifying ways—with men forced to watch while their wives and daughters were abused and mothers forced to watch while their babies were cast into the sea. It didn't matter if the stories were true—they were true to us. The only source of information about pirate atrocities came from interviews with survivors who made it to refugee camps and recounted their ordeals. Their stories were terrible, but there was no way to know if they were typical. Did all pirates commit violent atrocities? Our timid pirates didn't seem to want to harm anyone; were they the exception or the rule? Were all pirates monsters, or did they turn into monsters only when they were resisted? Some said that half of all refugee boats never made it to land—what happened to them? Did vicious pirates ram and sink them all, or were some of them lost in storms? Did some of them have second thoughts, turn around, and return to Vietnam, leaving those waiting for them to imagine the worst? Or did some of the leaky old boats that desperate refugees were forced to take to sea just gradually take on water until they disappeared beneath the waves? So little was really known, and the less that was known, the more there was to fear.

The men on our boat did nothing because they didn't dare. It wasn't what *did* happen that paralyzed them with fear; it was the thought of what *could* happen. That fear is something all refugees experience because refugees are forced to sail across pirate waters all their lives. So many things can go wrong for a refugee, but it's the fear of what could go wrong that haunts us.

Fifteen minutes after the attack began, the pirates scrambled back onto their trawler, carrying handfuls of stolen booty, and the ship roared its engines and sailed away. Everyone wondered if the pirates were really leaving, and we waited to see if the trawler would come back and ram us again and again until our hull cracked open and we sank into the sea. But they just continued on until they were once again a speck on the horizon.

When the attack was finally over, no one said a word. It was as though a bomb had gone off and sent a shock wave through the ship that left everyone stunned and mute. Those on the top deck were the ones who had been robbed and threatened, but the experience had been almost as terrifying for those below. All they could do was stare up helplessly at the open hatch, listen to the feet stomping on the planks over their heads and the women pleading for mercy, and imagine what was happening to their fellow passengers—and wonder if they would be next.

No one knew what to say because no one knew what to think or feel. What had just happened? We had been robbed, but we were alive and unharmed. The women had been traumatized, but no one had been assaulted. Our hull had been cracked, but the leak was repaired quickly. We had been attacked by Thai pirates, but our pirates turned out to be inexperienced amateurs. Should we celebrate or weep? Had we been blessed or cursed? We didn't even know if our ordeal was over. Were our pirates working alone, or were they part of a ring that would send other ships like a pack of wild dogs closing in on a wounded animal, each one tearing off a piece of our flesh until nothing remained?

What we did know was that if we had been attacked once, it could happen again—and if it did, there was nothing we could do about it. That was the realization that left us stunned: we were help-less. Even a bunch of skinny teenagers armed with nothing more than screwdrivers could walk onto our boat and take anything they wanted—and we didn't dare do anything about it.

My father looked at the horizon. There was no sight of land.

Sixteen

ONE MAN'S BURDEN

S TAN MOONEYHAM HAD PROMISED ED HILL THAT HE would look into the problem of the boat people, and to Stan "looking into" something meant studying it inside and out. He read everything he could find on the subject, and before long he had a thorough understanding of the situation.

Stan learned that when South Vietnam had fallen in April 1975, thousands of Vietnamese immediately left the country by boat, but those first-wave refugees had US Seventh Fleet ships, such as the carriers *Hancock*, *Okinawa*, and *Midway*, waiting to pick them up offshore, and those refugees were quickly resettled in other countries. Over the next two years the number of refugees declined, which made the refugee problem small enough for most nations to temporarily overlook. But by 1977, the number of refugees fleeing by boat was increasing again. Tens of thousands were fleeing every month, and because of Vietnam's growing animosity toward its Chinese citizens, 60 percent of all boat people were Chinese.

But the statistic that Stan found most alarming was that the death rate among boat people was reported to be as high as 50 percent—of every two refugees who left Vietnam, only one survived.

With those sobering facts in hand, Stan headed for Washington to meet with State Department officials and members of Congress to gather advice on the best way for World Vision to tackle the problem—but to Stan's dismay he was unanimously cautioned to do nothing. It was an international political minefield, they told him. Surrounding nations had been overrun by refugees and were refusing to accept any more; a foreign mercy ship on the South China Sea would be a slap in the face to those countries and would only create more hostility. It was an impossible situation, they said, and a young organization like World Vision that was still establishing credibility could not afford to have a colossal embarrassment on its hands.

Stan left Washington, feeling the same way he had felt that Sunday evening in Ed Hill's study. The congressmen and State Department officials were right; they had good reasons, logical reasons, practical reasons, for avoiding the problem entirely—but it didn't matter. The image of that refugee woman's face still haunted Stan, and he was bound and determined to do whatever he could to help.

Stan knew from his fund-raising experience that facts alone often are not enough to motivate people to take action; sometimes they have to *see* the problem, they have to *feel* it. That was not the kind of information Stan could get from books, so he decided to travel to Southeast Asia to witness the problems facing refugees with his own eyes.

He began by touring the refugee camps in Thailand, Malaysia, and the Philippines, and the conditions he found there were even more appalling than he expected. Refugees were packed into over-crowded shantytowns; there was an almost total lack of sanitation; the food was rat-infested; the water was fouled by sewage—they were the same problems World Vision was helping to alleviate all over the world; only here the problems were multiplied because of the sheer number of refugees in each camp.

In the Philippines Stan toured a cargo ship called the *Tung An* that was jammed with twenty-two hundred refugees who had been sitting in Manila Harbor for two months. Every inch of space on the ship was occupied, and a thousand of the refugees had been forced to remain in the cargo hold on top of a load of cattle feed that had gotten wet and had become a breeding ground for hundreds of thousands of worms and crawling insects. Stan had witnessed suffering all over the world, but when he emerged from that cargo hold, he could barely stand up.

After his travels in Southeast Asia, Stan had two kinds of facts at his disposal—the cold statistics that could appeal to the rational mind and the graphic firsthand stories that were able to reach the heart. Doubly armed and confident that he would find a warmer reception this time, he traveled not only to Washington but also to Geneva, Canberra, Ottawa, Bangkok, Kuala Lumpur, and Singapore in search of advice and support for his mission.

He found none.

Once again he was told to steer clear of the boat people problem. No country would agree to accept more refugees even if Stan found a way to rescue them. Thailand, Malaysia, and Singapore were especially hostile to his idea since they had already borne the brunt of the refugee problem. A government official in Canberra told him, "Don't give them enough gas to get here."

Stan returned from his travels discouraged but undeterred. "I came to this conclusion," he said. "Any idea opposed by seven governments with accompanying threats couldn't be all bad."

But he did have a dilemma: What was the point of rescuing refugees if there would be no place to drop them off?

The last stop on Stan's seven-capital tour was Singapore, where he met with the US ambassador, John Holdridge. The ambassador was sympathetic to Stan's cause, but he saw no way around the problem either. As long as surrounding nations were unwilling to accept refugees, he saw little point in rescuing them.

Stan rode back to his hotel completely discouraged. He felt a deep burden for the boat people, and he was willing to do anything he could to help them, but so far his efforts had been stymied at every turn. Stan was sharing a taxi with a World Vision colleague named Hal Barber, and Hal suddenly had an idea.

"Why do we have to rescue them?" Hal asked. "Why not just resupply them? We could load a ship with food, water, clothing—whatever they need to survive at sea. We could even offer to repair their boats or fix their engines if they need it. Then we could just send them on their way."

That was the solution Stan had been searching for, and it was so simple he couldn't believe he had overlooked it. They didn't have to rescue the refugees; they could just resupply them. And why not? That was exactly what World Vision was doing for the poor and hungry all over the world—they didn't remove people from their desperate situations; they just provided assistance for them while they were there. Stan knew Hal's idea did not solve the ultimate problem because as long as the refugees remained at sea, they were in mortal danger. But at least it was something. If they could help the boat people survive long enough to reach land, who knows how many might be saved?

Stan's burden was now a project, and he gave the project a name that suited its purpose: Operation Seasweep.

First they needed a ship, and the decision was made to charter one, rather than buy one, until their concept had proven successful. The ship they chartered was a 327-foot-long World War II relic called the *Cal Loader*. The *Cal Loader* was an LST, an awkward military acronym for "Landing Ship, Tank," which was designed with a flat bottom and a bow that could open like a pair of doors to allow tanks to roll out onto a beach. The ship had been designed to make amphibious beach landings, but it was adequate for World Vision's purposes since it was relatively inexpensive and had the facilities to house a crew and enough room to hold plenty of cargo.

Next a crew had to be recruited. A man named John Calder from New Zealand was named project director, and Burt Singleton from the US staff of World Vision became director of operations on the ship. There was an Indian doctor named T. N. Chandler, who had a two-room medical clinic at his disposal, as well as two Chinese nurses, Rosemary Ng and Regina Loh. The captain of the ship was Filipino, and the crew was a mix of different Asian ethnic groups, who were responsible for the daily operation of the ship. The cargo bay of the LST was loaded with food, water, diesel fuel, medical supplies, and even spare parts for the three-cylinder Yangma diesel engines that most of the smaller refugee boats employed.

It had been only six months since that moment in Ed Hill's study, when Stan first stared at that photo of a terrified refugee woman and her daughter. Now he had a ship, a crew, and a mission, and as the *Cal Loader* sailed out of Singapore Harbor he found himself wishing Ed Hill could be standing beside him.

When the ship left Singapore, it headed due east, and once it passed the hundred-year-old Horsburgh Lighthouse the British East India Company had set in place to mark the entrance to the Straits of Singapore, the *Cal Loader* was officially in the South China Sea.

It wasn't long before they encountered their first refugee vessel, a small boat with just twenty-one passengers aboard. When Stan and his crew saw it was damaged and taking on water, their instinct was to get everyone off the boat right away, but they knew they had to stick to their original strategy of resupply versus rescue. It was possible the boat could be repaired, and they had brought along tools and materials for exactly this kind of situation.

They towed the boat behind the *Cal Loader* while the ship's engineers attempted to make repairs; but the boat was damaged too badly, and by nightfall it was decided to take the fifteen women and children aboard the *Cal Loader* as a precaution. Around midnight the refugee boat suddenly broke apart and sank, and the six men aboard were thrown into the black water with it. The women and children aboard the *Cal Loader* began to scream and point at the water, where their husbands and sons had been standing moments before, and the ship immediately turned hard to starboard and swung its searchlight around to illuminate the area.

Five of the six men were located and pulled from the sea before they could drown, but the sixth man was nowhere to be found. He was the son of one of the women aboard, and she was so grief-stricken at the thought of losing her child that she tried to throw herself into the sea to join him in death. But the crew held the weeping woman back and continued to search; and after circling the area several more times, the crew eventually found the young man clinging to a plastic water container the *Cal Loader* had lowered to the dehydrated refugees when they first found them. It was a strange irony: Stan and his crew were supposed to resupply and not rescue, but by resupplying the boat with water, they had inadvertently rescued that young man from drowning.

Now there were twenty-one refugees aboard the *Cal Loader*, and there was no boat to which to return them. Stan knew he had a problem. This was exactly the kind of situation he was supposed to avoid, but he had had no choice. What was he supposed to do, just stand there and watch while twenty-one men, women, and children disappeared beneath the water of the South China Sea? Stan felt confident that he had a perfectly justifiable reason for rescuing these refugees—but that didn't mean the surrounding nations would agree with him.

And they didn't. Malaysia flatly refused to allow the refugees to come ashore, and it took two weeks of negotiations before Thailand finally agreed to take them—and only after the United Nations High Commissioner for Refugees promised to arrange resettlement. The refugees had nowhere to go during that time and were forced to remain aboard the *Cal Loader*, which put the ship out of commission fourteen days while the negotiations ground along. That was unacceptable to Stan. The twenty-one lives he had saved were priceless and worth every bit of his time and effort, but who could say how many other refugees might have perished while the system crawled along at a snail's pace?

He decided to try a different plan. John Calder was sent to buy a fishing boat in the Malaysian coastal town of Kuantan. He managed to find one for three thousand dollars that was capable of holding a hundred refugees, though he never let on to the sellers what the boat was intended to do. Fortunately fishing was one of the chief industries in Kuantan, and the boat could be left docked among hundreds of similar boats without raising any suspicions.

It wasn't long before the *Cal Loader* encountered another refugee boat, and that boat was in even worse condition than the first one and quickly sank. This time seventy-three refugees were taken aboard, and that was when the new plan went into action. The ship sent a coded message to Calder, instructing him to bring the fishing boat to a rendezvous point just outside Malaysia's twelve-mile limit in international waters. That was an important precaution because if anything went wrong, Stan didn't want to find himself and his crew at the mercy of an angry Malaysian court.

When the two vessels rendezvoused, the seventy-three refugees were transferred to the fishing boat. The boat had been outfitted with a compass, navigational charts, and enough food and water to take them just about anywhere they wanted, though it was learned later that the refugees decided to take their chances in Malaysia and managed to reach a refugee camp there.

It was not a bad plan, Stan thought. At least it seemed to be an improvement over the old plan because it had taken only two days for the *Cal Loader* to rescue the seventy-three refugees and let them find their own home, instead of two weeks to find a home for them. But it was an expensive plan—Malaysian authorities had confiscated the fishing boat, and three thousand dollars was a lot to pay for each new batch of refugees.

Stan and his crew continued to sail the South China Sea in search of refugee boats, but soon they encountered another problem. The *Cal Loader*, a World War II–era landing ship, was designed to sit shallow in the water so it could run itself aground and allow the tanks it carried to roll out onto dry land. When the *Cal Loader* was unloaded, its bow sat less than four feet underwater; the ship practically sat on *top* of the water, and that was a problem. The ship was just too small; a vessel that operates on the high seas needs a greater mass and a deeper draft to give it stability against the wind and waves. June to December was typhoon season in the South China Sea, when the winds could blow with hurricane force and the waves could be as tall as buildings. In seas like that the *Cal Loader* would roll over like an empty milk carton, which meant the ship would have to be out of commission for half the year.

By late 1978, Operation Seasweep had to be suspended for the remainder of the year. They had already been pushing their luck by continuing operations through the temperamental summer months; by fall, a typhoon could strike the area almost without warning, and it made no sense to take refugees aboard a ship that was in danger of sinking too.

At year's end Stan looked back on what Operation Seasweep had accomplished: 94 refugees in two different boats had been rescued from certain death and delivered to refugee camps; another 134 refugees in three other boats had been resupplied and probably saved from a slow death at sea. Those results were encouraging, but Stan knew they could do much better, and they would have to if they wanted to make even a small dent in the overall problem. More than two hundred lives spared in just a few months of operation—but how many more could be rescued if Operation Seasweep could continue throughout an entire year?

What Stan needed was a bigger ship.

Seventeen

LAND AT LAST

L AND!" SOMEONE SHOUTED, AND EVERYONE ON THE TOP
deck scrambled to their feet and pushed toward the bow to
stare in the direction he was pointing. It was just a dark line
across the distant horizon, and one of the men said it was probably
just a line of clouds and sat down again—but when details began to
be visible, we knew we had found land.

It was around noon on the third day of our journey, and for the
third day in a row, the skies were sunny and clear. But the beautiful weather had done nothing to lift the spirits of the passengers
on our boat; the general mood remained somber and fearful after
the pirate attack the previous day. An elderly man below deck had
begun to suffer from severe dehydration from the combined effect
of 145 bodies packed tightly around him and the hot, stagnant air
that the twin vents were supposed to relieve but didn't. We were
tired, we were hungry, and we were terrified into numbness by the
thought that the next pirates we encountered might have a lot more
experience.

But the moment land was sighted, everyone's mood changed.
We were not going to die at sea after all; we were going to make it.
Our boat was intact, our food and water had held out, and we had

managed to avoid the first typhoon of the season. Our endless journey suddenly became endurable, and everyone began to talk excitedly.

We had found land, but we had no idea what land we had found. It was definitely not an island because it spanned the entire horizon from east to west. It must have been some country's mainland, and since we had maintained a strict heading of south by southwest, it could only have been the Malay Peninsula—either the southern tip of Thailand or Malaysia itself. As we soon learned, we had found our way to the state of Terengganu on the east coast of Malaysia.

There were no houses or buildings anywhere in sight—just a wide strip of tawny sand bordered by a dense line of palm trees. The area looked desolate, and we couldn't help wondering how far from civilization we were landing. Someone suggested that we sail up and down the coast until we found a more promising site to land, but then we saw something that told us we had come to the right place: there was another refugee boat already there. It was beached bow-first on the sand and rested askew like a sunken shipwreck. The name on the stern told us that the boat had come from the city of Mỹ Tho in the Mekong Delta not far from our home in Soc Trang. They were fellow refugees from Vietnam, and the similar timing of their departure meant they were probably Chinese just like us. Suddenly our desolate landing site was beginning to seem like a family reunion.

We saw no sign of the other refugees as our boat approached the beach. We took that as an encouraging sign because it meant they had probably moved inland and possibly even found a refugee camp that would accept them. If we could land nearby, we might be able to pick up their trail and follow them. Picking a specific landing spot wasn't difficult because there were no docks or piers anywhere in sight. We had an entire beach to choose from, and all we needed to do was throttle up our little engine and run our boat up on the sand just as the other refugees had done. Speed was crucial because the deeper we managed to beach our boat, the shallower the water would be that we would have to wade through to get ashore; and for people who couldn't swim, that was an important consideration.

Everyone sat down and grabbed hold of what they could while

the captain coaxed the engine to maximum rpm, but as our boat approached the shoreline, local villagers began to pour out of the woods and rush toward our landing site. They shouted to us, but no one could hear them over the roar of the surf and the whine of our engine. When they waved to us, we all waved back, but the looks on their faces told us that this was not a welcoming committee.

The Malaysians were telling us to turn around and go back, but it was too late for that. Even if our feeble engine had possessed enough power to stop the boat's forward momentum and bring the boat around, where were we supposed to go? Back to Vietnam with no place to live? Back across the South China Sea without enough food or water to survive the voyage? Back into pirate-infested waters or into a summer typhoon that could swallow our boat, with a single wave? We had given up everything to get this far, and we had nothing to return to. Turning back meant death, so our only alternative was to run the boat aground and deal with the Malaysians later.

But we realized that even if we beached our boat, the Malaysians could still force us to turn back. We were arriving at midday when the tide was low; all they would have to do was wait until nightfall when the tide came in again and lifted our boat off the sand—then they could push us out to sea again. The only way to prevent that from happening was not only to beach our boat but scuttle it.

Some of the men rushed below deck and used any piece of metal they could find to hack away at the thick planks of the hull until cracks appeared and water began to trickle in. The men had to time the sabotage just right; if they scuttled the boat too soon, we would find ourselves in deep water, and if they waited too long, the Malaysians might see what we were doing—and they looked angry enough already.

When water began to gush into the boat, the lower-deck passengers grabbed their possessions and scrambled up the ladder to higher ground. While everyone was climbing up, my uncle was climbing down because he had hidden gold and jewels in a secret compartment below deck, and he wasn't about to let them go down with the ship. My mother and father never saw that hidden money and had no idea how much was there. As always, my uncle and grandmother controlled the family finances, and in their view the arrangement hadn't changed just because we had left Vietnam. My own family left the boat with only the money and jewelry that my mother had managed to hide on each of us, and it wasn't much.

Those who could swim preferred to take their chances in roiling surf, instead of a sinking ship, and they jumped into the water before we even reached the beach. The rest of us braced ourselves for impact, and we were all thrown forward when the boat hit the sand and ground to a halt. Then everyone began to pour over the sides of the boat; able adults went first, plunging into tepid, chest-deep water and struggling through the surf until they collapsed on the sand. Jenny, Bruce, and Yen jumped on their own, which was a dangerous thing to do, considering that Yen was only nine at the time and water that is chest-deep for an adult is deep enough for a nine-year-old to drown in. When their feet hit bottom, the water was well over their heads, and they came up spluttering and coughing. Some of the men remained in the water to assist anyone having difficulty by hooking their arms around them and hauling them to the beach.

For the older passengers the jump was too much, and they had to be lowered over the side of the ship into the water. That included Grandmother Chung, which was a lot like lowering a cat into a bathtub. Her throne went with her, of course, but at least she wasn't seated in it at the time. My mother's father was seventy-eight and one of the oldest people on board; he had to be lowered carefully because he walked with a cane and his bones were brittle enough to break.

When my father jumped into the water, he turned, held up his arms, and waited for my mother to drop the younger children down to him. She started with the oldest and worked her way down: first Nikki, then Thai, then me, and finally the twins. Deciding the right moment to let go of us was not easy for my mother because only the bow of our boat was resting on the sand; the rest of the hull was still floating, and the powerful surf rocked the boat back and forth like the pendulum of a clock. Our boat was designed to sit high in the water, and with the weight of more than 290 people removed, it sat even higher. It was a long way for a young child to fall, even into water. My mother had to hold us one at a time at the port side railing and wait for the boat to rock forward until the railing was closest to the water—then she had to let go.

Imagine dropping your children from the side of a rocking ship into pounding surf and hoping they come up again. I cannot imagine what was going through my mother's mind when she released each of us into midair and watched us drop like plummeting rocks into our father's waiting arms. But my father could not risk trying to catch us before we hit the water; we were going too fast for that. He had to wait and let us hit the water first, then scoop us up when we bobbed back to the surface like corks.

I have no memory of Bac Lieu or Soc Trang or our little farm with its ducks and geese and pigs. My very first memory in life is the moment I was dropped into that warm ocean water on the beach in Malaysia. One moment my mother was holding me under both arms; then suddenly I was weightless, drifting like a leaf through the noise and chaos all around me—then I plunged into a silent, blue haze of half-bodies wading through clouds of sand. I never shut my eyes. I just stared wide-eyed at this strange new world as my body slowly started to rise. A moment later I felt a pair of strong hands grab me by the arms and pull me from the water, and I found myself staring into my father's face. I thought I had forgotten the entire experience until twenty years later, when I stood on a beach for the second time in my life; as soon as I smelled saltwater, the memory came rushing back to me.

The twins were the last to go, and then my mother jumped after them. Within minutes my entire family was lying on the hot sand, shaken and panting but safely ashore.

The Malaysian villagers were like a gaggle of cackling geese gathered around us, shouting angrily as they pointed to the sea. We couldn't understand a word they were saying, which wasn't surprising, considering Peninsular Malaysians speak more than forty languages. But we knew what they were trying to say, and to be honest we really didn't care. We were too tired and too relieved to be standing on solid ground again.

The cold reception was more than a lack of Malaysian hospitality. In the four years since the fall of South Vietnam, more than 300,000 refugees had fled Vietnam and run their boats aground in "nations of first asylum" like Malaysia, Indonesia, Singapore, Thailand, and the Philippines. Malaysia alone took in 124,000 of them, and at first they were received with compassion and kindness—but their sheer numbers began to overwhelm the job market and social services of the country. Ordinary Malaysians like these villagers had borne the brunt of it because they were the ones competing for those jobs and social services. By the time our family arrived in Malaysia, the nation was suffering from what some have called "compassion fatigue," and our beach reception committee wanted to make it very clear that our kind were no longer welcome there.

My father considered telling them we were Chinese, hoping to play the ethnic exemption card that had worked so well for us in Vietnam, but when he learned the Malaysians hate the Chinese, he decided to keep it to himself. There had been a long and bitter conflict in Malaysia between capitalism and communism, and most of the communist insurgents had been Chinese. In their eyes we were not only social parasites but possible communist agents, and that made us the worst of all possible refugees.

When the boat had begun to founder, everyone had abandoned ship so quickly that they left many of their possessions behind—which were now underwater. Under the disapproving glare of the Malaysian villagers, some of the men began to return to the boat to salvage anything that might be useful on the beach. One man retrieved a combination ax-hammer, but it was no ordinary hand tool because the handle was hollow and filled with gems. Others retrieved cook pots, tarps, and any food or water they could find.

An hour later a military truck pulled up on the beach, and two dozen soldiers dressed in khaki shorts and green caps and armed with bolt-action rifles began to off-load and surround us. Apparently someone had tipped them off that another boatload of pesky refugees had arrived and sent for the soldiers to keep the villagers' displeasure from getting out of hand. The soldiers added to the confusion by trying to shout their orders above the din, and when they did we were surprised to find that they were speaking English. Malaysian was the official language of the country, but because of Malaysia's history as a British crown colony, English was a common language too. My father knew only bits of English, but my mother's younger brother, Uncle Lam, was fluent, and he became our official translator.

Uncle Lam told the officer in charge that our boat had been irreparably damaged and we had been lucky to make it to the beach before it foundered. The look on the officer's face made it clear what he was thinking: *Malaysia must be the luckiest country in the world.*

The officer waved off Uncle Lam's bald-faced lie and demanded, "Who's in charge here?"

Uncle Lam hesitated. The captain had guided our boat across the sea, but now that we had landed he was no longer in command. Our family was the majority shareholder in the boat, but that didn't mean we were in charge. Technically, no one was in charge—but that answer didn't satisfy the officer.

He divided our group into men and women and made us line up separately on the beach, then marched down the lines, demanding, "Who's in charge?"

He eyed my father and his older brother suspiciously because they were a head taller than anyone else, and in his mind height implied authority. When a few of the men began to nod sheepishly and point to the both of them, the officer's suspicions were confirmed, and he dragged my father and uncle out of line and forced them to kneel.

"Who else? Who else is in charge here?"

By the time the officer was finished, he had randomly selected five or six "leaders" from our group who knelt before him in the sand.

"You can't stay here!" the officer kept shouting, and the louder he shouted, the angrier he became until he lifted his rifle and brought the butt down hard on my father's shoulder. My father cried out and raised his arms to try to shield his head, but that only made things worse. The officer turned to my uncle and delivered the same blow, then started bringing the butt of his rifle down like a jackhammer until both men were barely conscious.

Then something happened that no one in my family had ever seen before. Grandmother Chung stepped out of the line of women, dropped to her knees in front of the officer, and begged him to have mercy on her sons. My grandmother was a fiercely proud woman, and that was probably the first and only time in her life that she had ever begged for anything. But as thick-skinned as she was, her sons were her whole life, and she knew that at the officer's whim both of them could die.

The moment the beatings began, our entire group had begun to shout and wail, and the officer was getting annoyed. He ordered us to be silent and emphasized his point by firing his rifle once into the sand—but the muzzle was so close to my father's ear when the shot was fired that for an instant he thought he was dead. The bullet missed him, but the blast was so loud my father temporarily lost hearing in one ear.

The officer eventually realized the beatings were accomplishing nothing other than allowing him to vent his frustration over the fact that yet another batch of annoying refugees had arrived on his beach and had become his responsibility. He needed time to consider what to do. The sun was setting by then, and he knew he had to contain our group before some of us tried to escape under cover of darkness. He ordered his soldiers to make a circle around us with a rope, and that enclosure became our world.

"No one crosses this rope," he ordered. "Cross the rope, and we shoot you."

Two hundred ninety-plus exhausted refugees spread out the handful of tarps retrieved from the boat, formed a crossword puzzle of bodies on the still-warm sand, and went to sleep.

Eighteen

BLOOD ON THE SAND

W<small>E WOKE UP HUNGRY AND THIRSTY. S</small><small>OME OF THE</small> fathers in the group stood at the rope perimeter and pled with the Malaysian soldiers, who were not particularly sympathetic after having to stand guard over us all night long. "We have children," the fathers said in broken English, and when they pointed back to our boat, the guards understood and began to escort them one at a time to retrieve any food or clothing the men could find. Unfortunately most of the food had been stored on the lower deck, which was now underwater, so they found very little that was still edible.

The skies were clear that first day on the beach, and the sunrise over the South China Sea had been breathtaking, but as the sun climbed higher in the sky, the sand underneath us began to grow uncomfortably hot. When my mother leaped from our boat, she had somehow managed to grab one small bag and take it with her. Along with a few other things, the bag contained a plastic tarp that she was now trying to rig into a makeshift tent to shelter us from the sun. No one knew how long we would be on that beach or what the next step of our journey would entail. The disgruntled villagers had returned to their kampong houses, the guards looked as bored as we were, and no one seemed to be in a hurry to do anything. Our exodus seemed to be turning into an extended camping trip.

My immediate family along with my mother's family set up camp on one side of the rope enclosure while Grandmother Chung and my uncle and his family chose the opposite side. That left my father caught in the middle because he was a member of both families. He spent his entire day hurrying back and forth to see what he could do to help both families, and my mother and Grandmother Chung took turns accusing him of disloyalty whichever way he went.

Our one consoling thought was that there was no sign of the refugees who had arrived on the boat before us, which gave us hope that the Malaysian authorities didn't plan to leave us here forever. With that thought to comfort us, we settled in and did our best with whatever we had to make our campsite more livable.

Then another boat arrived.

This boat was twice the size of ours and held five hundred refugees, which was enormous by our group's standards but not particularly impressive to the Malaysians. Transporting refugees out of Vietnam had become a lucrative business for regional smuggling syndicates, and the Malaysians were used to seeing fifteen-hundred-ton-steel-hulled freighters that carried two thousand refugees at a time. Those refugees were sometimes left to rot on board the freighters because the syndicates lost interest in them the moment they left Vietnam. But poorer refugees were forced to flee any way they could, and unscrupulous smugglers saw an opportunity to make a profit from them; that combination created a thriving business in human trafficking.

By the time the last of the new arrivals had waded ashore, our private beach had become a public parking lot. Ironically, the intrusion of a second group of refugees stirred some resentment in our own. This was *our* beach, and we were here first. Peninsular Malaysia had a five-hundred-mile coastline—did these people really have to land here? Our two dozen guards took one look at the number of new arrivals and realized that it would be impossible for them to maintain order in a group so large, so an hour later one of the guards shouted, "Let's go!" and began to coil up our rope enclosure.

We were leaving, and we had no idea where we were going.

Everyone carefully packed up the possessions they had managed to salvage from the boat and obediently followed the guards. They marched the entire group down the beach, then turned west into the palm trees and through some thick woods, then back onto the beach again. We marched for two or three hours under a midday tropical sun until some of the group were so exhausted they were ready to drop.

The worst part was the sand. In the process of abandoning our ship and struggling through the surf to the beach, almost everyone had lost shoes or sandals and was forced to walk barefoot, and by midday the sand was scorching hot. Yen had especially tender skin and had always been careful to wear shoes, even when she used to tramp through the mud on our farm. Without shoes her feet were blistering badly, and she could walk only a short distance before she had to stop. Whenever she did, my brother Bruce would take off his shirt and spread it out on the sand for her to stand on. To this day Yen tears up whenever she recalls her brother's act of kindness. Jenny carried Anh; Bruce and Yen took turns carrying Hon; and with everyone else's hands full, I had to walk on my own.

By nightfall we finally stopped. We were on the beach again, and the only difference we could see between our new location and the one we had left that morning was this one was occupied by five hundred fewer refugees. The guards herded our entire group down to the shore and into the saltwater, where we bathed without soap, but after the long day's march the water was a welcome relief. Even the guards joined us. There was nothing to dry off with, but it didn't matter because the evening was still hot; we all were dry in minutes. The guards used the rope to encircle us again, and we all spread out our tarps and readied our campsite for the evening.

We were too exhausted to sleep well, and the centipedes that crawled over us and tickled us with their hairlike legs didn't help. Throughout the day our one consoling thought had been that the previous group of refugees might have successfully arrived at a refugee camp; now we began to wonder if they were just camped like we were farther down the beach.

The next day was a repeat of the day before. We woke to the guards firing their guns in the air and waving for us to follow them. When we packed our belongings this time, we left a few of them behind; you discover which possessions are really important when you have to carry them around on your back all day. Again we marched for hours down the beach, and again the skies were clear, but by this time no one was giving thanks for the beautiful weather. Clear skies meant no relief from the sun, and it beat down and leeched the water out of us until our tongues clung to the roofs of our mouths.

Every day it was the same, for five days in a row—pack up our things, march for miles down the beach, stop at another random location, wade into the ocean for a quick bath, then collapse in exhaustion inside our rope corral. Each day we left a few more things behind until we carried almost nothing—even my grandmother's throne was eventually abandoned. Each day took a little more out of us, and the very young and very old suffered most. Somewhere along the way the old man who had struggled with dehydration on the boat died, and there was no choice but to leave his body behind.

What kept us alive during those five days of forced marching was a daily food delivery from the United Nations High Commissioner for Refugees. The UNHCR was an organization created by the UN General Assembly after World War II to help displaced persons in Europe, and their current mandate had been extended to include refugees in Southeast Asia. Each morning a white truck would pull up to the beach and a woman from the UNHCR would deliver food— not to us, but to the guards. A standard UNHCR ration pack was supposed to contain nine hundred grams of rice, condensed milk, meat, fish, vegetables, noodles, salt, sugar, and even two teabags, but by the time the rations reached us, the guards had removed most of it for themselves, and all we were left with was a little rice, saltine crackers, some dried food, and every child's favorite: lima beans. Bruce can't stand the smell of lima beans to this day.

Each ration was intended to last a refugee three days, but the stripped-down version we received was barely enough to get us through a day. The guards allowed us to gather driftwood from the beach to build small fires and cook the food that required it, and since most of us had left our pots and pans behind, we cooked in the tin cans the food came in.

By the fifth day all of us were exhausted, but my mother seemed especially tired and weak; she even began to weep as she trudged down the beach. My mother is an incredibly resilient woman who always seems to take life in stride, regardless of how difficult it is, and it was not like her to cry or even to complain. All of the children could tell that something was wrong with her, but we had no idea what it was.

Then we noticed she was bleeding.

Blood ran down her legs and left a trail behind her in the sand as she staggered down the beach. By nightfall she had lost so much blood that she was barely conscious, and when we finally camped, my father made her sit on a pillow to try to stop the bleeding. My mother had miscarried, and she didn't even know she was pregnant—the stress and exhaustion of the past few weeks had kept her from even noticing. Sometime in the last five days, she had passed two lumps of blood and kept it from everyone but my father, who secretly buried what might very well have been my mother's second set of twins.

And now she was hemorrhaging. Instead of being able to recuperate after her miscarriage, she had been force-marched for hours every day with barely enough food to sustain her and nowhere near enough water to replenish the blood she was losing. She lost so much blood that she finally passed out and lay unconscious on the sand while my father desperately tried everything he could think of to stop her from hemorrhaging—but nothing worked. There was nothing he could do but sit helplessly beside her and hope the bleeding somehow stopped on its own.

Then it started to rain.

And this was no summer shower—it was a torrential downpour from the southwest monsoons that inundated Malaysia from May to October every year. Lightning flashed all around us, and the wind blew so hard that the rain fell sideways and the drops stung our skin like needles. It rained all night long, and throughout that night Bruce and my father stood in that downpour and held a canvas tarp over my mother in a desperate attempt to keep her warm and dry while she slowly bled to death.

The monsoon stripped away just about everything that wasn't tied down. We went to sleep on tarps and woke up on sand. Everything we had salvaged from the boat and hauled like pack mules for the last five days was gone. We had the clothes on our backs, and we had each other—but we were terrified that we might not have our mother for long.

I believe that night was the beginning of my father's transformation. Less than five years before he had been a prince of Soc Trang, where he was rich, respected, and powerful. He owned rice mills, houses, cars, and even a luxury mistress; the world belonged to his family, and there was nothing he could not own or accomplish.

Then the wind began to blow.

The communists took the rice mills, houses, and cars; the mistress moved on; the Public Security Bureau took most of his money, and the government took the farm. Half of his luggage had been left floating in the Ganh Hao River, and half of our jewelry had been stolen by pirates. He had leapt from a sinking ship with just a few remaining possessions; most of them were scattered somewhere behind him on the beach, and now a monsoon had taken just about everything else.

Five years ago he was a prince, and now he owned a tarp.

The wind had stripped him of everything he owned, everything he had ever wanted—but as he looked down at his dying wife and his frightened children huddled around her, he began to realize that the only things he had left in the world were the only things that had ever mattered.

By morning my mother was conscious but so weak that she couldn't sit up on her own. Her bleeding had slowed a little but only because she had not moved a muscle all night long. Now she would be forced to march for hours again, and my father knew she would never make it through the day.

He squatted down and pressed his back against her, then wrapped her arms around his neck like a sweater and stood up. He took one of her legs in each hand and carried her piggyback to the nearest guard, and we could see drops of our mother's blood trailing in the sand behind her.

When my father came to the rope, he stepped over it.

The guard pointed his rifle and shouted at him.

"My wife is dying!" my father pleaded. "She needs a doctor!"

The guard took one look at my mother and knew he was not exaggerating. He pointed to a spot farther up the beach near the trees. "There's a truck there. Tell them she needs to go to the hospital. H-O-S-P-I-T-A-L."

My father nodded and hurried off.

The truck was a military cargo vehicle with an open back like a pickup. The truck bed had no cushion or pad; it was just bare corrugated metal, painted the same color as the truck. My father set my unconscious mother on the truck's gate and gently laid her back, then climbed onto the truck bed, and dragged her in the rest of the way. She lay on her back in the center of the truck bed with her arms limp at her sides. There were no benches on the truck, so my father squatted down beside her, and when he knocked on the cabin window, the driver took off.

The roads were rough, and the soldier driving the truck drove fast; he was used to hauling cargo and apparently didn't think that human cargo deserved any different treatment. My mother's head banged against the corrugated truck bed every time the truck hit a bump. There was nothing my father could do but watch and wince every time it happened.

It was a long and jolting ride to the hospital. When they finally got there, my father helped transfer my unconscious mother to a stretcher, and when he lifted her head from the truck bed, the back of her hair was soaked with blood. He was allowed to help carry her into the hospital, but the moment he set her down, he was told he would have to leave. They were willing to accept my mother, but they made it clear that this was a hospital and not a refugee camp. My father had no choice but to climb back into the truck and drive off again, and by the time he made it back to the beach, it was already starting to get dark.

On the way to the hospital, he at least had my unconscious mother to keep him company; on the way back all he had was a puddle of her blood and all the terrible thoughts it brought to mind. Would the hospital really treat her, or was it just providing a comfortable place for her to die? Had he taken his wife to a hospital or a morgue? Would a worthless Vietnamese refugee receive the same quality of care that a Malaysian would? Would anyone even bother to look at her?

And the most terrible question of all: *How will I raise eight children by myself?*

For some reason our group was not forced to march that day. The guards allowed us to remain camped where we were to try to pick up the pieces after the previous night's storm. My brothers and sisters and I had all watched that morning as our father lifted our mother onto his back and carried her up the beach to the truck, and even after they disappeared into the palm trees, we stared after them for a long time. We spent the entire day hoping they would both come back, but that evening when our father stepped out of those palm trees again, he was alone.

Nineteen

SHELTERING ANGELS

THE LAST THING MY MOTHER COULD REMEMBER WAS sitting on the beach and a vague sensation of being lifted— after that everything was a blank. Now she found herself lying on her back on a comfortable bed, staring up at a man who was speaking a language she could actually understand, and that had not happened since she left Vietnam.

Where could I possibly be? she wondered, but she was too weak to even open her mouth to ask.

"I need to do a procedure on you," the man told her. "I'm going to give you something to make you sleep." And with that, he slid a needle into her arm, and everything went black.

When she woke up again, she was finally clearheaded enough to understand she was in a hospital room, but she had no idea how she got there or how long she had been gone from her family. She had no sense of elapsed time at all; to her, it seemed as though she had closed her eyes one minute and awakened the next.

A man entered the room and walked up to her bed—the same man who had spoken to her before. Now she could see that he was a doctor and that the reason she had been able to understand him was because he was Chinese.

"You miscarried," he said bluntly. "I performed a D & C, and you should be all right now. But you can't have any more children—your blood is too thin." And to make certain she followed his advice, he informed her that while she was unconscious, he had taken the liberty of implanting an IUD, free of charge.

To the doctor's credit, he allowed my mother to remain in the hospital until she recuperated, and she had lost so much blood that recovery was a slow process. Nine days passed before she was strong enough to leave, and when she was finally released and went to get dressed, she discovered that the blood-soaked clothing she had worn to the hospital had turned putrid. The nurses had to scrounge up something for her to wear back to the beach, and the clothes they gave her would have fit loosely on a woman twice her size.

The same military transport that had brought her to the hospital returned to take her back again, and as she climbed into the back, she realized she had no idea where the hospital was located or how far it was from the beach. Since the driver didn't bother to ask her for directions back to her family, she assumed he knew where to take her, and if he didn't know, there was nothing she could do to help.

The trip back took far longer than she expected, and the longer they drove, the more worried she became. The driver didn't seem to know where he was going. From time to time he pulled over and stared at the trees for a moment, then drove off again. To make matters worse, it was already evening and getting dark fast. If the driver couldn't find her family in the daylight, he wasn't going to do any better in the dark.

My mother began to see patches of sky through the palm trees, which told her they must be nearing the beach. A few minutes later the driver abruptly pulled over, tapped his horn, and pointed to a small break in the trees. Thirty seconds later he roared off again, leaving my mother on the side of the road. She almost ran to the beach, eager to see the looks on all of our faces when we first spotted her walking toward us.

But when she stepped out of the palm trees, she saw nothing but sand and sea. She looked up and down the beach, and as far as the eye could see, there were no groups of refugees anywhere in sight.

It was the wrong beach.

Her stomach began to twist into a knot. She had no idea where she was or where her family was. Each day our family had been forced to march farther down the beach, but it had always been a random distance, and each place we stopped looked exactly like the one before. There were no distinguishing landmarks anywhere—just water on our left, palm trees on our right, and sand in the middle. And our group could have been moved several times in the last nine days—we could have been anywhere by now.

Then another thought occurred to her: A boat of refugees had arrived before we did, and a second boat arrived the day after. That meant we were not the only refugees wandering up and down the beach—there were hundreds, maybe even thousands, and locating one family among them could be like finding the proverbial needle in a haystack. And even if she did know where we were, how was she supposed to get to us? This wasn't Soc Trang, where she could just wave down a pedicab and tell the driver, "Take me to my family." The truck was gone, and she was stranded.

Nine days ago she was part of a refugee family. She knew all the dangers her family might encounter when they left Vietnam, but she always thought they would face them together. This was a situation she had never even considered. She was alone, and the thought terrified her.

The sun disappeared below the trees behind her, and the tall palms covered her in deep shadow. In a few more minutes she would be alone in the dark.

Then she heard sounds from somewhere behind the palm trees, and in the deepening darkness she could make out lights. She followed the lights through the trees and discovered a large warehouse-type building in a gravel-covered clearing. The light she had seen was coming from the building's windows, and when she stretched up on her tiptoes and peeked in, she saw row after row of wide bunk beds lined up from one end of the building to the other. It was a military barrack, and it was temporarily housing a large group of refugees.

She felt a surge of hope as she opened the door and stepped in— but when she scanned the faces of the refugees, she didn't see a single face she recognized. She began to wander around the room, asking if anyone had seen or heard about her family, and before long she ran across two sisters in their early twenties who were from her hometown of Bac Lieu.

"Where are you going?" my mother asked them.

"To France," one of them said. "We have sponsors there."

"When are you leaving?"

"Tonight, at ten o'clock. You can come with us."

"I can't," my mother said. "I have to find my family."

"Well, you can't stay here."

"Why not?"

"Because you're alone. Sometimes the soldiers come and take women at night. There won't be anyone here to protect you, and if you're alone you're going to get raped."

My mother stared in disbelief. In just a few hours this entire group was going to leave for France, and she would be left at the mercy of the Malaysian soldiers. There was no law to protect her—the soldiers were the law. As a refugee her life was worth nothing, and the soldiers could do anything they wanted. They could even kill her when they were done with her, and one refugee among thousands would never be missed. She was thirty-seven, attractive, and barely healed from a hemorrhage that had almost killed her. She couldn't just abandon her family and board a plane for France, but she couldn't find her family either; she couldn't bear to go, but it wasn't safe to stay. What was she supposed to do?

Then the second sister said, "Only Jesus can protect you now."

My mother looked at her. She had heard of Jesus before but only as one enlightened being among many. Household shrines in Vietnam commonly included an image of Jesus along with the Buddha and honored family ancestors. But this young woman spoke of Jesus as if

He were God himself, a powerful and loving being who strengthens the weak and protects the defenseless—and considering my mother's situation, it was no surprise that she found herself eager to listen. The young woman's words touched something deep inside her, and before long my mother was on her knees, praying for protection and deliverance.

At ten o'clock the soldiers came—but only to notify the group that plans had changed and they would not be leaving for France that night after all. My mother was greatly relieved and wondered if the last-minute change of plans was her first answered prayer.

An hour later one of the soldiers announced, "Lights out!" and promptly switched off the lights, throwing the entire barrack into darkness. Everyone immediately found their way to their beds, and my mother was left standing alone in the middle of the barrack.

"Come with us," she heard a voice say. A man and woman who looked to be in their midfifties, motioned for her to follow them and led her to a lower bunk, where two other figures were already reclining. They were the two young sisters from Bac Lieu, and the man and woman were their parents.

"Take the middle," the man told her. "You'll be safe there."

My mother lay down in the center of the bunk while the two sisters reclined on either side of her. The woman lay down beside one of her daughters, and her husband took the opposite side—five adults in one narrow bed. My mother spent the entire night with a compassionate Christian family surrounding her like human parentheses—the mother and father protecting their daughters and the daughters protecting her.

My mother didn't sleep much that night. From time to time the door would squeak open, and a few minutes later some young woman would be heard whimpering, "No, no," followed by silence when the soldier dragged her off or just climbed on top of her in her bunk. No one dared to intervene, and the next morning everyone wondered who last night's victims had been—but the poor souls refused to identify themselves out of shame. I'm sure that event haunted each of them for years to come—not only the brutality of the rape itself but the sense of utter powerlessness that a refugee feels when she learns that sometimes even her body is no longer her own.

To my mother's great surprise, early the next morning the driver who had mistakenly dropped her at the wrong beach returned for her. He told her through a translator that he had only left her there because he had been ordered not to return with her and had to leave her somewhere—but he had been searching ever since and had managed to find our family and returned to take her to them.

Before she left, my mother thanked the family of sheltering angels who had slept surrounding her the previous night. She never saw that compassionate family again; she never would have met them at all if not for a driver's poor sense of direction. It was a mistake, an error, an accidental encounter. She was there for only a single night, but that night was a turning point in my mother's life, just as my father's loss of wealth and power was a turning point in his. The simple prayer she prayed the night before was more than a desperate cry for help—it was a response to something beyond her, the beginning of something that would stay with her for the rest of her life.

My grateful mother was told she would soon be reunited with her family, but the driver failed to mention that one day earlier her family had been loaded onto fishing boats to be towed to an island refugee camp—without her.

Twenty

THE BEACH

W HEN MY FATHER RETURNED FROM THE HOSPITAL, he told us our mother would have to remain there until she was well. He did not know how long that would be, but he was sure she would be fine and would come back to us soon. That was what he told us, but I wonder if he was really thinking something more like, *Your mother bled the entire way to the hospital, and she was unconscious when I left her. I didn't know a woman that size had that much blood in her. She could be dead by now, and I would have no way to know. If she does die, I'm not sure if anyone will even bother to tell us.*

But that would not have been a very good way to comfort eight frightened children, so he just reassured us that everything was going to be okay.

For nine straight days my brothers and sisters and I stood at the edge of the rope and watched anxiously for our mother to return. We were worried about her, but we had other concerns that helped distract us—like staying alive. Our family had marched so far down the beach that the UNHCR no longer made regular food deliveries and we had to scavenge whatever we could to eat. My aunt walked up to the rope one day and beckoned for one of the guards to come closer, then pulled off one of her gold rings and handed it to him while she gestured to her mouth. The guard weighed the ring in his hand and held it up to examine it, then nodded his head and walked away—and a few minutes later he returned with a loaf of bread and a few bananas. It was extortion, but when you're starving, a loaf of bread is worth its weight in gold.

Someone donated three big sacks of rice, but the rice had been stored so long it had turned hard and yellow with age. We ate it anyway. We ate anything given to us and stretched it as far as possible; whatever it was and no matter how small the portion, it had to feed eight children and an adult. Whenever we complained to the guards that we didn't have enough food, they just pointed to the children and said, "Eat them."

Water was a bigger problem. It continued to reach ninety degrees every day, and we desperately needed water to replace what we were losing to sweat. The soldiers began to escort us to a small well where we could draw water, which was little more than a hole in the sand near the palm trees where we could lower a can attached to a long rope and dredge up whatever water we could find. The water was always dirty and hot, and with 290 people drawing from the well, it sometimes went dry. The guards quickly tired of escorting individual refugees back and forth from the well, and instead set a specific time period each day when everyone was allowed to draw water. People waited in long lines, hoping to get their chance before time ran out. Jenny and Bruce had the job of fetching water for our family, and they waited in line each day with Jenny holding one of the twins on her hip while Bruce stood behind her in his red-checkered shorts. When the allotted time ran out, the guards just shouted, "Go!" They fired their guns into the air, and everyone scattered, whether they were still thirsty or not. Go was the first English word Bruce and Jenny ever learned. Apparently it meant, "Run, or I'll shoot you."

On the morning of the ninth day, the guards fired their rifles to get our attention and announced we were leaving. That concerned my father because we had not been forced to march since he took our mother to the hospital, and he had been hoping we would be allowed to remain where we were until she returned. If we moved, how would she find us? The thought of our mother dying had terrified him, but the thought of her living and never finding us again didn't seem much better.

But when a line of trucks pulled up to the beach, my father realized we were not going to march—we were being taken somewhere by truck, and that meant it would probably be more than just a few miles down the beach.

"Everybody on the trucks!" the guards shouted.

But the sudden change of routine was so unexpected that no one moved.

"Where are we going?" my father asked.

The guards were not interested in discussion. "On the trucks!" they shouted again, and when they started to aim their rifles at us, everyone jumped to their feet and began to gather anything they had managed to collect since the storm.

"Leave everything," they ordered. "You won't need it. We're taking you to a refugee camp a few hours away, and you'll have everything you need there."

At that news everyone began to talk excitedly. We weren't just moving down the beach; we were leaving. After fifteen days of useless waiting, we were finally being taken to a refugee camp where our lives could start again. Everyone was thrilled—except for my family.

"My wife is still in the hospital," my father pleaded with one of the guards. "She hasn't come back yet."

"Nobody stays," the guard said with a shrug, and then he raised his voice so everyone could hear: "Leave everything—there won't be room for it. We'll take an inventory of everything you have and give you a receipt. You'll get it all back later. But you have to report everything—money, jewelry, personal possessions—*everything*. If you fail to report one single item and we find out about it, you won't go— we'll leave you here to die."

The threat of being left behind to die was an effective incentive, and everyone began to reach into secret pockets for lumps of gold and jewelry they still concealed. To look at our haggard and sunken-faced group, you wouldn't imagine there was a dollar between us, but it was astonishing how much money was produced once life itself was on the line.

The guards went from person to person and catalogued every item they received. Each family was given a written itemization and was instructed that without their receipt they would be unable to claim their possessions later on. At that point, a single piece of paper became the most valuable item that any of us owned.

My family took one last look at the palm trees in hopes that our mother would show up at the last moment, but she didn't. We had no choice but to join the others on the trucks and pray that she would catch up with us later.

The trucks drove for a long time before stopping again, and when they did we realized we were still at the beach and there was no refugee camp anywhere in sight.

The guards banged on the sides of the trucks and ordered everyone out.

"Where's the camp?" someone asked.

"We're taking you to the camp," one of the guards replied.

"In *those?*"

Lined up side by side in the water were four derelict fishing boats that looked battered and worn and probably hadn't been used in years—and for good reason. Paint flaked off everywhere, revealing patches of weathered gray wood. One of them had a crack in its stern so large, we could see through it into the boat.

"What happened to our boat?" someone called out.

"We heard it sank," a guard called back. "You should be more careful next time."

There was nothing we could say. We had scuttled the boat ourselves to avoid being pushed back to sea, and consequently it was unavailable—but even if our boat had been in perfect condition, it was doubtful the Malaysians would have returned it to us. Our boat was worth money, and these fishing boats clearly were not.

"The refugee camp is on an island," one of the guards explained. "It isn't far—only two or three hours. But there won't be much room, so again—leave everything behind."

Our group of 290 divided by four—each of the fishing boats had to carry more than seventy people, and none of the boats was more than thirty-five feet long. A fishing boat that size was probably designed to carry a crew of half a dozen men. How would seventy people ever fit? And how many people could it hold before it sank like a rock?

"Load up!" the guards shouted, but instead of heading for the boats, everyone began to scurry around like ants, waving and shouting to each other. This was not a group of strangers; it was a group of families and in-laws and distant cousins, and everyone wanted to make sure that all of their personal connections boarded the same boat. The guards couldn't have cared less about our family connections—all they wanted was to make sure the boats were weighted evenly. We were just heights and weights to them.

As everyone divided into families and scrambled aboard the boats, my father had to make a decision. He was a member of two families, one by birth and the other by marriage. On my mother's side were her mother and father, her younger brother, his wife and their two children, and one of her younger sisters who was still single. That made just seven on the Truong side of the family.

On my father's side of the family was Grandmother Chung, my uncle, his wife and children, and my three aunts, along with their husbands and children. The Chung family was more than twice the size of the Truongs, and numerically it only made sense for our family of nine to balance out the numbers by boarding with my mother's family. But loyal son that he was, my father chose to stay with Grandmother Chung, and the nine of us squeezed into a boat along with my father's family and took up almost half the available space.

It took quite a while for everyone to decide on a boat and board. Some had connections to several families and could not decide between them; they kept jumping back and forth between boats until the guards finally ordered them to stay where they were, and even then one or two of them made last-minute changes.

When the boats were fully loaded, there was barely room for anyone to breathe. Everyone sat cross-legged, wedged in like matchsticks in a box; no one had room to lie down or stretch out, regardless of size or age. Older children sat beside their parents while toddlers sat on their parents' laps. We were all hot and miserable, but at least we could be comforted by the thought that the trip would only last a couple of hours.

My entire family kept staring at the beach, hoping against hope to see one more truck roll up at the last minute and let our mother out. But that truck did not come, and we kept glancing at our father and wondering if he would really leave without her. He had no choice; no one was allowed to remain behind except to die. We were really going without her, and we cried when we thought we might never see her again.

Everyone else sat looking out to sea, waiting for something to happen. So did the guards—but apparently something went wrong. A connection wasn't made, or a phone call was never received, or someone wrote the wrong date on a calendar. We were never told exactly what the foul-up was, but a couple of hours later we were ordered to get out of the boats and load onto the trucks again. The guards drove us back to the same spot we had left from that morning, and once again we flopped down on the sand while the guards roped us in for the night.

Everyone was tired and disappointed, but the eight Chung children couldn't have been more relieved.

Twenty-One

BETRAYED

THE MOST BEAUTIFUL SUNRISE I HAVE EVER SEEN occurred on the morning of July 3, 1979. There wasn't a cloud in the sky that morning, and when the first sliver of sun appeared over the South China Sea, the world burst into color. The black water took on its first hints of blue, the dull gray sand sparkled with light, and the horizon caught fire and burned upward into the sky. But it wasn't the dramatic lighting that made that sunrise so memorable; it was the fact that when the first rays of sunlight fell across our beach, my brothers and sisters and I saw our mother walking toward us.

It would be a gross understatement to say that we were happy to see her. We were thrilled, we were overjoyed, we were complete again—but the emotion we felt most was relief. Less than twenty-four hours earlier our family had been sitting on a fishing boat, expecting to put out to sea, and if we had been forced to leave without our mother, there would have been no way to know when we would be reunited again—if ever. The problem was more than logistical; if our mother had remained on the beaches without us, she would have been a young, unattached female refugee—and at that time there was no more vulnerable person on the planet.

Compassion fatigue is understandable—when hearts grow tired and cold after repeated attempts to offer help. What I find impossible to understand is how fatigue can descend into assault, abduction, and brutal murder. That was the fate of many women who sailed into the South China Sea, and the violence didn't end when their boats reached shore. Women were particular objects of violence during that period, just as they have been throughout history. Man's inhumanity to man can be appalling, but it's nothing compared to man's inhumanity to woman.

Within an hour of our mother's arrival, the trucks returned and the guards ordered us to load up again. That was when our sense of relief turned to awe. If our mother had returned a single hour later, we would have missed her and possibly never seen her again. After nine days of separation she rejoined us within sixty minutes of our departure—and only because the previous day's departure had been mysteriously cancelled. That kind of incredible coincidence is enough to make even a hardened cynic think about Providence.

The trucks returned us to the same location as the day before, and once again the four derelict fishing boats were lined up waiting for us—only this time an enormous Malaysian navy patrol boat sat anchored just offshore. This time it was easy for everyone to decide seating arrangements because everyone had had a dry run just the day before—except for my mother. My father had made the decision yesterday that our family would accompany *his* family, but yesterday my mother had not been there to cast her vote. This time when my father got off the truck and started toward the Chung boat, my mother decided it was time to make her opinion known. Maybe she felt sorry for her own family when she saw them outnumbered by the Chung clan two-to-one, or maybe she considered the prospect of being wedged into a tiny boat alongside Grandmother Chung; whatever her reasons, she made it very clear to my father that our family was going with *her* family, not his.

There is a very wise Chinese proverb that says, "Never strike a flea on a tiger's head," and I think my father sensed that this was not the time to challenge his wife's wishes. We were going with her family—end of discussion. Besides, he thought, what did it really matter? My father knew it was only a journey of two or three hours, and when we reached the refugee camp, we would all be together again anyway. It seemed like a good idea to yield to his wife on such a minor point.

But to my mother it wasn't a minor point. When we were on the beach, the Chung family had not seen fit to associate with the Truong family, and for five straight days my mother had to watch her husband shuttling back and forth between families, trying to play the role of both faithful husband and loyal son. In my mother's eyes it was time for her husband to choose. All her married life she had felt her husband's divided loyalty. One of the reasons she wanted to leave Vietnam was to put an ocean between her husband and his mistress, and now she wanted to put some ocean between his family and ours. She knew that his choice would be mostly symbolic since we would all soon be reunited anyway, but to her it was an important choice because it meant that her husband was deciding where his heart really belonged.

So instead of heading for the Chung boat, my parents chose to join the Truongs, and I'm sure the last-minute change of venue earned my father and mother a few smoldering glares from Grandmother Chung. But my mother ignored her, and my father complied, and before long everyone was once again loaded and waiting to depart.

Sailors aboard the Malaysian patrol boat tied four large ropes to the stern and cast them to us, one for each fishing boat. We understood then that the patrol ship wasn't there as an escort—it was there to tow us, which we were glad to see since the patrol ship's engines were far more powerful and reliable than the ones on our rickety boats. The guards helped tie the ropes to the bow of each boat, and again we waited for something to happen.

This time something did.

It was about ten o'clock in the morning when we were finally cleared to leave, and we were all getting impatient because we were eager to reach the refugee camp and settle in. The Malaysians didn't tell us which specific refugee camp they were taking us to, but we had heard there were several island refugee camps just off the Malaysian coast, and we were probably headed for one of those.

The most famous of the island camps was Pulau Bidong, a rocky one-square-mile island about thirty miles from the coastal city of Merang. Just three years earlier Pulau Bidong had been a deserted tropical paradise, but when the Vietnamese exodus began, a refugee camp was established there, and it quickly became a tropical ghetto. The camp was called Bidong for short, but the camp's unfortunate occupants called it Bi Dat—the Malay term for *miserable*.

Pulau Bidong was expected to house only five thousand refugees, but just five weeks after it opened, it was home to twenty-five thousand refugees and eventually held more than forty thousand—all packed into one filthy, overcrowded shantytown along the coast. The camp was officially run by the UNHCR but in reality was left to fend for itself. Building materials were in short supply, so refugees were forced to live five or ten to a makeshift shack constructed entirely from discarded items—cardboard, plastic tarps, tree limbs, rice sacks—anything they could manage to find. The only sanitary facilities were Asian squat toilets in tin sheds, and the only showers were drums of water with ladles. The beach was littered with garbage that rotted in the tropical heat, which made the island an ideal habitat for rats—and they were everywhere. The refugees once caught eleven thousand of them in a desperate attempt to ward off an outbreak of plague.

Pulau Bidong was a dangerously overcrowded slum, where refugees were forced to live with limited food, polluted water, overwhelming stench, and disease-carrying mosquitoes. They survived any way they could until they could find a sponsor and leave, and some never did. They thought their stay would be only temporary—that was the thought that kept them alive—but few of them knew how long their stay would last or how bad the conditions would be.

My parents had heard about refugee camps like Pulau Bidong, but details about the deplorable conditions there did not become widely known until later. Maybe it was best they didn't know because my family was forced to go wherever the Malaysians chose to take us anyway. To my parents, a refugee camp was just the next stop on the road to a new life, and regardless of the conditions they encountered there, they would just have to endure it as best they could.

The big ship's engines finally started to rumble, and the ship inched forward until it had taken the slack out of the ropes—then the engines roared and we took off. We moved slowly at first until the ship made certain that the ropes were holding and our fishing boats had cleared any sandbars near the beach. Everyone cheered when the ship finally accelerated and we were really under way, but our enthusiasm didn't last.

When the big ship gunned its engines, its stern sank low in the water and generated an enormous wake. Our little fishing boats were dwarfed by the patrol ship, and its wake was almost big enough to swamp us—Jenny remembers reaching over the side of our boat and being able to touch the upswell of the wake. Our boats rode four abreast and sometimes banged together as they cut back and forth across the wake, and we had to constantly bail to keep water from filling the boats. But the ship settled into a constant speed, and as our boats followed more or less in a straight line behind it, we managed to keep the flooding to a minimum. It was an exhausting and nerve-wracking trip, but we knew we could handle anything for two or three hours.

But a few hours later the ship had not stopped, and there was no sign of an island anywhere. When we left the beach, the patrol ship had taken us straight out to sea and had not veered a single degree to port or starboard since. No one could be certain that we were even headed for Pulau Bidong, but if we were, we should have been there by now.

We felt even more uneasy when we looked behind us and saw nothing but water. All we could do was grip the sides of the boat, hold on to each other, and wait to see what would happen next. Once again we were powerless, unable to control our direction or destiny. The Malaysians had the big ship, and we were consigned to the tiny boats; we danced behind them like wooden puppets on strings. They could take us anywhere they wanted, at any speed they wanted, for as long as they wanted, and we had no way to stop until they allowed us to.

They towed us until it was completely dark, but even then they didn't stop; the patrol ship still maintained its speed and course, taking us deeper and deeper into the South China Sea. Another hour passed, then two, then four—they towed us for twenty straight hours and didn't stop until just before dawn. When they finally cut their engines, the big ship lurched to a stop while our momentum bumped our lighter boats up against its stern. When the wake washed past the ship and flattened out, the night fell eerily silent. We were too exhausted to say anything, and we were all numb from the deep-bass rumble of the twin diesel engines.

My father still wasn't sure what the Malaysians had in mind. Maybe there had been a last-minute change of plans; maybe we were never headed to Pulau Bidong at all; maybe they decided to take us to the big refugee camp in the Anambas Islands far to the south— that would have accounted for the extended voyage. The night was so black that the sky blended seamlessly into the sea, and my father stared into the darkness hoping to see some sign of land nearby.

Then some Malaysian sailors lined up along the stern of their ship and looked down at us.

"You're on your own now," one of them shouted down, and with that they cut the four ropes and dropped them into the water.

We stared up at them in shock. Even then my father had a hard time comprehending what was happening to us; he wondered if the Malaysians might have made a navigational error.

"This isn't the place!" he shouted up to the sailors. "We're not there yet!"

There was no reply.

Another man on our boat was beginning to catch on. "You're leaving us here?"

"You're not our problem," the sailors called down. "Go back where you came from."

Another man on our boat, an engineer by trade, stood up and shouted, "We need diesel fuel! Give us some fuel for our engines!"

One of the sailors yelled back, "Here's your fuel!" and cracked the man over the head with a long oar. The blow sent him tumbling over the side of the boat into the sea, and we had to drag him back in to keep him from drowning.

"At least leave us water!" someone else pleaded, but he kept his head down to avoid a similar fate.

This time the sailors responded by firing rifles into the air, and when they had our attention, one of them said through a megaphone, "Don't ask for help. You have to take care of yourselves."

Take care of yourselves—the Malaysians picked a fine time to return control of our lives to us. It's not easy to "take care of yourselves" in the middle of an ocean without food, fuel, or water. But that was not the Malaysians' concern. A moment later their diesel engines roared again, and the ship veered hard to port and headed back in the direction we had come from.

The most depressing sunrise I have ever seen occurred on the morning of July 4, 1979, because when the sun came up that morning and illuminated the sea, it revealed to us what a terrible predicament we were in. We had been abandoned in the middle of the South China Sea, and there was no sign of land in any direction. We all sat in stunned silence for a few minutes, unable to comprehend what had just happened. We knew the Malaysians didn't like refugees, but we did not know they despised us so much that they would tow men, women, and even children out to sea and leave us all to die.

There were lots of things we didn't know at the time. We didn't know there were ten thousand refugees just like us back on the beaches of Malaysia. We didn't know that in the previous three years more than a hundred thousand Vietnamese boat people had landed in neighboring countries, such as Malaysia, and already more than sixty thousand refugees were waiting for sponsors in overcrowded refugee camps all over Southeast Asia. We didn't know just how hostile the Malaysians had become or that it was now common practice to tow refugee boats at high speeds until the boats overturned and everyone drowned. On islands such as Pulau Bidong, the bodies of drowned refugees washed ashore almost daily, and the camp's residents were left to bury their kin. We learned later that the refugees from Mỹ Tho, who had arrived on the beach before us, had received the same treatment we did—only when they were towed to sea, some of their boats capsized, and the passengers drowned.

Malaysia's deputy prime minister had even publicly announced that if any more refugees attempted to come to his country, "We will shoot them on sight!" But shooting was such an unsightly way to deal with the refugee problem; the Malaysian government apparently decided that drowning was much quieter, and the sea offered the added bonus of not only killing the refugees but burying them too.

Because our fishing boats had been towed to sea, no one had thought to test the boats' engines, and when some of the men did, they found them fouled with seawater—our engine even had a cracked block. A couple of the engines actually started up but quickly sputtered to a stop, and the hope of sailing under our own power was quickly abandoned. Someone suggested that our boats might be more stable if we used the ropes that were still attached to our bows to tie the four boats together into one giant raft. We tried that, but the sea that morning was rolling in big, undulating waves, and our boats kept slamming together until we finally had to cut them loose out of fear that the fragile old hulls might break apart. No engines, no sails—not even an oar. These were not boats; they were floating coffins.

Because there were several children on our boat, we carried more passengers than any of the others—ninety-three in all, packed together in one mass of human flesh. There was nothing we could do all day long but sit in our little boat and watch each wave carry the other boats a little bit farther away from us until by nightfall we could no longer see them at all.

Then we were *really* alone.

Twenty-Two

SEASWEEP SETS SAIL

I N EARLY 1979, STAN MOONEYHAM WAS MAKING preparations for the *Cal Loader* to set sail again in search of refugees adrift in the South China Sea. He was committed to the work of Operation Seasweep, but he knew that to improve upon the previous year's efforts there were two problems he would have to solve. The first was the ship itself: the *Cal Loader* was sufficiently large but too light to operate safely in anything but calm seas. The second problem was the bigger one: after witnessing two refugee boats sink without warning the year before, Stan knew it was no longer enough just to resupply them and send them on their way—for all he knew, the three boats that the *Cal Loader* had only resupplied last year could have sunk the very next day. The only way he could guarantee the safety of the boat people was to rescue them, and to do that Stan would have to find a way to get some country to agree to resettle any refugees he managed to pluck from the sea.

That was not going to be easy. He had already experienced blunt and sometimes hostile rejection from half a dozen countries when he first presented his plan, including his own United States. But two things had happened since then that were about to change everything.

First, World Vision's efforts were becoming internationally known. Refugees who were fleeing Vietnam and safely arriving in other countries were beginning to report that they had heard about Operation Seasweep on radio broadcasts from the BBC, Radio Australia, and the Voice of America prior to leaving Vietnam and that World Vision's compassionate efforts had given them courage and hope.

The second thing that happened was more subtle but even more important. Operation Seasweep was helping draw international attention to the boat people crisis itself, and when the rest of the world saw that a small handful of dedicated people were willing to risk their own lives to rescue another country's refugees, they were shamed into changing their policies and taking action themselves. In Washington, President Carter issued a presidential directive that any refugees picked up by a US-owned or US-registered vessel would be guaranteed resettlement in America if the refugees so desired.

That gave Stan an idea. World Vision didn't have a US-owned ship—they had been chartering the *Cal Loader* from a company in Singapore. But what if they did? What if World Vision bought a ship of its own? President Carter's directive was addressed to currently owned and registered vessels; would the presidential directive apply to ships that would be purchased in the future?

Stan immediately flew to Washington to seek a ruling from the State Department, and he was elated when the ruling came back: any ship owned by an American entity, including World Vision US, would fall under President Carter's directive—and that included ships that would be purchased in the future.

Washington's unexpected change in policy had just solved Stan's biggest problem. Now all he needed was a ship, one big enough to handle the unpredictable weather in the South China Sea. A suitable ship was soon found—a fourteen-hundred-ton cargo freighter currently being used to haul coconut meat from the Solomon Islands to Singapore, where it was processed into coconut oil and copra cake to feed livestock. The *Cal Loader* had barely tipped the scales at 345 tons, but this ship had more than four times the bulk and a deep enough draft to allow it to stand up to the worst weather the region could throw at it. The ship was purchased for $200,000, and it took another $100,000 to completely overhaul it and make it ready for its new use.

The only detail that remained was to get the ship registered because every ship operating in international waters was required to fly the flag of some country. If it failed to do so, the ship could be considered derelict, and according to international maritime law, it could be seized and sold for salvage by anyone who wanted it. Even if Stan had been willing to take that risk, the port authorities in Singapore would never have allowed the ship to leave port without a flag, which meant that Operation Seasweep was on permanent hold until the ship could be registered.

The ship was too old to be registered in the United States. It would never have met US Coast Guard requirements, and it would have been too expensive and too time-consuming to try to bring it up to standards. Besides, a US-registered ship was required to employ a crew of all US citizens, and American salaries were astronomical compared to those in Southeast Asia at the time. No country in the region was willing to register the ship for fear that granting approval to the ship might be mistaken for granting approval to its mission, so it was eventually decided that the ship would sail under a "flag of convenience," which essentially meant that some small country would be willing to ignore the ship's poor condition in exchange for a hefty fee.

The ship was eventually registered in Honduras, and that made Operation Seasweep a truly international venture. It was an American-owned ship flying a Central American flag with an Indonesian captain, an Indian doctor, Chinese nurses, and an Asian crew—all they were lacking was a French chef.

The ship had to be given a name, and since Operation Seasweep was already achieving international recognition, it was decided to christen the ship with the same name: *Seasweep*.

But *Seasweep* had been purchased in Singapore and would dock and sail from Singapore Harbor, and that made the Singaporean authorities acutely aware of the ship's mission and purpose. The United States had guaranteed resettlement to any refugee that *Seasweep* picked up, but that did not mean that Singapore, Malaysia, Thailand, or any other nation of first asylum actually believed that promise. Those nations knew that even if America made good on her promise, it would still mean more refugees for them to deal with on a temporary basis, so to avoid that problem, they began to apply pressure to the Singapore-based members of *Seasweep*'s crew: the captain, doctor, nurses, and several crew members were privately warned that if *Seasweep* attempted to return to Singapore with any refugees aboard, the ship would be refused entrance to the harbor, which meant none of them would be allowed to return to their homes and families. Stan wasn't sure if he would end up stranded in the South China Sea with a shipload of refugees that no one wanted, and his crew wasn't sure if they would even be able to return home.

So it was with fear and trepidation that on the afternoon of July 6, 1979, Stan Mooneyham took a launch from Clifford Pier to join his crew aboard a converted cargo vessel named *Seasweep*, waiting at anchor in Singapore Harbor to begin their second year's mission—this time not only to resupply the boat people but, he hoped, to rescue them.

No one knew exactly what to expect this year. It was not the best time to put to sea since they were leaving in July and the typhoon season had already begun. *Seasweep* was supposed to be large enough to handle a typhoon, but no one on board had actually experienced a typhoon, and no one particularly wanted to.

But it was an ideal time to go fishing for refugees with sixty-five thousand ethnic Chinese pouring out of Vietnam every month. Since the beginning of the year, the Malaysian government had towed more than fifty-five thousand refugees back out to sea, which meant *Seasweep* would be able to rescue boat people coming and going.

Seasweep left Singapore Harbor just before midnight on July 6, and once it passed Horsburgh Lighthouse, it turned to port and followed the Malaysian coastline, being careful to remain in international waters outside the twelve-mile limit. The crew stood watch in four-hour shifts around the clock because, unlike commercial vessels, the derelict refugee boats rarely carried lights and would be easy to miss in the darkness. *Seasweep* itself carried a bright flashing beacon atop its forward mast to make it easily visible to other ships and avoid collisions. Ted Agon, who was aboard that night and would eventually become *Seasweep's* project chief, would have to climb that mainmast two weeks later to replace a burned-out bulb in the middle of Super Typhoon Hope, the worst typhoon to pass through the South China Sea in almost a decade. The typhoon's waves were so enormous that they swallowed an entire boat carrying four hundred refugees off the coast of Macao, and no trace of the boat or the refugees was ever found. *Seasweep* was caught in violent seas on the western edge of that typhoon, and whenever the ship dropped into a trough, the surrounding water was taller than the mast and rendered the ship invisible. Because *Seasweep* operated near major shipping lanes, there was a very real danger that a massive container ship or tanker could cut *Seasweep* in half before anyone knew the ship was there. In that kind of weather it was absolutely imperative to have a working masthead light; but in the hurricane-force winds, *Seasweep's* mast was whipping back and forth like a metronome, and no one in the crew was willing to climb the mast to replace the bulb. Ted Agon had to do it himself, and he will never forget clinging to the mast with one hand while he desperately tried to pry the beacon's rusted lamp housing open with the other.

But the seas were much calmer on the night of July 6, and as *Seasweep* steamed northwest at a conservative eight knots, everyone on deck stared into the darkness and hoped to be the first one to spot a refugee boat—but no one did. From time to time *Seasweep* would turn aside to take a closer look at some small vessel that couldn't be positively identified at a distance, but none of them turned out to be refugee boats.

The next day they continued to follow their course up the Malaysian coast, but even in the daylight there were no refugee boats to be found. *Seasweep* encountered all kinds of commercial vessels: container ships, cargo freighters, oil tankers, auto carriers, and fishing trawlers of every imaginable shape and size. Half of the world's commercial shipping passes through the South China Sea, and it seemed incredible to the crew of *Seasweep* that so many ships would pass by dying refugees without stopping to help. But statistics confirmed it: with all the refugee boats leaving Vietnam during the first seven months of that year, only forty-seven boats had been rescued.

The following day brought similar results—commercial ships everywhere, but not a refugee boat in sight. It was discouraging to the crew that with so many refugee boats at sea, they had encountered none, and Stan began to wonder if *Seasweep* had journeyed so far up the Malaysian coast that it had moved out of the path most refugee boats followed from Vietnam to Malaysia. That night the skies were cloudy, and the stars were unavailable for navigation, so under cover of darkness *Seasweep* headed west toward Malaysian territorial waters to take a location bearing from the lighthouse near Kota Bharu. Just as he thought, *Seasweep* had traveled almost to the border between Malaysia and Thailand, so Stan gave the order for the ship to head northeast in the direction of Vietnam and pick up speed. That was a wise strategy since the Malaysian coastline was more than five hundred miles long, and a refugee boat could land anywhere along it. Five hundred miles was a lot of water for *Seasweep* to have to search, but its new course would allow it to focus on a much smaller area by intercepting refugee boats not long after they left Vietnam.

By dawn on July 9, *Seasweep* was directly south of the Mekong Delta and headed east across a strip of water that had come to be known as "refugee alley."

Twenty-Three

ENDLESS SEA

NINETY-THREE PEOPLE PRESSING SKIN AGAINST SKIN made the boat unbearably hot on our first day at sea. No one said much that day because everyone was still in shock from the realization of what had been done to us the day before. The Malaysians had lied to us. They had never intended to take us to a refugee camp at all, and they told us the trip would take only two or three hours in order to convince us to leave everything behind. Food, water, additional clothing—everything we now desperately needed we had abandoned back on the beach. The Malaysians' last-minute inventory had been nothing but a ruse to rob us of anything else of value, to keep us from taking it with us to the bottom of the sea. The receipts they gave us were worthless pieces of paper. They were just like the worthless receipts the Nazis gave the Jews when they stripped them of their possessions before packing them into boxcars like cattle. The Nazis understood that bureaucracy has a calming effect when people feel out of control.

No one knew what to do next because there was nothing to do. Our engine didn't work, and even if it had, we had no fuel. There was no sail to unfurl or even an oar to row with. There was no compass, and even if there had been one, it couldn't have told us how far we were from land. Without engine or sail the tiller was useless, and without power our boat was at the mercy of the shifting tides and rolling sea. Even if someone aboard had possessed the foresight and navigational skill to take a bearing from the stars the night before, the knowledge would have been useless. Our boat drifted, turned, slid silently down the side of the swells, and turned again. We were pointed in every direction and headed in none of them.

We could have been anywhere. A twenty-hour tow at even a modest nine knots would have put our boat more than two hundred miles out to sea, and once the sun dropped below the horizon, we had no way to tell which direction we were traveling. The South China Sea was a 1.3-million-square-mile body of water, and all we knew for certain was that we were somewhere in the middle of it.

The only food we had was the scraps a few people had stuffed into their pockets, and the only water was a few small cups and containers that some had thought to grab as we left the beach. There was nothing on the boat that could help us survive. It was a fishing boat, not a lifeboat, so it carried no emergency supplies—no food, no water, and no flares or dye markers to help make our tiny speck visible against an infinite sea.

The night we set sail from Ca Mau and journeyed down the narrow Ganh Hao River, irritating black flies had circled our heads and picked at us all night. We had hoped to escape them when we reached the open sea, but we were disappointed to discover that flies inhabit the oceans too. Now they appeared again, and the annoyance only added to our anger and frustration. On the voyage from Vietnam to Malaysia, some of the passengers had become seasick, and that boat was much larger and far more stable than this one; our tiny fishing boat bobbed in the water like a cork, and it wasn't long before people began to double over and retch.

The other three boats had disappeared from view the previous day, and we could only hope that one of them was having better luck than we were. Maybe one of them would manage to repair their engine, or maybe they would drift to land and send someone back to search for us. We knew it was a remote possibility, but any hope is important in a life-and-death situation.

By the end of the first day, all the water and food had been consumed. Most of it had been given to the children, who suffered most from the heat and couldn't understand the reason for their misery. My mother tried in vain to nurse the twins, but her body was thin and frail, and the stress of the last few weeks combined with her recent hemorrhage and hospital stay had caused her milk to dry up completely. At eighteen months old the twins needed more than milk to survive, but milk had been a significant addition to their meager diet, and now it was gone.

All we could do was sit and wait, and the heat that slowly increased through the day turned the boat into a floating slow cooker. The children found it intolerable to have to remain seated for long hours in a rigid and cramped position, and they longed to move and stretch their legs—but there was no room to move and no place to go. The elderly moaned because of their stiff limbs and aching joints, but there was no relief for them. The real agony was that no one knew how long we would have to endure these conditions or if rescue would ever come at all. No one dared to say what everyone was thinking—that we were all just waiting to die, and the process could be long and terrible.

We had no relief at all until sunset that first day. Even then the temperature dropped only a few degrees, but at least we had a brief reprieve from the baking sun. When the sun disappeared below the western horizon, the blue-gray sea turned inky black, and the sky settled over us like a shroud. During the daytime, the sea had looked infinite and made us feel that we were nothing but a microscopic speck of living dust, but at night the darkness closed in around us and somehow made us feel larger but even more alone—as though we were floating in a dark room with no way to reach the walls. Our sleep was fitful and constantly interrupted by the cries of children and the shifting of aching bodies struggling to change positions.

We began the second day exhausted and weak from the day

before, which shortened tempers considerably. Everyone stared at the horizons, hoping to spot a passing ship that could help us. Maybe the Malaysians had abandoned us somewhere near a commercial shipping lane; that would have been the compassionate thing to do though the night before the Malaysian sailors had not demonstrated much compassion. If our boat happened to drift near a big commercial shipping lane, like the Singapore–Bangkok line, a passing freighter might spot us and come to our rescue. But the odds were against us because we were just a flyspeck in the middle of an endless sea. A crewman standing on a freighter's deck thirty feet above the water could see only about seven miles to the horizon, and seven miles is a microscopic margin of error in the vastness of the South China Sea. And even if a ship did happen to pass within seven miles of us, these were commercial ships with schedules to keep and cargo to deliver. Why would they be any more compassionate than the Malaysians had been?

Still, it was possible that a ship would pass by, and searching for one at least gave us something to do. But no ship ever appeared, which added a feeling of hopelessness to our fear, frustration, and anger.

On our third day at sea, we spotted a rocky outcropping, about twice the size of a house, protruding from the water. It was much too small to be called an island but more than large enough to reduce our boat to tinder if we happened to crash into it—there was a strong wind that day driving our boat directly toward it. We assumed our boat had been floating almost motionless for the last two days, but the rock was a true stationary point; when we saw it, we realized that our boat actually had been drifting fast.

Our boat had been abandoned in an area known as the Sunda Shelf, a region of the South China Sea so shallow that geologists wonder if it was once a land bridge that allowed ancient travelers to walk dry-footed between Southeast Asia and the Malay Peninsula. When the *Titanic* went down off the southern coast of Newfoundland, it sank in two and a half miles of water, but the water under our boat was fewer than a hundred feet deep in some places. That was more than deep enough to drown in but shallow enough to allow rocks like this one to poke up from the bottom. Our boat began to rush directly toward the rock, but for some reason we would veer off at the last moment and pass by unharmed; then the strange current would turn us around and force us to make another pass. Each time we thought we were about to crash into the rock, our boat would narrowly miss it and drift on. It was a strange experience that added a touch of terror to an otherwise monotonous day.

By the fourth day people were so hungry and thirsty and weak from constant exposure to the sun that they just slumped against each other in exhaustion. Some began to hang over the sides of the ship and stare into the water, where they saw slender silver fish gliding back and forth beneath the boat. One man came to the conclusion that the fish were tiny sharks; and he warned us that if there were baby sharks near the surface, there must have been a monstrous mother shark lurking down below that was waiting to eat us. No one bothered to argue with the man because by that time none of us was thinking any more clearly than he was.

My mother and father began to have fantastic nightmares that bordered on hallucination; my mother had a vision that the eighteen-month-old twins were rowing our boat and working as hard as they could to rescue the rest of us. My mother started to display the first signs of heatstroke, and nine-year-old Yen actually passed out from the heat. My father had to slap her to bring her out of it, and my mother had to pry her mouth open and place tea leaves on her tongue to help her produce saliva. Bruce sat farther forward in the boat than the rest of us, and because he was a growing boy, he struggled the most with hunger. When his hunger pangs became unbearable, he would beg our mother or grandmother for nonexistent food, and the only way he could get to them was to crawl around the railing of the boat. My mother was always terrified that he would slip and fall into the sea.

Then someone shouted, "Look! A ship!"

On the horizon we saw two ships, a larger one and a smaller one, and they seemed to be traveling together. A few of the men struggled to their feet and summoned all the strength they had left to wave the ships down—and to our indescribable relief the ships saw us and turned in our direction. The larger boat came first; it was a big commercial fishing boat, almost the same size as the boat we were in when we left Vietnam and more than large enough to take all of us aboard. It had two pairs of booms that pointed to starboard and port and trawl lines that were dotted with cork-colored buoys. As the ship drew closer, we could see some of its crew standing along the ship's railing, watching us. One of the men was enormous; he had a huge potbelly, and he was wearing a colorful sarong. He was shouting something to us that no one could understand—and then he opened his sarong and exposed himself.

They were Thai pirates.

Everyone sat down in shock. No one could imagine what pirates could possibly want from a boat as small as ours. We had nothing they could desire: food, water, fuel, money—even our women were emaciated and near death from four days without water or food. The attack was beyond our comprehension, and all we could do was sit and wait for them to tell us what they wanted.

But they never said a word to us.

The smaller ship was much lighter and faster than its partner. The two ships were most likely working together using a fishing technique known as "pair trawling," in which two ships sail side by side, hauling a net between them and catching everything in their path. The larger ship carries the net and stores the catch while the smaller ship serves only to drag the other end of the net.

The smaller ship pulled out from behind the trawler and began to circle our boat quickly. As it sped around us, we could see that it was towing a large rope behind it and that the other end of the rope was tied to the trawler. By the time the small boat had made a half circle around us, the rope had slid under our bow, and when the rope was directly beneath us, the small ship gunned its engines and turned away from us, pulling the rope taut and lifting the bow of our boat out of the water.

Everyone began to scream and cry. I was too young to understand what was happening, but when I heard the screams and saw the looks of terror on my family's faces, I began to cry too. Jenny looked over the side of the boat and could see daylight between our bow and the water. We were tipping over backward; and if the overloaded hull didn't break in half from the strain, it would dump us all into the sea and slam down on us like a massive wooden mallet.

There was no time for anyone to try to jump clear; all we could do was hold on and wait to be poured out like rice into a boiling kettle. The children would be the first to die because they would hit the water and sink like rocks. The adults who had no ability to swim would struggle for a few seconds before they slipped beneath the surface, and those who were able to swim a few strokes, like my father, would last the longest—just long enough to watch his entire family perish before he succumbed to exhaustion.

Then something happened that no one expected: the rope snapped, and our boat came crashing back down to the surface and plunged so deep that it looked as if water might pour over the sides of the bow and sink us. There was utter panic because no one knew exactly what had happened, and we feared that the boat had broken in half. As everyone gradually realized our boat was still intact, we began to stare up at the pirate trawler and wonder what would happen next.

But nothing happened next, for at precisely the same moment that the rope snapped, the smaller ship's engine broke down.

There was no apparent reason for the breakdown. The smaller ship's engine had been working just fine a few seconds before, and considering our distance from land, it must have been working for the last several hours—but the moment the rope broke, the ship's engine shut down and refused to start again.

It was hardly remarkable that the rope broke when it did. I'm sure the rope was never intended to lift the combined weight of a fishing boat and ninety-three passengers; it probably just reached its breaking point and snapped—no explanation necessary. What *is* remarkable is that the ship's engine broke down exactly when it did. If the smaller ship's engine had not broken down, the pirates could have tried again with another rope—or with a chain. But it takes two ships to accomplish what they were trying to do, and the moment the smaller ship's engine died, they were out of luck. If that engine had waited just fifteen minutes longer before dying, the pirates would have had time to try again, and their second attempt might have proven successful. When the rope broke, we were only given a temporary reprieve; it was the perfect timing of the two events that saved the lives of everyone on our boat.

There are times when an apparent coincidence is so incredible and so perfectly coordinated that it forces us to wonder whether there must have been purpose behind it. My father considered that event a true miracle, and it wasn't the only one my family witnessed during our journey. To my father, that event was just one more indication that something or someone seemed to be guiding our family's fate.

When the smaller ship broke down, the pirates lost interest in us and turned their attention to repairing their engine. Fortunately for us they were unable to repair it. They used the broken rope to tie the two ships together, and we all sat and watched the trawler tow the smaller ship away while the fat man in the sarong cursed at us at the top of his lungs.

Twenty-Four

THE PRAYER

THE WOMEN DID THEIR BEST TO RELIEVE THE MISERIES of the children while the men stared blankly at the horizon, hoping to see some sign of land—but even if they did spot an island on the horizon, there was no guarantee our boat could reach it. Without power we would probably sail right past it; the prevailing current wasn't likely to deliver us directly to a tiny spot in the middle of a vast sea. Some of the men fashioned makeshift sails from T-shirts and tarps they found on board; but there was very little wind moving, and the pathetic sails hung as limp as retired flags.

After yesterday's encounter with the Thai pirates, no one was particularly eager to encounter another ship because there was no guarantee it would have any better intentions. Yesterday's pirates were the most cold-blooded kind of all. They didn't want to rob us or assault our women as did most of the predators who prowled the Gulf of Thailand and the South China Sea; these pirates just wanted to overturn our boat to watch us drown, and if their rope hadn't broken at the last possible moment, they would have succeeded.

In the seclusion and anonymity of the South China Sea, the human heart was free to turn its darkest, and predators knew that even the worst atrocities could be hidden beneath the water. Those

Thai pirates were trying to kill us just for the pleasure of doing it, which seems like an incomprehensible thing for one human being to do to another. But refugees were not human beings; when they left their home, no list was made of who they were, when they left, or where they were headed. No nation mourned their departure, and no country awaited their arrival. There was death at sea but no death toll; there was heartbreak but no history. Refugees were unwanted, unclaimed, and unnamed—invisible people. They were just some country's former problem, and the moment the problem was gone, they were forgotten—out of sight, out of mind.

If the pirates' rope hadn't broken, we would have died; if their boat hadn't broken down, they would have tried again. That was two minor miracles in a single day. But that was yesterday; it's hard to give thanks for yesterday's grace, and no one on our boat was feeling grateful today.

We were dying of thirst.

We left Malaysia without food or water, but food was not the critical concern. If necessary we could have endured for more than a month without food, but the human body requires water to survive— a lot of it. Every cell of our bodies contains it, and every day some of that water is lost. In a temperate climate the body loses between two and three quarts of water per day, but our boat was adrift just a few hundred miles north of the equator. In that kind of tropical climate, the body perspires, but sweat won't evaporate. The body loses water but can't cool down, and hyperthermia can occur. The very young and very old are especially susceptible, and my family included both the oldest and some of the youngest aboard; my grandfather was well into his seventies while my twin brothers Anh and Hon were only eighteen months old.

On the South China Sea in July, the temperature can reach a sweltering ninety degrees with 90 percent humidity, and the sun shone brightly every day we were at sea. There was never a cloud in the sky to block its rays and grant us a few merciful hours of relief, and despite the suffocating humidity, there had not been a single drop of rain. In those extreme conditions at least one member of my family should have died two days ago—yet there we were, still hanging on to life after five long days at sea.

There was a pregnant woman on board who suffered greatly from the heat. I cannot imagine what the ninety-degree temperatures must have added to the incubator she already carried inside her. There was a young man on board, probably in his early twenties, who seemed to have been afflicted by some form of mental illness. He occupied his time by grabbing at the black flies that swarmed over our boat like a cloud, and whenever he caught one he ate it—a revolting habit that made the children frightened and nauseous.

Not that nausea was a cause for concern; after five days without food or water, there was nothing left to vomit. That had not been the case for the first day or two, when plastic bags filled with vomit and feces had to be passed from the center of the boat to the gunnels, where they could be emptied into the sea. The stench on board was unbearable at first, but after five days we had grown almost immune to it. During those first days at sea the adults sipped seawater and let the children drink their urine, but after five days there was no urine left to pass and the saltwater only leeched more fluids from our bodies and made the dehydration even worse.

Mild dehydration begins when the body loses 1 or 2 percent of its water reserves. We reached that point after a single day at sea, when everyone began to complain of thirst and headache and fatigue and the mood on board changed from one of fear to anger and irritability.

Moderate dehydration occurs when the body's water loss reaches 5 or 6 percent, and general irritability gives way to lethargy and extreme sleepiness and people begin to complain of dry mouth and a swollen tongue that cleaves to the roof of the mouth.

Severe dehydration takes over when the body's water loss reaches 10 to 15 percent. At that point the muscles begin to contract involuntarily, vision dims, and delirium begins.

After 15 percent, you're dead.

By the fifth day we had clearly reached severe dehydration. Anh and Hon became increasingly agitated; they began to bite at my mother while one of them banged his head against the boat rail in frustration. They kept moaning the term *mum mum* over and over, a Vietnamese child's way of asking to eat or drink, and my mother had to hold them tightly to keep them from crawling over the side of the boat and into the sea. They couldn't comprehend why their own mother would not let them slake their thirst when they were surrounded by water as far as the eye could see.

My elderly grandfather turned to my grandmother and said, "I'm going to the kitchen for a glass of water."

"That's not a kitchen," she told him. "That's the ocean, and if you go out there you'll die."

"Let me go to the kitchen," he kept pleading, and they began to argue. His water-deprived brain had begun to hallucinate; fortunately for him my grandmother was still a bit more clearheaded.

One man had almost gone blind. His corneas had been scorched by the unrelenting sun, and his eyes were crusted over with a yellowish excretion that oozed and ran down his face. My sister Nikki had a similar experience. Every morning when she awoke, she found her eyes sealed shut by a crust from the salt spray that constantly misted over the boat; she had to scrape the crust away and pry her eyes open before she could see.

Though almost everyone on our boat left the beach without food or water, one family had the foresight to grab a gallon jug of water as the Malaysian soldiers were hurrying us aboard. That family concealed the jug of water from the rest of us, and when it was eventually discovered, they refused to share. My uncle Lam began to plead with them—not for himself but for the younger members of our family.

"These are children," he told them. "They need water or they'll die. You have to share."

So they did. They removed the cap from the jug and carefully filled it, then passed the tiny capful of water across the boat—one capful for each of the children.

When I think back on this event, I can't help but marvel at the selfishness of the human heart. You would think that our common suffering would have bonded all ninety-three passengers into one devoted family—a true band of brothers. But hearts are not always softened by difficult circumstances; sometimes they are hardened into stone. Though everyone on our boat faced the same likelihood of death, for some inexplicable reason one of our families was determined to hang on to life just a few hours longer than everyone else.

Others aboard the boat were more humane. Some of the mothers began to quietly make arrangements for the care of any children who might survive the voyage.

"If you die, I'll take care of your children," they told one another. "If I die, you must promise to take care of mine."

Some of the women, having lost all hope of survival, began to discuss the possibility of drowning their children to spare them further suffering. *"If death is a foregone conclusion, why let the children suffer? And why put ourselves through the torment of having to watch them die? Wouldn't the loving thing be to end their misery now?"* They began to consider the unthinkable: wrapping the youngest children in strips of cloth to bind their struggling arms to their sides and slipping them into the sea.

Then something happened to my father—something none of us could see. A thought presented itself in his mind, like the flare of a match in a dark room. It could have been just a hallucination of his own, but he didn't think so; he described it later as a moment of clarity. Something had spoken to his soul, and he knew what he needed to do. He picked himself up from his cross-legged position and, to everyone's surprise, knelt down near the center of the boat and began to pray aloud.

"I know there is a Creator God," he called out. "I know You created us and don't want us to die like this. So if You're listening, please send rain."

Then he sat down again.

It was not the first time my father had ever prayed, but there was something very different about this prayer. There were no memorized words, no ritualistic postures, no petitions for help from enlightened beings or benevolent ancestors. It was an elemental prayer, stripped of all pretext and formality, just a creation speaking to its Creator. Thanh Chung had never prayed like this before, but something within him—or something from without—had told him that the only one who could help him was the Creator God.

Within minutes of his prayer a dark line appeared on the southwestern horizon. Some thought it might be land because the peaks and valleys looked like a range of mountains, but the peaks began to rise and grow and reach out toward our boat like fingers, darkening the sky as they came.

Then, without lightning or thunder, the heavens opened and it began to rain.

It was a torrential downpour. Everyone's first instinctive response was to lean back and open their mouths to the sky to feel the first cool drops of water on their swollen tongues. But drops of water were not enough to satisfy, and everyone began to scramble to find something, anything, that could capture and store this gift from above. My father and my brother Bruce grabbed a dirty canvas tarp and spread it out, hoping to catch the rain and direct it into something that could hold it, but the soft canvas absorbed more water than it channeled—so each of the children leaned back like baby birds while my father twisted and squeezed the water from the tarp into our waiting mouths. The tarp was so filthy that the water that came out of it was almost black, but none of us cared. It was water, and after five days that was all that mattered.

There wasn't an empty bucket or container anywhere on board, so the best we could do was to drink all we could while the rain continued. We could drink, but we couldn't store; we had water for today, but as soon as the rain stopped, there would be no more. But no one was thinking about tomorrow because we were too busy enjoying this manna that fell from the sky today.

Until the boat began to sink.

The rain came down so hard our boat began to fill with water, and when that happened, everyone stopped drinking and began to bail furiously. "Too much of a good thing" has never been a better description. If the rain hadn't started, we would have died, but if the rain wouldn't stop, we were going to die. Sometimes you just can't get a break.

To make matters worse, the sudden storm brought violent seas. The swells began to rise until they looked like dark hills that rose and fell around our boat. Then we were facing two threats: water from above and water from below. Our boat was shallow; when Jenny dangled her arm over the side of the boat, her hand could touch the water. All it would take was one good wave to spill over the side of our boat, and we would all be headed for the bottom. Everyone began to panic.

When my father saw what was happening, he knelt down again.

"Creator God, I know that You heard me because You sent rain," he prayed aloud. "If You hear me again, please make it stop."

Within minutes the sky lightened, the storm moved on, and the seas became calm again.

Now everyone began to pray.

Buddhists appealed to the Absolute Refuge, Taoists invoked the immortals, and ancestor worshipers sought the intervention of loved ones long since dead. Some tried to cover all the bases—my grandmother admitted later, "We prayed to Buddha; we prayed to our ancestors; we prayed to Jesus. We prayed to anyone who would listen."

Apparently Someone did.

Our fifth day at sea ended with a ray of hope—not because we now believed we would be rescued but because we had begun to hope that maybe, just maybe, there was Someone out there who actually cared whether we lived or died.

But a single rainstorm cannot replace the lost 15 percent of a body's water. We were refreshed but not replenished; we were hopeful but far from healed. The next day would bring the sun again, and with it the heat and humidity. Tomorrow would be our sixth day at sea, and it was likely to be our last.

Twenty-Five

RESCUE

B
Y OUR SIXTH DAY AT SEA, MOST OF US HAD LOST hope and with it the will to live. There is an ancient proverb that says, "Hope deferred makes the heart sick" (Prov. 13:12 ESV), and our hopes of rescue and deliverance had been dashed so many times that the only prayers we still offered were requests for an end to our suffering. A twelve-year-old girl aboard our boat would later recall, "I knew I was going to die. I prayed only that my death would be quick and merciful."

My father was confused to the point of despair. His family had endured so much suffering, so much loss, yet at the same time he had seen hints of divine protection all along the way. The communists had taken everything we owned, yet we had been allowed to live and even leave the country. We had been attacked by Thai pirates, but we had been spared the horrific rape and mutilation that had befallen so many other refugees. Again we were attacked by pirates, this time attempting to overturn our boat for the sheer pleasure of doing it, but their rope had broken at the last possible moment.

What did it all mean? Why had there only been hints of divine protection—why not outright deliverance? Were we really being protected, or was it all just a stay of execution? If there really was a Creator God, was He for us or against us?

My mother was thinking the same thoughts. She had miscarried and probably lost two precious children whom she would never see, but her own life had been spared. She had been returned to the wrong refugee camp late at night, a helpless sheep among ravenous wolves; but a compassionate Christian family had surrounded her and shielded her from harm. She had been separated from her beloved family for nine straight days, but she had been returned to them within minutes of their departure. If there really was a compassionate God who cared for her family and protected them, where was He now? For every terrible danger her family had faced, there seemed to have been a remarkable deliverance, but what was the point if it all ended this way? Moreover, my mother was still haunted by the dream she had experienced just before leaving Vietnam—the dream about the man in the marketplace who had pointed to her family and brought them all back to life. What did the dream mean if her family was to die like this?

Yesterday's rain had brought a brief respite from heat and thirst, but it was almost worse than nothing at all. It seemed like a cosmic tease—not enough to save us, just enough to prolong our agony another day. My father had prayed for rain, and his prayer had been miraculously answered—but the storm that immediately followed almost sank our boat. Even our blessings turned out to be curses; even the answers to our prayers were denials. Nothing made sense. We felt hopeless, helpless, abandoned by God and man—and my father was certain that this was the day we would all die.

———

When *Seasweep* entered refugee alley, the watch was doubled with crew members spaced along the railings so that no sector of the horizon would be overlooked. Stan took the noon to four o'clock watch, scanning the sea with powerful binoculars but so far finding nothing. At about three thirty, he heard someone calling to him; he looked up at the bridge and saw project director Burt Singleton waving for him to come up. The bridge was the highest point on the ship, aside from the forward mast and rear stack, and the extra elevation made it possible to see a mile or two farther out to sea. Burt pointed to a dark spot on the port side horizon, and when Stan trained his binoculars on that spot, he could see that it was definitely a boat.

On the journey up the Malaysian coast, there had been several sightings of possible refugee boats, but on closer inspection they had turned out to be nothing but small pleasure craft. Stan wanted to spare the crew any further disappointment, so he decided to just observe the boat for a while before deciding whether to take a closer look.

The boat didn't seem to be moving, which would not have been unusual for a recreational boat within sight of the shore, but Stan checked the ship's charts and estimated that *Seasweep* was 120 miles off the southern tip of Vietnam. A boat that far from land had to be going somewhere, especially during typhoon season on the South China Sea, but this one wasn't moving. As small as the boat was, it was difficult to estimate its actual size at a distance, but Stan thought it looked no more than thirty feet long. In the rough swells the boat rocked like a seesaw from bow to stern, with the two ends of the boat taking turns peeking up above the waves. Then Stan noticed something else: as he squinted through his binoculars, he could make out shapes above the boat. He had seen those shapes before—they were shirts or plastic sheets rigged as makeshift sails.

That was the giveaway—it was definitely a refugee boat.

Stan immediately gave the order for *Seasweep* to come about, and he alerted the crew to get ready.

———

By late afternoon the temperature had peaked around its usual ninety degrees. No one on the boat could sleep anymore, nor was anyone fully awake; we just existed in a constant state of heat-induced torpor, mentally drifting with the rolling swells.

Then someone called out, "Ship," but with far less energy and enthusiasm than at the previous sighting two days ago. Still, we all sat up and looked, and this time things looked different. This time it was a single ship, and it was clearly not a fishing trawler. It was a real cargo ship, a big one, and most encouraging of all was the fact that it was painted white. The color of the ship meant nothing, really, but the pirate ships that had attacked us were dark and dreary, and we interpreted the cheerful appearance of this one as a positive sign. The ship was definitely heading toward us, approaching on our port side.

"Everyone lie down!" someone shouted. "Act like you're sick and dying!" That was strange advice, considering most of us *were* sick and dying, but the logic was easy to understand: "Try to look as desperate as possible to merit all the compassion we can." I can remember lying back in the boat, doing my level best to look dead but still squinting up at the ship to see what would happen next.

———

When *Seasweep* was less than a mile away, Stan could finally see the boat clearly, and what he saw astonished him. The boat wasn't much larger than it had appeared at a distance, and it was packed with more bodies than he could count. He had never seen such an overloaded refugee boat, and when he saw how low it sat in the water and noticed that the stern was broken open, he wondered what was keeping the thing afloat. Because the boat was just over a hundred miles from Vietnam, Stan figured it had probably only been at sea for a single day. *Thank God,* he thought. *There's no way that death trap would have stayed afloat a second day.*

The crew hurried around the deck, making preparations. White plastic five-gallon containers of water spiked with glucose were readied and boxes of saltine crackers were opened to give the refugees something light to eat; as far as the crew knew, it could have been hours since their last meal.

Stan looked down at the rickety boat and realized there was another problem: *Seasweep* had to approach very carefully because in rough seas the ship's steel hull could crush the fragile wooden boat like an eggshell. Stan gave the order for *Seasweep* to slowly circle while he figured out the safest approach.

———

Our eyes all widened as the ship approached. It was the size of a building—at least it looked that way to us. It was five times longer than our little boat and ten times taller. As the ship drew nearer, we could see figures lined up along the ship's railing, just as we had seen on both pirate ships—only this time we were relieved to see no one holding a knife and no sarong wrapped around a big potbelly.

An Asian man in a maroon Windbreaker and a floppy white boat hat was holding a bullhorn, and when we saw him, we were even more relieved to see an Asian face that wasn't Thai. The man smiled and called down to us in Vietnamese, "Friends! We've come to help you!" But the word he used for *friends* was a word that is often translated *comrades*, and that made everyone fear that this was a Russian ship that would only tow us back to Vietnam. But at that point no one cared; even returning to Vietnam would have been preferable to a slow death at sea, and my brothers and sisters tried to encourage one another by saying how nice it would be to return to Bac Lieu and eat ice cream and sugarcane again.

But when the man in the floppy boat hat saw our dejected faces, he immediately turned around and showed us the back of his Windbreaker, which bore a bright yellow rectangle with three red horizontal stripes—the flag of South Vietnam. At the same moment a man on our boat spotted the name *Seasweep* on the bow of the ship and shouted, "Our savior!" The man said he had read about this mercy ship in an American magazine prior to leaving Vietnam and told us we were in safe hands—and that was when everyone began to applaud and grin and wave to the people lined up along the ship's railing.

———

The crew of *Seasweep* threw ropes over to the boat and gently drew it up alongside, and once the boat was safely secured to the ship's port side, the five-gallon containers of water were lowered to the boat by rope. Some of *Seasweep's* crew had assisted with World Vision's land-based relief efforts, and what they saw here took them by surprise. In Africa, when an airdrop of food was made, the people waiting below would scatter everywhere, and whenever a bundle broke apart, there was complete chaos. But these refugees did nothing; they just watched as the containers were lowered down, without moving a muscle, almost as if they didn't believe it was real. They were so dehydrated and so close to death that the sight of water floating down to them from the sky must have seemed like a hallucination.

The refugees gradually realized their deliverance was real, and the crew smiled and watched with satisfaction as they began to gulp down water from plastic cups and empty tin cans. The crackers were sent down next, and the children eagerly devoured them.

The next order of business was to send down *Seasweep's* chief engineer, Mr. Choi from Hong Kong, who was assigned the task of examining the boat's engine and determining whether the boat was seaworthy. Stan's hope was that Singapore would be willing to accept these refugees simply based on President Carter's promise that America would resettle them, but he knew it was a good idea to have a backup plan. If the refugee boat was not considered seaworthy, Stan could tell the Singaporean authorities that according to international maritime law he had been required to take them aboard in order to save their lives.

After Mr. Choi climbed down the rope ladder to the boat, one of the refugees climbed up—a young man who spoke English fluently—and recounted the story of the boat's journey. Stan was astonished to learn the boat had not come directly from Vietnam as he had thought—it had been towed from Malaysia six days prior. Stan looked over the railing at the boat again. *Six days* in that thing? And Malaysia was 230 miles away! The story defied imagination—it was a miracle the boat was still intact and no one aboard had perished.

The young man also told Stan that this boat was not the only one that had been towed to sea from Malaysia. He told them there had been four boats in their original party of 290 refugees, but the other three boats had drifted apart after their first day at sea and had not been seen since. Stan immediately sent word to the bridge to search the horizon for the others, but none was found. The other three boats must have been more than ten miles away, and each one could have drifted in a different direction. If they looked anything like this one, Stan wondered if they were still afloat.

Mr. Choi soon returned with his engineering report: The engine's cylinder head was cracked, he announced, and it was impossible to repair it at sea. He added that the crack appeared to be old, which meant that the engine probably had not been working for a very long time, and he also noted that the boat was leaking badly. In Mr. Choi's professional opinion the boat was definitely unseaworthy; so with international maritime law on its side, the crew of *Seasweep* began to bring the refugees on board.

A basket stretcher was lowered first, to assist four refugees who were either too sick or too weak to move; they were taken immediately to the ship's medical clinic, where Dr. Chandler and the two nurses could tend to them. The babies came next; they were placed in white pillowcases and pulled up by rope, like sacks of groceries. The younger children were lifted, using a rope sling, and the older children rode on their parents' backs as they climbed the rope ladder to the ship's deck. Stan took a head count as the refugees were brought aboard: he counted an unbelievable ninety-three refugees, including fifty-six adults, seven elderly, twenty-seven children, and three pregnant women. He could not believe the age range—from a six-month-old baby to a feeble old man. Stan felt humbled by their courage and the risks they were willing to take to gain freedom—men, women, and children alike.

———

Anh and Hon screamed at the top of their lungs when they were dropped into pillowcases to be hoisted up to the ship. The first time the method was tried, the pillowcase tipped backward and almost dumped a baby into the sea. But the people on the ship figured out the problem before anyone was lost, and we all applauded as each one made it safely aboard. I rode up on someone's back, hanging around his neck like a human cape, and so did Bruce, Yen, Nikki, and Thai.

The family who had hoarded a container of water and kept it from the rest of us now realized their leftover water was unnecessary, and before they left the boat, they dumped the remainder into the sea.

My father was the last to go aboard, and Jenny waited beside him until everyone else had taken his or her turn. As always, Jenny played the role of second mother and made sure the rest of us were safely aboard before she followed. She was the last child to leave the boat, and she climbed the rope ladder all by herself.

While Jenny was waiting, a large, black butterfly suddenly appeared out of nowhere and settled on my father's shoulder. Jenny smiled; she couldn't imagine what a fragile creature like that could be doing in the middle of an ocean. What did it eat? How did it live? Where did it come from, and where was it going? She searched the evening sky to see if there were any more of them, and she wondered if she was the only one who knew they were there.

———

Stan watched each refugee as each one reached the top of the rope ladder and was helped aboard by one of *Seasweep*'s crew. Some of the refugees were so weak and exhausted after six days at sea that climbing the ladder took every bit of energy they had left; and when they reached the deck, they just slumped down and sat there in a stupor. The children had the opposite response; they were thrilled by this new adventure and could not wait to explore their new environment. After six days of inactivity they had legs to stretch and energy to burn.

The last refugees to come aboard were a young girl and her father, and by the time the boarding process was completed, it was dark, and the decks had to be illuminated by spotlights. The refugees were escorted below deck to the number-two cargo hold, where they would be served dinner. Stan knew that the ship's cook would take good care of them because the cook was a refugee himself, with a wife and two sons who were still in a refugee camp somewhere in Malaysia.

Stan gave the order for the empty boat to be tied behind *Seasweep* so it could be towed back to Singapore. He thought it might be wise to bring "Exhibit A" along with them and let the authorities back in Singapore take a look for themselves. Mr. Choi was a professional ship's engineer, and in his professional opinion the boat was unseaworthy, but Mr. Choi was also a member of *Seasweep's* crew, and the authorities in Singapore might have considered his opinion less than objective.

Stan wanted to stay and search for the other three boats, but he knew it would have been impossible to find them at night. To even begin a search, *Seasweep* would have had to wait until morning, and then the search could have taken days. He was now responsible for the safety of not only his crew but ninety-three others, and the weather clock was ticking on the South China Sea. He knew his first responsibility was to return the refugees safely to port, so he reluctantly gave the order for the ship to start its engines and head south by southwest. He comforted himself with the thought that *Seasweep* might still have a chance of spotting one of the other three boats on the way back to Singapore.

———

The stairway down to the ship's cargo hold passed under a metal beam so low that even ten-year-old Bruce had to duck his head to get under it. The cargo hold was nothing but a cavernous storeroom with a floor made of rough wooden planks where blankets had been spread out for us to sleep on. The room looked as big as a soccer field to us, and part of it was occupied with stacks of supplies and food. There was a large opening in the deck over our heads where pallets of cargo could be lowered down to the hold; the opening allowed lots of fresh air into the room and kept us from feeling claustrophobic.

At the far end of the hold was a long table lined with serving kettles, and that was where all the children headed. Sleep could wait—it was dinnertime. My brothers and sisters can't recall many details about the cargo hold and its appearance, but they all clearly remember the menu that night: steamed rice with pork and eggs. Each dish was prepared to perfection since the Asian cook knew the way we would like it. Ever since we left Vietnam we had been eating dried, tasteless, preserved food that sustained our bodies but never satisfied us, and in the six days since we left Malaysia, we had eaten nothing at all. It was the best meal any of us had ever eaten, and no future meal would ever be able to compare with it because that meal went past our stomachs and directly into our souls.

Around midnight the ship's engines started up for the first time since our rescue, and as we dropped off to sleep on our blankets, we could feel the floor rumbling beneath us.

Twenty-Six

SINGAPORE BOUND

T HE NEXT MORNING WATER LINES WERE OPENED ON *Seasweep*'s decks, and they gushed like fire hydrants while the refugees gratefully bathed in freshwater for the first time since arriving in Malaysia more than three weeks ago. Three weeks without a bath—it was every parent's worst nightmare and every child's dream. Clotheslines were strung everywhere to allow clothing to dry; before long the deck corridors looked like laced tennis shoes, and the cargo hold closely resembled a Chinese laundry.

When my father learned that *Seasweep* was headed back to Singapore without searching for the other three boats, he was heartbroken. His mother and other family were on one of those boats, and he didn't know if they were even still alive. He thought back to our boat's six days at sea, and he wondered if things had been as terrible for his family as they had been for us. Grandmother Chung, his brother and sisters, his nephews and nieces—would he ever see any of them again?

Now that we were all safely aboard *Seasweep*, Stan Mooneyham had to figure out what to do with us. It was not an easy decision. He was sailing toward Singapore simply because that was the ship's home port, but the authorities there had made no promise that they would accept his new passengers. The Singapore-based members of

Seasweep's crew had been threatened with fines and penalties if they attempted to return with refugees, and Captain Samudra had even been told that he would lose his pilot's license—and that would have meant the end of his career.

There were places other than Singapore where Stan could have dropped us off, but there were not many, and none of them was certain. There was one port in Thailand that was a possibility but not a very good one. Guam was a good option because it was a US territory; but it would have taken fourteen days to get there, and the ship didn't have enough fuel, so Guam was rejected. That turned out to be a very good decision because exactly fourteen days later Super Typhoon Hope was spawned just southeast of Guam; it was a Category 4 typhoon with winds that eventually reached 150 miles per hour.

Hong Kong contacted Stan at sea before the refugees had even been taken aboard to warn him that *Seasweep* would not be allowed to enter Hong Kong Harbor with refugees aboard, and if their warning was ignored, the ship would be confiscated and the captain and owner would each be fined $20,000 and sentenced to five years in prison.

That crossed Hong Kong off the list.

That left only Singapore; and after a couple of hours of soul-searching and discussion, the captain and crew agreed to take their chances at their home port while Stan agreed to do everything he could to negotiate with the authorities en route.

It took four days for *Seasweep* to make it back to Singapore. The adults spent most of their time resting, recovering, and tending to daily necessities while the children spent their days exploring the ship and being entertained by the crew. Stan's seventeen-year-old son, Mark, was aboard, and he was a favorite among the children because he organized games and activities for us and could do magic tricks and make balloon animals. My sister Nikki especially liked Mark; on our first day aboard, he accidentally kicked her and made her cry, and he felt so bad about it that he carried her around for the rest of the trip. My brother Thai remembers the bread that was served on board because it was so thick and fluffy. Someone dropped a piece of it on the filthy deck, and Thai hurried over to pick it up and eat it, but before he could reach it, a crew member tossed it overboard. Thai was shocked—he couldn't imagine how anyone could throw away a piece of food.

The crew handed out Vietnamese-language magazines that had been brought along just for the refugees, and small, blue Vietnamese-language Bibles were offered to anyone who wanted one; after three weeks of monotony and boredom, the refugees devoured everything they could read. A worship service was held on deck one day, and anyone who wished to could take part. My mother was busy below deck with the children, but my father decided to attend, along with most of the other refugees.

My father was not a particularly religious man, and he wasn't sure why he attended that service. It was mostly because someone in *Seasweep*'s crew had invited him, and he thought it might have seemed like an insult if he declined after these people had been so kind to his family. There was another reason he attended: he hoped these people would explain why they would go to so much trouble and expense to save the lives of people whose own country didn't want them and the rest of the world valued less than dirt.

Stan Mooneyham spoke that day, and the same man who had first greeted our boat with the South Vietnamese flag on his Windbreaker translated the sermon so everyone could understand. To my father's surprise, Stan didn't talk about his noble organization or the selfless crew of *Seasweep* or even the details behind the rescue. Instead, he talked about Jesus: about His love for the unloved, His compassion for the helpless, and His heart for all those whom society sweeps into the gutter. He healed the lame and blind, He wept over the dead, and He wrapped His arms around the untouchable. His greatest act of love was to die for us, Stan said, and He returned from the dead to offer love and forgiveness to everyone who would accept it. It was that great love that brought *Seasweep* here, Stan told everyone. His great love compelled His followers to love and care for others. He loved, so we love; He gave, so we give back.

My father was riveted by those words. It was as though Stan Mooneyham was explaining his own life to him in a way he had never understood before. He suddenly recognized that all the seemingly random events of his life had a purpose, and the terrible and bewildering events of the last few weeks all had meaning. He had no way to articulate that meaning and purpose or even to fully comprehend it, but the assurance that it was there gave him an overwhelming sense of peace.

There is an expression the Chinese use when asking for forgiveness: "Let's drop it in the ocean." At that moment my father felt his entire past had been dropped into the South China Sea—he was free; he was released; he was forgiven. Now he knew the Creator God had a name and a face, and my father knew he would never be the same again.

At the conclusion of Stan's sermon, someone suggested singing a hymn, but none of the refugees knew any Christian hymns, so instead, they sang the South Vietnamese national anthem, which includes these words:

No danger, no obstacle can stop us.
Our courage remains unwavering in the face of a thousand dangers.
On the new way, our look embraces the horizon.

The words could not have been more appropriate to the occasion, and I doubt any song could have better expressed what was in everyone's heart.

That night, when we were about to go to sleep, someone called down to the cargo hold, "Whoever wants to see the boat one last time come on up!" Most of us were already sound asleep, and those who were still awake couldn't have cared less about our old boat now that we were safely off of it. But Bruce was curious, and he went topside to see what was going on.

He followed the crew to the stern of the ship and looked over the railing. Our boat was being towed behind *Seasweep* exactly as it had been towed behind the Malaysian patrol boat, but Bruce had never seen the boat from this vantage point. *This is how our boat must have looked to the Malaysian sailors*, he thought. For six days Bruce had been jammed into that little boat, but as he watched it bobbing up and down in the ship's huge wake, he found it hard to believe it had ever happened.

Then as Bruce looked on, the boat began to fill with water until it quietly slipped beneath the surface, and *Seasweep* was left towing nothing but a rope.

Stan Mooneyham was also watching as the boat filled with water, and when it finally disappeared, he shook his head in disbelief. That boat had managed to stay afloat for six entire days, supporting the weight of ninety-three human beings, yet with no one at all aboard, it sank. The Vietnamese translator had told Stan the boat had been towed behind a Malaysian naval ship for twenty straight hours—how was that even possible?

To Stan, it was nothing less than miraculous, but the miracle wasn't just that the boat had stayed afloat—it was the fact that *Seasweep* had managed to find it at all. After three solid days of searching more than six hundred miles of ocean, this was the only refugee boat the crew had been able to find. Only one pair of eyes had managed to spot it—Burt Singleton's—and only because he happened to be standing on the bridge, where he could see a mile or two farther than anyone else. Ten miles to the horizon—that was as far as you could see from the tallest point on the ship. A ten-mile margin of error in a body of water twice the size of Alaska—what were the odds? If the boat had drifted just a few miles farther, if *Seasweep* had varied its course by a single degree, if Burt Singleton had even *blinked* . . .

On the fourth day *Seasweep* passed Horsburgh Lighthouse at the entrance to the Straits of Singapore. The ship dropped anchor outside Singapore Harbor because we didn't dare enter until Stan received official permission to do so. The Straits were named after Singapore alone, but the ten-mile-wide waterway is actually bordered by both Singapore to the north and Indonesia to the south, and both countries take an active interest in any foreign ship that wants to pass through. Two hours after we anchored we were buzzed by two different patrol planes and approached by an Indonesian customs ship and three coastal patrol boats from Singapore, one of which was heavily armed and kept circling us like a hungry shark.

As soon as the ship anchored, Stan took a launch ashore to meet with Singapore's foreign ministry to try to obtain permission for *Seasweep* to enter the harbor and off-load her ninety-three refugees. Negotiations had not gone well for Stan en route; he hoped things would go better when he could negotiate face-to-face, but the fact that we had arrived on Friday the thirteenth should have tipped him off that things would not go as smoothly as he hoped. It took three days of negotiation and an actual letter from the American Embassy, promising the United States would take full responsibility for the resettlement of all ninety-three refugees before Singapore's foreign ministry would relent and allow us to enter the harbor.

Late at night on July 16, *Seasweep* finally sailed into Singapore Harbor. All incoming vessels had to be cleared at anchor by separate boats from Immigration, Customs, and Quarantine. When we were finally cleared to go ashore, slow-moving launches shuttled back and forth between the ship and the pier until all of us had disembarked. It was an incredible thrill for the children to ride the launch across the harbor with the wind blowing in our hair; and the breathtaking sight of thousands of glittering lights from downtown Singapore reflecting off the water made us feel as if we had just sailed into Neverland.

Stan Mooneyham was there to watch as we boarded a row of chartered buses that were waiting to take us to a refugee camp. At the time, we were all too preoccupied to think about shaking his hand or thanking him for what he had done; but looking back, it almost seems like a crime that we didn't. Operation Seasweep was an international effort that involved the labor and sacrifice of hundreds of individuals, but it was the compassion and tireless dedication of one man who got it started and saw it through to the end despite the enormous obstacles he faced.

There is a Vietnamese proverb that says, "When you eat the fruit, remember who planted the tree." We owe our lives to Stan Mooneyham, and so do hundreds of other grateful refugees.

Twenty-Seven

25 HAWKINS ROAD

MY BROTHER BRUCE HAS ALWAYS BEEN A BIG EATER, yet for more than two weeks on the beaches of Malaysia, he had been forced to survive on little more than crackers, lima beans, and uncooked rice. When the Malaysians abandoned us at sea, there was nothing to eat at all, and Bruce spent the entire six days begging for something to fill the aching void in his stomach. We were all starving, but Bruce seemed to feel the pangs of hunger more than anyone, and the moment he set foot on *Seasweep*, he started making up for lost time.

By the time we reached Singapore, Bruce was almost eleven, and looming adolescence was stoking the furnace of his metabolism. He ate anything he could find, and it didn't much matter what it was; if it was edible, Bruce ate it. That kind of indiscriminate palate can get a boy into trouble, which is why less than one day after we arrived in Singapore, Bruce was close to dying from food poisoning.

After clearing Customs, Immigration, and Quarantine, it had taken the buses about an hour to drive us the fifteen miles from the docks of Singapore Harbor to our refugee camp on the north side of the island. Singapore is an island nation-state that sits at the tip of the Malay Peninsula, like the dot at the end of an exclamation point;

the entire nation is smaller in area than Lexington, Kentucky. On the northern side the island is bordered by the Johor Strait, and just across the water is the nation of Malaysia. Ironically, after being towed out to sea by the Malaysians and left to die, my family found the Malaysians living just a stone's throw away.

Our refugee camp was known as 25 Hawkins Road, and it was located in the suburbs of an area known as Sembawang. The camp had once served as a British army barrack, which was easily recognized by the stone memorials and cannons that dotted the grounds. When Singapore declared its independence from Great Britain, the facility had been abandoned and left unoccupied until it was opened again in 1978, to serve as a refugee camp. Aside from our miraculous rescue by *Seasweep*, my family's assignment to 25 Hawkins Road was our first good break since leaving Vietnam five weeks previously. The conditions in refugee camps throughout Southeast Asia varied widely, from the horrific cesspools of island camps such as Pulau Bidong to decent camps like 25 Hawkins Road.

We were assigned to Camp 14, which was one of many pleasant-looking two-story buildings with narrow white siding and red tile roofs. Because our building had formerly served as a barrack, it was laid out to suit that purpose: the bottom floor was a single open room that had once been lined with rows of metal bunk beds for enlisted men, and the upstairs was divided into separate rooms for officers. The upstairs rooms lined one side of the building, and across a long hallway there was a communal bathroom with showers and a bathtub that everyone had to share.

A single upstairs room was assigned to my entire extended family—the ten members of our immediate family, my maternal grandmother and grandfather, Uncle Lam and his wife, their five-year-old daughter and four-year-old son, and my unmarried twenty-two-year-old aunt. My mother had two sisters, but only the older one was accompanying us as the younger sister had left Vietnam on her own in the first wave of refugees back in 1975, when she was only eighteen.

Seventeen people sharing a room that measured eighteen-by-eighteen feet—and there was nothing in the room. No furniture, no beds, no kitchen—just an empty space barely big enough for every-one to lie down, but we were grateful for it because it was the first time we had slept under a real roof in five weeks.

When we first arrived, my family signed in at the office, and we were required to register by male heads of household. My father signed for our household, and my grandfather and Uncle Lam each repre-sented their own. Our group of ninety-three was assigned the name Seasweep One, which apparently meant that we were the first group of refugees rescued by *Seasweep* to be taken to 25 Hawkins Road.

As soon as we were assigned a room, my brothers and sisters all raced upstairs to see it, and because Bruce was the fastest, he got there before everyone else. He found the room empty, but on the window ledge Bruce saw a couple of unopened cartons of orange juice and some cookies someone had left behind—apparently for good reason. But Bruce didn't know that, so he immediately downed the orange juice and gobbled the cookies.

By the next morning Bruce had severe diarrhea and uncontrol-lable vomiting, and before long his skin grew clammy and cold, and his body began to stiffen. When Bruce's fingers started turning blue and his eyes rolled back in his head, my father decided it was time to get help, so he hoisted Bruce onto his back and ran to the camp office with Jenny right behind him. He was hoping to find a nurse or at least some kind of medicine that might be able to help him, but the office staff took one look at Bruce and told him, "You have to take this child to the hospital." But no one in the entire camp had a car to drive him there, so they just led him outside and pointed to the road.

My father started running toward the road with Bruce jostling half-conscious on his back. "Wake up! Wake up!" he kept shouting over his shoulder, but Bruce did not respond. My father had no idea how far away the hospital was or how long it would take him to run there with the weight of a ten-year-old on his back, but he had no choice—he didn't have enough money to even take a bus.

On the way to the road, my father passed a woman he had never seen before. She stopped him, took a look at Bruce, and said something to my father in a language he didn't understand but recognized as French. Then the woman opened her purse, handed my father a few dollars, and without a further word went on her way.

My father had no idea who the woman was or why in the world she would hand him money—but he didn't care. Money was exactly what he needed right then, and he waved down a taxi to rush him to the hospital and used the French woman's money to pay for it.

My father was hoping to have Bruce treated as an outpatient and return home with him because he had no money to pay for a hospital stay. But the moment the doctors saw Bruce's condition, they admitted him, and within minutes they had a bottle of saline dripping into his veins, and they were rolling him into an elevator—which was the first elevator Bruce had ever seen.

Hypovolemic shock was the probable cause of Bruce's condition—a serious decrease in blood volume that can be caused by excessive diarrhea and vomiting. Without enough blood reaching the body's extremities, they can turn purple or blue; in extreme cases, the patient can even die. Bruce's condition was serious enough to require a three-night hospital stay. My father returned to 25 Hawkins Road to take care of the rest of us while my mother took his place at the hospital. Officially, family members were not allowed to stay overnight, but they bent the rules for my mother, and she slept in a chair beside Bruce's bed every night until he was allowed to go home.

The hospital was at the top of a tall hill, and when Bruce was released, he was still so weak that my father had to carry him. At the bottom of the hill, a kind-looking Chinese man walked up to my father and began to talk to him, but my father doesn't speak Mandarin and couldn't understand the man. Once again, a perfect stranger handed my father some money and walked away—this time a US five-dollar bill. And once again, my father used the money to take a taxi home.

My father remembers those two unexpected acts of compassion, not because the gifts were so large but because the timing of the gifts was so perfect. He was given exactly what he needed, precisely when

Grandmother Chung sits on her wicker throne.

Her glare makes people clear the streets. Nobody messes with Grandmother Chung—not even the communists.

My mother, Hoa, the second-most beautiful woman in Bac Lieu.

My father and mother marry in 1966. The second-most beautiful woman in Bac Lieu marries the luckiest man in Soc Trang.

We celebrate with the other refugees on board our boat when we are told *Seasweep* will take us aboard.

We wait and applaud as each one of us is lifted onto the ship. My father and Jenny are the last to be brought on board.

Life on *Seasweep*: my mother sits surrounded by seven of her children (Bruce is off running around the boat). L to R (front): Jenny; Thai; cousin Ba; and Nikki, drinking from cup. L to R (back): my mother, holding twins Anh and Hon; me, standing behind her; and Yen.

We are happy on board *Seasweep*. I'm standing shirtless behind my mom, surrounded by my siblings

We stay in the cargo hold, a cavernous storeroom that becomes a refuge. That's me, looking on as a girl reads.

We spend our days exploring the ship. Thai (left) still remembers the thick, fluffy bread they served on board.

Laundry time on *Seasweep*: the deck begins to resemble a Chinese laundry.

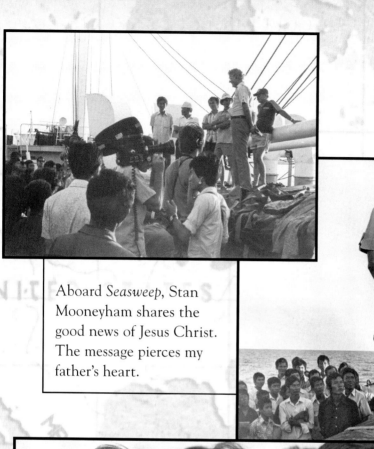

Aboard *Seasweep*, Stan Mooneyham shares the good news of Jesus Christ. The message pierces my father's heart.

We do not know any hymns, so we all sing the national anthem of South Vietnam, which includes the words, *On the new way, our look embraces the horizon.*

Clifford Pier in Singapore, as it looked when
Seasweep is permitted to off-load its ninety-
three refugee passengers.

A family photo taken at the Singapore refugee camp 25
Hawkins Road: I am dressed in blue and white, standing in
front of the fence.

My family remains in Singapore for one hundred days, awaiting a sponsor. I'm in the bottom left-hand corner.

My mother is holding one of the twins, and I stand directly in front of her, wearing my new *moldy* clothes.

he needed it, from sources he never expected, and without even having to ask. To my father, that seemed like more than coincidence.

When Bruce came home from the hospital, life returned to normal—at least, as normal as life in a foreign refugee camp can be. My mother's day was spent taking care of the children and managing our one-room apartment. There was a bathtub in the communal bathroom across the hall, and since none of us had ever seen one before, my mother used it to wash dishes. When we first arrived at 25 Hawkins Road, we had no money at all, and to make ends meet my mother had to sell off the few pieces of jewelry she had managed to save, most of which she was wearing. She had also crocheted a black handbag before she left Vietnam and concealed a necklace and bracelet in the handle, and while my obedient father had surrendered the last of our family's money to the Malaysian authorities, my defiant mother held on to that handbag—which she still has to this day. None of her jewelry was expensive—mostly just bits of jade in settings of gold—but there were pawnbrokers in Singapore who visited the camp regularly because they knew refugees often fled with jewelry. The gold used in Asian jewelry was purer than most, and it was profitable to resell as jewelry or just melt down.

My father went to work right away doing a variety of jobs: farming, plywood fabrication, asphalt roofing, finish carpentry, grocery work—anything he was offered. Every morning a labor organizer would drive a bus into camp and ask the men if anyone wanted to work. My father always received $10 for his day's labor, regardless of what the job actually paid, and the organizer pocketed the rest as his fee.

After a while, the UNHCR began to give us $1.50 per person, per day, to help with living expenses, and that's where a large family came in handy. We were given $15 every day, and though that amount didn't go a long way with a family of ten, it more than doubled my father's daily salary. Before long my father had enough money to begin to buy things in preparation for our trip to America, and the shrewd merchants in Singapore offered him lots of helpful advice.

"Everything is more expensive in America," they told him. "You'd better buy it now because you won't be able to afford it there." It was the taxes, they told him. America taxed everything—that was why everything was so expensive. But there was no sales tax in Singapore, so if my father was smart, he would buy everything he could before he left.

My father took their word for it and bought everything he thought he might want but would not be able to afford in the United States. He bought the biggest boom box he could find, a high-end rice cooker, some very fancy watches, and sunglasses for all of us. My mother bought a sewing machine, hoping to do part-time work as a seamstress when she got to America, and my father even bought two bottles of Hennessey cognac though he didn't drink. Might as well, he figured, because he was being paid in Singapore dollars and wouldn't be able to spend them in the United States.

The children just had fun. There were twenty-seven children among our group of ninety-three, and some of them were the same age as we were and became our regular playmates. There was a playground at the bottom of a hill that we liked to play on, but we had even more fun rolling down the hill to get to it. We spent hours playing tag, but none of us really understood the concept of the game, so we just ran up to perfect strangers, touched them, and ran away. We had a favorite toy too: a small straw with a tube of some kind of plastic goo. We rolled some of the goo into a little ball, stuck it on the end of the straw, blew into it, and presto—a plastic balloon. It may not sound like much when I describe it now, but it provided hours of entertainment for us then.

There were vendors who visited our camp every day, and once my father had an income, he would give each of us a few cents to buy something. Our favorite was the ice cream man, who sold ice cream and flavored snow cones—always a treat in a tropical climate. The ice cream man was Chinese and actually spoke Cháo zhōu as we did, so we were able to converse with him and tell him exactly what we wanted. There was also a grocery store nearby, where we used to buy bread and condensed milk, and sometimes sympathetic locals would even give us vegetables and apples free of charge.

There was a single-room building in the camp filled with donated clothing that any of the refugees could take for free. The room was dark and damp, and the clothing was old and out of style; some of it was even stained and moldy, but we were glad to have it. If whatever we grabbed actually fit, we were lucky; if it was too small, we gave it to a younger sibling; and if it was too big, we just grew into it. "One size fits all" was the Chung family motto, and we lived by it until I was eighteen.

The UNHCR was responsible for running 25 Hawkins Road, and it also coordinated the details of resettlement for each individual or family. No refugee was allowed to leave the camp without having a sponsor in another country who would take responsibility for them when they arrived and help them adjust to life in their new home. Some in our group were lucky enough to have friends or relatives in other countries willing to sponsor them, and they were able to leave 25 Hawkins Road right away. Others—such as my family—knew no one overseas and could only wait until some anonymous person or group heard about them and agreed to be their sponsor. Some did not even know what country they would be going to; the only reason my family knew we would be going to the United States was because that arrangement had been made even before *Seasweep* rescued us.

Though we knew we would eventually be going to America, we had no idea where or how long it would take before someone would agree to sponsor us. There was an intercom system in the camp, and when a refugee family had found a sponsor, the UNHCR would ask that family to come to the office. Whenever that intercom came on, everyone in the camp held their breath, and when the name was announced, everyone cheered for that family—but also felt bad that it wasn't them.

Imagine sitting by an intercom, waiting for your name to be called, knowing the sponsor assigned to you would determine not only where you might live for the rest of your life but also what language you would speak, the traditions and activities you would take part in, and the culture your children would adopt. The consequences of that one decision are so far-reaching, they boggle the mind, yet the decision was often made without the refugee's slightest knowledge or consent.

Individuals and small families seemed to find sponsors quickly, and my father and mother began to worry that no one would want to sponsor a family as large as ours. Day after day we heard other names called and said good-bye to those families as they left for their new homes. My parents had heard horror stories about refugees who had floundered in refugee camps for years without ever finding a sponsor, and they hoped our family would not become one of them.

Gradually everyone left, except for us. Even my mother's family left for America before we did. My grandparents had a distant relative in Falls Church, Virginia, who agreed to sponsor them, and Uncle Lam, his family, and my aunt asked to go with them. The relative in Falls Church was sponsoring seven Truongs, and it was too much to ask him to take ten Chungs, too, so our family decided to remain in Singapore to wait for a sponsor of our own.

Exactly one hundred days after our arrival at 25 Hawkins Road, we heard the intercom crackle and a voice say, "Thanh Chung, please come to the office."

Then we really cheered. Somewhere in America, someone had been kind enough and generous enough and maybe even crazy enough to sponsor a family of ten refugees who didn't have a dime between them and didn't speak a word of English. Whoever they were, they had no idea what they were getting themselves into.

But then, neither did we.

Twenty-Eight

ACROSS THE PACIFIC

W HEN MY FAMILY LEFT OUR HOME IN THE MEKONG Delta of Vietnam, none of us had ever seen the ocean, another country, a cargo ship, an elevator, or even a bathtub—so imagine what it was like for us to board a 747.

The date assigned for our departure from 25 Hawkins Road was October 25, 1979. On that day we dressed in our best moldy clothes and our flashy new sunglasses, loaded up all the treasures my father had shrewdly purchased in Singapore, and boarded a bus for Paya Lebar Airport, about ten miles away. Since we were the last ones to leave the camp, no one was there to say good-bye to or bid us a fond farewell, but we felt no disappointment because we were going to America.

Paya Lebar Airport was sprawling and modern, big enough for even the Concorde to land, but the airport itself was nothing compared to what we saw when we stepped out onto the tarmac and beheld our waiting transport. The 747 was even longer and taller than *Seasweep*, and when they told us it could fly, we knew anything was possible. The 747 had room for more than four hundred passengers, but when we boarded the plane, we were surprised to find we were the only ones there. The plane's cabin was the size of a subway tunnel, and the children all ran around until a flight attendant pointed to our seats to let us know it was time to buckle up for takeoff.

You would think my brothers and sisters and I would have been frightened to fly for the first time, but we didn't give it a second thought. After all the wonders we had already witnessed, we just took for granted that a 190-ton chunk of metal could hurtle across the sky at five hundred miles per hour carrying us in its belly. Why not? If the pilot had told us we were going to make a quick stop on the moon, we probably would have believed him.

Since no one spoke our language, no one could tell us how long our flight would be, so we were surprised when the plane started down again, less than an hour after takeoff. We were landing in Malaysia—we just couldn't seem to get away from that place. In Malaysia a large group of refugees boarded the plane and joined us. This time when we took off, we looked out the windows and saw water below us. We knew then we were finally on our way.

Actually, we were only on our way to Japan, where we had to refuel before making the long hop across the Pacific to the West Coast. The flight from Malaysia to Japan took about seven hours. No additional refugees boarded there, so as soon as the plane was refueled, we took off again. Everything about flying was fun for us, but the best part of all was the food—they kept bringing it to us on little plastic trays. One of the entrees was pizza, which my father had never seen before. He took one look at it and said, "What's that mess?" But the rest of us loved it. I don't think my brother Bruce would have cared if we never landed.

The flight from Japan to the United States took almost eleven hours; we landed at Travis Air Force Base, about fifty miles northeast of San Francisco. Due to the bizarre mathematics involved in flying east across the International Date Line, we actually arrived in America five hours before we took off from Japan, which our minds found fascinating but our bodies found unconvincing. The clock on the wall told us that we had been flying for only six hours, but our exhausted bodies insisted that we had really been flying for twenty-one.

For refugees arriving in America from Southeast Asia, Travis Air Force Base served the same purpose Ellis Island had for immigrants from Europe a generation before. At one point in time, five hundred refugees were arriving at Travis every day to meet with immigration officials, make sure all their papers were in order, and most important of all, find out for the first time where they would be living in America.

We were given boxed lunches when we arrived, and each one was packed with exotic American delicacies we had never tasted: fried chicken, a biscuit—none of us knew what it was—and even a big, beautiful red apple. An apple for each of us—we couldn't believe it. In Vietnam an apple was a luxury that would have been cut into small slices and savored by an entire family. Everything tasted so good; we couldn't have felt more welcome if the governor of California had shown up to shake our hands.

The refugees from our plane gathered in a group while a Vietnamese-speaking translator announced each family's assignment, and my father noticed that regardless of the location, the translator always added the same comment:

"Oh, that's a wonderful place. You'll like it there."

The translator wasn't just trying to encourage us; that was what he believed. He told my father later, "In America, to make money is difficult, but to starve is even more difficult." In other words: "You're in America now. How bad can it be?" Most refugees had very little knowledge of America before their arrival; their goal was only to get here, and after that one city or state was the same as another. They were all just names on a map to us, and the only names that sounded familiar were the places that had large Vietnamese populations, such as Los Angeles, Houston, Philadelphia, and New York. Those were the assignments everyone hoped for though no one had the slightest idea what the climate was like there or whether the landscape would look anything like Vietnam. Those things didn't really matter because for an unemployed refugee with no language skills, community meant a lot more than geography or climate.

We finally received our assignment: Kansas City, Missouri— though the translator pronounced it *Misery*. We had no idea what the word meant, so we were elated—we were going to live in Misery. But we had barely begun to celebrate when we were informed that, for some reason, our assignment had been changed. We were not going to spend our lives in Misery after all; we were going to Fort Smith, Arkansas.

Where?

After completing all the necessary paperwork, we were taken by bus to a small hotel near the San Francisco airport, where we were told we would spend the night before flying out the next day. The ten of us were assigned to a room with one king-size bed, which looked luxurious to us after our empty room at 25 Hawkins Road. My brother Thai turned on the television and saw the first of many wonders we would see in America: a commercial that showed slices of bacon flying through the air from a frying pan to a plate. Who would have known—in America even the food could fly.

My father had just taken off his shirt when there was a knock at the door. It was the same man who had just dropped us off.

"Let's go," he said to us. "We have a plane for you now."

We were rushed to the San Francisco airport and told we would be taking an American Airlines flight to some strange place called Dallas. We had never heard of Dallas before, but we liked the name of the airline and remembered it because the flight attendants gave us all little plastic wings to wear on our jackets.

While we were hurrying to the gate in San Francisco, a strange man stopped me, smiled, and slipped a piece of paper into my jacket pocket. At the gate I said to my father, "Look what someone gave me," and pulled from my pocket an American hundred-dollar bill— another mysterious act of compassion by a perfect stranger.

It took another three hours to fly to Dallas, and the moment we stepped off the plane and into the terminal, we were told that we had to hurry to catch another flight at the opposite end of the airport. A gate agent pointed the way, and we hurried as fast as a family of ten could—which wasn't very fast at all because Anh and Hon were almost two years old by then, and after twenty-four hours cooped up on an airplane, they insisted on walking while my parents insisted on carrying them. We must have made quite a sight: ten frustrated and exhausted Chinese arguing with each other in Cháo zhōu while we hurried across the airport like a column of army ants.

The terminals in Dallas were shaped like two half circles with a long straightaway in between, which made us feel like hamsters on a treadmill. We managed to get lost once along the way, and that made my mother very anxious because the closer we got to our final destination, the greater her fear that something would go wrong at the last minute—an emotion I would feel many times over the next years. We finally found the correct gate and boarded the flight—our fifth for the trip and, mercifully, our last one.

Our final flight lasted less than an hour, and with every mile our anticipation grew because our next stop would be more than just another connection—it would be our new home. Each step of our journey had presented us with another wonder: Paya Lebar with its two-mile runways; the flying cargo ship called the 747; a flight across the world's widest ocean; the sprawling city of San Francisco glistening below us; and the Dallas airport with its Texas-size terminals. If those were just the wonders along the way, what would our final destination be like? It had been almost five months since we left Vietnam, and we had journeyed more than eleven thousand miles. At last we were coming to the end of the Silk Road, and we were about to see the Imperial City of Fort Smith, Arkansas, for the very first time.

It was late October, and we arrived around eight o'clock at night: it was dark and cold when we stepped off the plane. The temperature had reached eighty degrees that day, but it would drop to thirty-nine before the night was over; that was the coldest temperature any of us had ever experienced, and we were wearing only light jackets. The Fort Smith airport was just one small building with a single door marked A on one side and B on the other; after successfully navigating DFW, we had no trouble finding our way inside.

The night was cold, but the reception we received inside the terminal more than made up for it. Our family had been sponsored by a small Lutheran church on the south side of Fort Smith, and fifteen of the church's members showed up that night to welcome us. Neither party could understand a single word the other was saying, but our grateful smiles and their welcoming handshakes covered just about everything that needed to be said.

When Vietnamese refugees first began to pour into the United States in 1975, nine voluntary agencies, or *volags*, helped to find individuals or organizations who would agree to sponsor them. One of those volags was the Lutheran Immigration and Refugee Service in New York, which contacted the pastor of Our Redeemer Lutheran Church in Fort Smith, a gracious and compassionate man named Fred Hagemeier. Fred did a lot in those early years to help those first refugees adjust to their new lives in America, and when Fred and his congregation of 160 at Redeemer Lutheran heard about our situation, they agreed to do what no one else would: take on the ten-member Chung family.

It was the sponsor's responsibility to find housing for us; provide enough food, toiletries, and household items to get us started; and orient us to our new community. Those were the basics, but some sponsors took it upon themselves to help register their refugees for school, shop for clothes, find employment, and even give English lessons. The range of a sponsor's duties was really up to them, but anything they chose to do took a lot of work when they were doing it for a family of ten.

From the airport they escorted us to a waiting luxury stretch limousine—at least it seemed like one to us. In reality it was a twelve-passenger conversion van with swiveling captain's chairs, wooden cup holders, and most impressive of all, wall-to-wall shag carpet. Shag carpet is hard for some people to appreciate, but after three months on a bare wood floor, we thought it was like sitting on 1,000-count Egyptian cotton sheets.

We all piled into the van, and the man who was driving handed us each an enormous chocolate chip cookie. I bit into mine and gagged. I wasn't used to eating things so sweet, and to me it tasted terrible. Jenny liked hers, but I collected the cookies from everyone who didn't and left them in a neat little stack with a single bite missing from each one.

We were driven to our new home, a three-bedroom, two-bath house where we would be allowed to live rent-free for the next six months, courtesy of Our Redeemer Lutheran Church. The house was located on South Seventeenth Street in a spot now occupied by a parking lot. When we pulled up in front of the house, my brothers and sisters and I scrambled out of the van and ran to the door while the grown-ups took their time. The house looked palatial; 1,100 square feet of space for only ten people—that was almost four times larger than our room at 25 Hawkins Road. Such luxury—did everyone in America live like this?

The man who drove let us into the house and handed us the key—and with a warm good-bye that we didn't understand, he left us to settle in. The house was completely empty except for a folding table and ten folding chairs leaning against a wall. My mother and sisters headed straight for the kitchen, which was decorated in a color that can only be described as guacamole-gone-bad. But Jenny loved that kitchen because on the farm she had to cook with leaves and wood and charcoal; in this kitchen all she had to do was turn a plastic dial and an electric element glowed orange-red—and there was no ash to clean out when she was done cooking. The kitchen came outfitted with flatware and dishes and even a set of beautiful red cook pots—everything we could possibly need.

There was a refrigerator, too, and when we opened it, we found that the church had thoughtfully stocked it with food. They left plenty of milk for the eight children, but we couldn't drink milk because we were lactose intolerant. In Vietnam children drank only goat's milk or powdered milk, and adults didn't drink milk at all. The church left beef for us in the freezer, but Asians rarely ate beef because the taste and smell were too strong. There was canned tomato sauce and canned green beans, which was a real novelty to us because we had never eaten canned vegetables in Vietnam; they tasted so bad that Yen still can't stand the taste of canned green beans.

The church was even thoughtful enough to leave five pounds of rice, which probably would have lasted a year for any American family but would last only about three days for my family. It was the wrong kind of rice too. American rice was hard and had a different texture than we were used to. My family came to call it "Sam's rice" because it was the kind that was always sold in big sacks at Walmart and Sam's Club.

By the time we finished exploring the house, it was almost eleven o'clock. My mother decided it was time for bed, so we divided up bedrooms. There was a master bedroom with its own bath on the right, which my mother and father claimed for themselves and shared with me and my two little brothers. The other two bedrooms were on the left side of the house and shared a bathroom between them. My brothers and sisters were supposed to divide those two bedrooms, with the girls in one and the boys in the other. But there was a problem: the back bedroom had glow-in-the-dark owl stickers on the walls, and in Vietnam the owl was considered an evil omen. No one wanted to sleep with an evil owl glaring down at them, so Jenny, Bruce, Yen, Nikki, and Thai all crowded into the remaining bedroom that, for some odd reason, had carpet not only on the floor but also on the walls. Since there were no beds in any of the rooms, we all just curled up on the floor, and since we didn't know how to turn on the heat, the house was cold, so we just snuggled up together, closed our eyes, and waited for sleep to come.

Unfortunately eleven o'clock in Fort Smith was six in the morning in Singapore, so our hours were completely reversed—it was time to wake up, not go to sleep, and we were still too excited to sleep anyway. We ended up playing most of the night, and when exhaustion finally overtook us the next morning, we just dropped wherever we were and went to sleep.

Part Three

*Life can never give security; it can
only promise opportunity.*
—CHINESE PROVERB

ARKANSAS

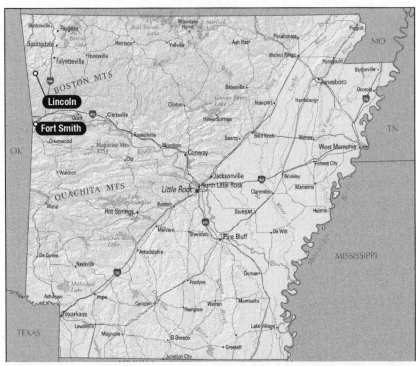

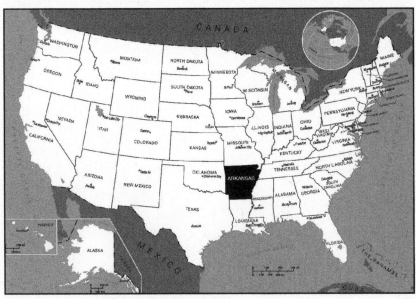

Twenty-Nine

WAKING UP IN AMERICA

TWO DAYS AFTER ARRIVING IN FORT SMITH, WE RAN out of food and needed to buy more, and that meant we would have to shop in an American grocery store. My father had not taken a job yet and had no income, but he did have a hundred dollars, courtesy of a generous stranger at the San Francisco airport. The good people at Our Redeemer Lutheran had also had the foresight to register our family for food stamps, so when it came time for us to go shopping, the problem wasn't money—the problem was we didn't speak English.

At the end of our street, there was a small grocery store, and since we had no transportation, it was the only place we could go to buy food. My father took the older children along with him the first time, and they got to watch as he tried to find all the items on the grocery list my mother had given him. In the marketplace back in Vietnam, nothing was packaged, and everything was easy to recognize; the chicken had feathers, and the pork had a head. But in America all the food was hidden behind boxes and bags and jars, and the only way to guess what was inside was by the image on the label. We heard about one Asian family who was frustrated and confused when it bought a can of Crisco shortening only to discover the can did not actually contain the fried chicken pictured on the label. I can't even imagine what the family thought the first time it saw a jar of Gerber baby food.

My father had to point to the things he wanted, and the clerk would gather them for us and set them on the counter. My father could read a few words of English, and he tried his best to read some of the labels instead of just pointing. Sugar came out "shoo-gah," and flour sounded like "fla-wah," but the clerk understood well enough to give us most of the right things. We needed pork, too, but my father didn't know that word; instead he tried his best to pronounce "pig" and "meat," but the clerk just looked at him blankly. Bruce was the artist in the family, so the grocer gave him a sheet of brown butcher paper and a pencil and Bruce drew a picture that vaguely resembled an animal with a curly tail. The clerk shouted, "Oh! Pork!" and everyone learned a new word that day.

We bought sugar, flour, and eggs so my mother could bake things, but the flour was different in America, and everything she baked came out coarse and grainy. Not that it mattered to us kids—we ate everything she made and asked for more. My mother had to learn to cook with American ingredients and spices, but she picked it up quickly and continued to employ her supernatural ability to make any amount of food stretch to feed a family of ten. My father couldn't wait to try out his brand-new rice cooker, but when he went to plug it in, he discovered that Singapore used a different voltage and his rice cooker would not work in America—a fact the merchants back in Singapore had somehow forgotten to mention. Oh well. At least he could listen to his boom box.

Oops.

My mother's biggest struggle was loneliness. She felt isolated in America. In Soc Trang her house was also a place of business, and every morning she rolled open the big double doors and neighbors wandered in and out all day—there was no separation between her home and her community. But in America people kept their doors closed and locked, and they only opened them if someone came by to visit—and no one wanted to visit a woman who couldn't speak a word of English.

For the first few days after our arrival, we wondered if the Lutheran church had abandoned us because no one had contacted us in almost a week. Then a Vietnamese man from the church stopped by one day and asked, "Where have you been?" We didn't understand; we hadn't gone anywhere. As it turned out, people from the church had been visiting us every day, but because our bodies were still adjusting to the new time zone, we had been sleeping all day and staying up all night. We were all asleep every time they came to visit, so when no one answered our door after they knocked several times, they just left whatever they brought us and went home.

That explained why mysterious things kept showing up on our doorstep—like a large bag of candy. We had no idea what the candy was for, and until my father got an explanation, none of us were allowed to touch it, so he just set the bag in the entryway and left it there. A couple of days later we heard the doorbell ring, and everyone ran to the door to greet our first evening visitor. When my father opened the door, there was a group of children wearing costumes and hideous masks more frightening than any owl we had ever seen, and they were holding out paper sacks and shouting something. Anh and Hon burst into tears and started screaming, and my father just stood there, staring at them—and then he shut the door. *Crazy American kids!*

A few minutes later the doorbell rang again. This time when my father opened the door, the group of costumed children spotted our bag of candy in the entryway and rushed into the house uninvited, which made Anh and Hon scream even louder. Each of the children grabbed a handful of candy, shoved it into his sack, and ran out the door again, and no one in my family could figure out what was going on—except for Bruce. Bruce hurried back to one of the bedrooms and found a square cardboard box with some of our belongings in it. He dumped everything on the floor and got my father to help him cut two eyeholes in the box, and then he put it over his head and ran out the door.

Bruce ran across the street while Yen, Nikki, and Thai followed at a distance, and the rest of us peeked through the blinds to see what would happen. A few minutes later Bruce came back with a handful of chocolate bars and a grin on his face.

He proudly held them out to my father. "Dad! Look at this!"

My father counted them. "Do it again," he told him, and three houses later we all had big smiles and chocolate-covered faces.

That was our first Halloween, and Bruce went dressed as a box. His costume may not have been fancy, but Bruce had a knack for figuring things out and getting the things he wanted, and those skills would come in handy for him later on. We thought Halloween was a wonderful American custom, and the next night we waited by the door for more costumed children to come—but to our disappointment no one did. Our costumes didn't improve much over the years; they were usually just paper plates with faces drawn on them and tied around our heads. Somehow I don't think the neighbors had much difficulty guessing who we were.

Our Redeemer Lutheran continued to be generous to us by dropping off donated items for the house: first mattresses, then a couch, then end tables, and even a small black-and-white TV with rabbit-ear antennas. My brothers and sisters preferred the carpet to the mattresses and ignored them. They wanted to spread out and use the second bedroom, but not as long as the evil owls were roosting there, so they asked my father if they could remove the glow-in-the-dark stickers from the walls.

"No," he told them. "Don't touch anything—this is not our house."

That feeling ran deep for my father: "This isn't our house; this isn't our country; this could all be a mistake, so be careful—they can always send us home."

There were houses on both sides of us and one across the street. There was a boy who lived in the house across the street who was flying a kite one day and came over to ask if Bruce could play with him. My father said no—he was afraid that Bruce could get into a fight with the boy and we would all be sent back to Vietnam. What an ironic reversal: when we were wealthy back in Soc Trang, the poor neighbor children were afraid to play with us—now we were the ones who were afraid.

Though we were not allowed to play with the neighbors, there was always someone to play with in a family of eight children. Our house had a deep backyard and there was plenty of room to run and kick a ball. When we first arrived in Fort Smith, I was too young for kindergarten, so while my brothers and sisters were in school each day, Anh and Hon and I were free to play in the backyard. One day I was squatting under a large tree, picking up nuts from the ground, when an insect buzzed in front of me and I swatted it. Unfortunately the insect turned out to be a wasp, and when it stung my hand, my entire arm immediately began to swell up. The Vietnamese folk remedy for a bee sting is to roll a hardboiled egg on the skin to draw out the poison, but when my mother saw that my arm had swollen so large that it was about to rip my shirtsleeve, she knew I was way beyond the egg method. She rushed me to Sparks Hospital, just a few blocks from our house.

My allergic reaction was so serious, I had to spend two nights in the hospital; my mother stayed by my side as much as she could. I enjoyed the hospital because I got to eat Jell-O and drink Coke whenever I wanted. The first English word I ever learned was *Coke*, which didn't turn out to be very useful but did come in handy when I was thirsty. When the hospital brought my meals, I didn't have much of an appetite—probably because of too much Coke and Jell-O—so I just picked at the food on my tray and left most of it. When I was finished, my mother ate everything that was left—not because she was hungry but because just a few months ago she was starving to death, and it was unthinkable to let good food go to waste. When the nurse came back for the tray, she would always say, "My, what a good eater you are," then make a note in my chart that my appetite was returning nicely. I lost five pounds in that hospital, but my mother gained ten to make up for it.

For my family, adjusting to life in America was no harder than it would have been on any other distant planet. That was what

America was like to us: a different planet. The terrain, the climate, the flora and fauna, the weird aliens who lived there, and their incomprehensible language—everything was strange and new to us, and we were going to have to learn to do everything in a completely different way.

Thirty

ALLIED GARDENS

AFTER SIX MONTHS IN FORT SMITH, WE HAD TO MOVE
from our rent-free home on Seventeenth Street that the
Lutherans had generously provided, but on our father's paycheck we could not afford to rent another house. Instead we took
an apartment in a complex called Allied Gardens. Today Allied
Gardens is called Allied Gardens Estates, a beautiful gated community of well-maintained apartments and manicured hedges and
lawns—but when we moved there, it was a bit different. Most of the
units at Allied Gardens were Section 8 housing, a government-sub-
sidized program that made housing available to the poor by limiting
the rent to no more than one-third of the renter's income. Based on
my father's income at the time, we were able to move into a four-
bedroom apartment for just over a hundred dollars per month.

Allied Gardens was made up of separate C-shaped apartment
buildings, each of which had two floors and six individual apartments. Our apartment was on the ground floor and was about the
same square footage as the house we just left—close to 1,100 square
feet. Unlike our house, the apartment had no carpet; the floor was
covered in square vinyl tiles, and instead of trying to sleep on the
cold, hard floor, we threw down mattresses and slept on those.

The apartment had a gas stove, and my mother completely covered the top of it with aluminum foil, either to keep it clean or to keep from seeing how dirty it was. The cabinets above the stove were so caked with grease from thousands of previous dinners that we had to use a butter knife to scrape it off. The bedrooms were not much better. At night my brothers and I had a favorite game: whack-a-cockroach. The rules were simple: sit on the floor in the dark, holding one of your flip-flops, then switch on the lights and smash as many cockroaches as you could before they disappeared into the woodwork. No matter how many times we switched the lights off and on, there were always more cockroaches—hours of fun for the entire family.

Because Allied Gardens was so affordable, it attracted other low-income families and soon became a minority ghetto. There were Hispanics, blacks, Caucasians, and even a few Laotians. Each group occupied its own building, not because Allied Gardens segregated them but because each ethnic group preferred it that way. Like us, they were all looking for community, and community was easier to find among people they knew and understood. All six units of our building were occupied by Vietnamese families, and their children became our friends and playmates.

A Vietnamese neighbor owned a TV and a VCR, and all the Asians at Allied Gardens used to squeeze into his tiny apartment to watch the same kung fu movies over and over again—everyone's favorite was *The Way of the Dragon*, where Bruce Lee beat up Chuck Norris in the Roman Colosseum. We couldn't afford our own VCR, so we used to peek through the neighbor's window to try to watch his—another ironic reversal of our lives in Vietnam.

All the kids had nicknames, and it wasn't always clear how they originated. Some were obvious enough; Bruce was called Crab because he ran so slowly, and another boy was called Rabbit because he ran so fast. But a boy who lived upstairs was called Fat Dog, and none of us ever knew why. Fat Dog had a hot temper and used to pick fights, which wasn't hard to understand, considering the nickname he had to live with.

There was a boy in another building who was missing a leg, but none of us ever had the courage to ask him how he lost it. Since he was from Laos, it wasn't hard to figure out. During the Vietnam War, more bombs were dropped on Laos than on Germany and Japan combined during World War II, and children at play often discovered the unexploded ordnance. Mercifully, that boy was never given a nickname.

With buildings divided by ethnic group, conflict was unavoidable. It would start with some kid throwing dust; then dust turned into rocks, and before long it escalated into an all-out fistfight. Once a little Vietnamese boy was beaten up on the playground, and when his older brother heard about it, he ran back to his apartment and grabbed a butcher knife from the kitchen. He was just heading out the door when an adult Vietnamese neighbor spotted the knife and yelled to him, "Where are you going with that? Put it back right now!" The boy obeyed even though the neighbor was a stranger to him; Asian culture is authority-based, and the boy recognized the man's authority over him simply because of his age. It was a good thing he did because there was no telling what would have happened if he had returned to the playground with that knife.

An ethnically diverse apartment complex was a great place to begin learning about different people and cultures. There was a mailman who used to come by each day, dressed in his regulation blue shorts and shirt, carrying a leather shoulder bag full of letters. He was a nice man, and we always looked forward to his coming, and all the kids used to swarm around him and tug at his clothing until he finally laughed and handed out bubble gum to everyone. But one day when we tugged at him, he turned and shouted, "Stop it! Go away!" I didn't understand. I thought he liked it when we tugged at him. Why did he get angry this time, and more important, why didn't he give us any gum? I knew I was missing something, but I didn't know what it was.

What I was missing was the fact that it was a different mailman, but I couldn't tell because to me all Caucasians looked the same. That was an educational moment for me. The truth is, all Caucasians do look the same to Asians, and all Asians look the same to Caucasians—at least at first. It takes time to develop the sensitivity to subtle facial differences that allows us to distinguish one person from another within our own ethnic group; and when we take our first good look at a different ethnic group, we're starting all over. Prejudice begins with ignorance, and whenever one culture first meets another, there is ignorance. At Allied Gardens, the Caucasians didn't like the Vietnamese because their food smelled funny, and the Vietnamese didn't like the Laotians because they were dirty. I'm not sure who the Laotians didn't like, but I knew one mailman who didn't like me.

My parents allowed us to roam free—not that they had much choice. My father was always at work, and my mother was responsible for eight children, and the youngest two required her full attention. The rest of us just came home from school, dropped off our books, and ran out to play. There was a playground with a swing set and a merry-go-round for the younger kids, and we played kickball endlessly. We played hopscotch on the sidewalks and roller-skated on the streets, using cheap metal skates my mother bought at a flea market. They were the kind that clamped onto your shoes with a key, and if you jumped the curb the wrong way, they could rip the soles right off your shoes. My feet were too small for skates, so I used a pair of plastic Playskool buses; I discovered that if I took out all the passengers, I could just fit my feet into them, and I skated after my brothers and sisters just as fast as my two little buses would go.

We played until midnight if there was no school the next day, and in the summers we played all day because there was nothing else to do. There were no camps, no programs, no babysitters— just dozens of kids and room to run, which was all we needed to have fun.

My family lived at Allied Gardens for two years. We were surrounded by children very much like us, even when they came from different countries. Most of us were new to America, so no one could laugh at anyone else's manners or customs. No one felt stupid because all of us were ignorant, and no one owned anything to envy because no one had any money. Allied Gardens was our own little Vietnamese hamlet, and we were safe and comfortable inside our familiar minority bubble.

But when we stepped out of that bubble, things were different.

Thirty-One

STARTING SCHOOL

THE FIRST DAY IN A NEW SCHOOL IS HARD FOR ANY child, but try to imagine what it's like for a refugee who doesn't speak a word of English. The teacher tells everyone to take out a piece of paper, but you have no idea what she's saying, and the only reason you take out a piece of paper is because that's what everyone around you is doing. You nod a lot, not because you understand but because you don't want everyone else to think you're stupid. You smile at everyone, not because you're happy but because you're terrified by the thought of making someone angry. You sit by yourself in the cafeteria and wish someone would approach you, but you don't dare approach someone else.

On the first Monday following our arrival in Fort Smith, Jenny, Bruce, Yen, Nikki, and Thai all began their American educations at Belle Point Elementary School, starting classes almost two months into the school year, which put them behind in every subject. Jenny was in sixth grade, Bruce in fifth, Yen in fourth, Nikki in first, and Thai in kindergarten. Almost everything they had been taught in Vietnam was useless; in America no one cared if they were able to recite songs of praise to Uncle Ho.

I was too young even for kindergarten, but at Allied Gardens there was a program called Head Start that was funded by the Department of Health and Human Services to help children from low-income families get ready for kindergarten. My parents loved Head Start because the program was free. I loved it because all we did was play and eat doughnuts, and if we wanted another doughnut, all we had to do was ask for more. *More* was the second English word I ever learned, which gave me a two-word vocabulary: *Coke* and *more*. If I ever wanted more Coke, I was ready.

I only spoke Vietnamese and Cháo zhōu, so when they had story time, I listened without understanding; and when they sang nursery rhymes, I lip-synched so no one would know I didn't understand the words. There were a couple of other Vietnamese kids in my Head Start program, so I didn't feel completely alone—I just couldn't talk to anyone. But there wasn't much need to talk with a mouthful of doughnuts anyway, and I was too busy enjoying all the activities to care much about conversation.

When I advanced to first grade, I was in school only a couple of weeks before an error was discovered on my enrollment record. On American calendars the New Year always begins on January 1, but on the Chinese calendar the start of the New Year varies each year from late January to mid-February. I was born on January 1, and according to the American calendar the year was 1976. But on the Chinese calendar the New Year did not begin that year until January 31, so according to that calendar, my birth year was 1975. My parents had used the Chinese calendar when they recorded my birth year on official documents back in Singapore, and that gave everyone the impression that I was five years old when, in fact, I was only four. When the error was discovered, the school decided I was too young to be in first grade and should be in kindergarten instead. The decision to move me back a grade level meant nothing to me at the time, but it was to have a major impact on my life later on.

Kindergarten was new to me, and it had its challenges. On the very first day the teacher announced that everyone should bring a towel to class the next day for nap time. The teacher knew I wouldn't understand, so she gave me a note to take home to my mother that would explain everything—but my mother didn't know any more English than I did, and the note didn't help at all.

Yen helped her decipher the note, which is something she always did for our family. Whenever there was a note or letter for my parents to read, Yen helped them figure it out; whenever there was a report card or a permission slip for my parents to sign, Yen signed it for them. Yen managed to figure out that I was supposed to bring something to school the next day, but even Yen couldn't understand what the item was. It was the word *towel* that confused them; *towel* sounds like the Vietnamese word *thao*, which means "wash basin," and my mother couldn't understand why in the world the teacher would want me to bring a wash basin to school. It finally dawned on Yen what the word must have meant, and she explained it to my mother.

The next day when the teacher asked everyone to take out their towels and spread them on the floor for nap time, I watched as the other kids unrolled enormous beach towels with He-Man or Malibu Barbie printed on the front—then I reached into my pocket and pulled out a little washcloth. Everyone laughed at me, and while they were all napping on their fluffy beach towels, I had to curl up on the carpet.

Coke, more, and *towel*—my vocabulary was expanding fast.

In grade school I also learned my first lessons about racism and discrimination. My elementary school was predominantly white, and my brothers and sisters and I stood out like beacons there. In my first-grade class we were all sitting on the floor for story time one day when a boy raised his hand and asked in front of everyone, "Why does Vinh have a flat nose?" I lost count of the number of times I was asked, "Do you know kung fu?" and each time I was asked that question, I wished I did. We were called "flat-faced," "fat head," and sometimes names that didn't even make sense.

I was in second grade before anyone called me "gook," and I had no idea what the word meant. Another Vietnamese boy had to tell me, "Don't you know what that means? That's the worst thing anyone can call you!" and I had to make a mental note that the next time I was called gook, I should get very angry. That's the strange thing about discrimination: it has to be learned, on both the sending end and receiving end. In a fistfight no one has to tell you if you've been punched or not, but you have to learn when you've been insulted in a conversation—and I was given plenty of opportunities to learn.

My biggest struggle was that I didn't speak English. I got into a pushing match with a boy in first grade, and we both had to go to the principal's office. The principal listened while the other boy explained his version of the story first: yes, the boy admitted, it was true that he pushed me first, but only by accident. The principal turned to me and asked, "Is that true? Did he push you by accident?" I had no idea what he was asking me. *Accident*—that word was not in this week's vocabulary lesson. What did it mean? I don't remember what I said to the principal in reply, but whatever it was got me punished and allowed the other boy to go free.

It happened again in second grade. I got into a pushing match with another boy, and this time my teacher asked me, "Don't you think you owe him an apology?" I just stared at her. I didn't know what an apology was, and I wasn't sure if you could owe one or not—so I told her no and got in trouble again.

In both cases I clearly remember thinking, *That's not fair.* I wasn't being punished for pushing someone—I was being punished for not knowing the words *accident* and *apology.* If I had possessed a better command of the language, the other boys would have been punished and I would have gone free. That was when I first began to understand the power of language. I could use it to attack, and I could use it to defend but only if I knew the right words.

Though school was difficult for us all, it was hardest for Jenny. She was twelve when we arrived, and though she may have been the brightest of all of us, she had the hardest time learning the English language. When I was only four, Jenny brought a book home from school one day. She always took immaculate care of her books; she saved the nicest wrapping paper from previous holidays to wrap them in, and it would have been unthinkable for her to ever make a mark in one. But she left her book on the coffee table that day, and I not only opened it but tore a page—and when I did, she slapped me so hard that I almost passed out. Jenny feels terrible about that to this day, but I understand. Jenny loved school back in Vietnam, and she suffered more than any of us when the communists took over and her dream of one day becoming an engineer was shattered. In America she saw a second chance, and the opportunity to get an education was far more precious to her than it was to the rest of us. The book I tore was sacred to her because education was sacred to her. When I tore that page, I think she felt her dream being torn away from her for a second time.

We all struggled when we first started school, and unfortunately the challenges did not go away as the years went by. The lessons just got harder—the lessons in math, science, English, and also racism and discrimination. We had a lot to learn about what it took to succeed in America, and the most important lessons they didn't teach in school; we had to learn those lessons somewhere else.

Thirty-Two

GRAND AVENUE

THE TOWN OF FORT SMITH IS ONLY ABOUT 5 PERCENT Asian, and there were only two types of places where Asians could mix and mingle: a few small Asian grocery stores and the occasional Chinese restaurant. But while we were living at Allied Gardens, we discovered a third place, and that one changed our lives.

One of our neighbors at Allied Gardens told my parents about a Vietnamese church that had recently been started in Fort Smith, and he said there were about thirty or forty Vietnamese who attended every week. Thirty or forty Vietnamese all in one place—to my parents that sounded like Saigon. When our neighbor told us the service was translated into Vietnamese, we were sold, and the following Sunday the neighbor's unsuspecting nephew dropped by. He expected to drive a small family to church but found ten of us waiting to pile into his pathetic little car.

When the smoking car limped into the church parking lot, we were all amazed—the church building was enormous. My father was the only one who could read the sign, though he didn't understand all the words: *Grand Avenue Baptist Church.*

The Vietnamese church at Grand Avenue Baptist became the single most powerful influence on my family in Fort Smith. My father made sure we attended that church without fail, regardless of weather or circumstances. Bruce once sprained his ankle and thought he had the perfect excuse to stay home. He told my father, "Dad! I can't walk!" but my father just said, "Put on your shoes and get dressed. We're going to church." The reason my father was so adamant about church attendance was that the church played a far more important role in our lives than it does for many natural-born Americans. For my parents, it completed a spiritual journey that had begun long before they ever reached America.

My mother had never been able to understand the vivid dream she'd had shortly before leaving Vietnam—the dream about a long-haired, bearded man in a white robe who pointed to our family and brought each of us back to life. No one was ever able to explain it to her or help her identify the mysterious figure who had the power to raise the dead. But the first time she walked into the lobby of Grand Avenue Baptist Church, she saw a portrait of Jesus hanging on the wall—the first image of Jesus she had ever seen—and she took one look at it and said, "That was the man in my dream."

I have asked my mother about that experience many times, and she makes it very clear that the portrait of Jesus did not remind her of the man in her dream—He *was* the man. For my mother, walking into that church solved a mystery that had puzzled her ever since she had left Vietnam. She felt as if the portrait were saying to her, "I am the one who delivered your family from death. Welcome to America."

The church completed a spiritual journey for my father too. After six days adrift on the South China Sea and nearly dead from thirst, he had cried out to the Creator God for rain and minutes later found himself frantically bailing water. Onboard *Seasweep*, when he had heard Stan Mooneyham speak about Jesus, the Creator God was given a name, and my father made a commitment to Him. There were other refugees aboard *Seasweep* who had made that same commitment, but as soon as they reached Singapore, many of them returned to their former rituals and the worship of their ancestors. My father couldn't understand how they could so quickly abandon a commitment they had made, a commitment he fully intended to keep. When he walked into Grand Avenue Baptist, that was what he was doing: following through on a commitment he had made to the faithful Creator God.

There was another reason my parents were so adamant about their children attending church: fear. Not fear that God would punish us if we didn't—that has no place in Christian belief—but fear of all the things that could go wrong for us in America. Fear is one of the most powerful influences for a refugee; it is often the hidden motivation behind obsessive discipline and drive. There are so many things that could go wrong for the refugee, so many mistakes that could be made, so many things to be afraid of—and there is no margin of error. I walked a path two inches wide and eighteen years long, and my parents were determined their children would not step off that path the way other children often did.

I have asked my parents what their image of America was before they came here; their answers seem humorous now, but they were no laughing matter at the time. My father thought all of America was like Las Vegas: morally loose, self-indulgent, and superficial—which is understandable when you consider that many foreigners only know America through television shows such as *Baywatch* and *All-Star Wrestling*. My father had been misled by American media too. Back in Vietnam he had seen photographs of Marilyn Monroe and Elizabeth Taylor and assumed they were typical American women.

My mother thought America was all big cities, where everyone smoked and drank and hung out in bars all day. Since she didn't smoke or drink, she had no idea what she was going to do with her time once she got there. She had no idea what Americans themselves would be like because in Vietnamese comic books Americans were always drawn with long noses and hair like a porcupine's quills, and they were portrayed as so dimwitted that a Vietnamese child could trick them into doing anything he wanted.

Those were groundless fears, but there were others that were all too real. We constantly heard stories about other refugee families and all the things that went wrong for them: sons who joined gangs or became criminals and went to prison, and daughters who got pregnant and ran off with their boyfriends never to return. Those were not imaginary stories; they were real ones, and my parents constantly related them to us to graphically illustrate the world that awaited us if we ever dared to step off that two-inch-wide path.

One of the values my parents tried hard to instill in us was to never forget where we came from. There is a Vietnamese expression for it: *Mất Gốc* (pronounced *Mutt Goch*), which means "to lose root." Our language, our heritage, our traditions, our ethnicity—it was all part of our root, the centuries-old source material that defined who we really were. Losing root was a risk for every refugee trying to adapt in America, though not every refugee thought it was a bad thing. Some believed their best chance of success in America was to assimilate as quickly and completely as possible—to just erase their past and blend into the American culture. That was certainly the easier way to go. For my family, "keeping root" meant living in two worlds at the same time—learning to be American while at the same time trying to remain Chinese.

I had a Vietnamese friend growing up whose parents decided to take the assimilation route. They changed their son's Vietnamese birth name to David, and they abandoned their original language completely and spoke only English at home. As a result, David learned English a lot faster than I did, and he was able to blend in better too. I envied David, and I wished that my parents would let me choose a cool American name.

My brothers and sisters wished it even more than I did because their names were a source of difficulty for them all throughout school. Jenny's birth name was not "Jenny"; it was Yen Nhi, which is pronounced *In Nyee*. No teacher reading her name from an attendance list ever guessed the correct pronunciation. Yen's name was originally Yen To, and because she used to go everywhere with her older sister, people used to tease, "Here come Knee and Toe!" Nikki's birth name was even harder for people to pronounce: it was Nga, which is pronounced *Nya*; and Bruce was originally Luong, pronounced *Loong*. Thai and I were the lucky ones because our names were easy for our teachers to figure out, and Anh and Hon, who came after us, were fortunate as well.

Jenny, Bruce, Yen, and Nikki eventually adopted Anglicized versions of their names: Yen Nhi chose the similar-sounding Jenny; Yen To shortened her name to Yen; Luong took the name of his boyhood hero, Bruce Lee, and Nga just picked Nikki because she liked the way it sounded. But none of them changed their names until later on. Jenny and Bruce were in college before they did, and part of the reason was Mất Gốc—their names were part of their root.

Our language was a big part of our root too. David learned English quickly, but in the process he also forgot Vietnamese. In our home we spoke only Cháo zhōu and Vietnamese because my parents knew that our schools would teach us English, and they didn't want us to lose our native tongues. But I left Vietnam at the age of three and a half, so I had only a rudimentary knowledge of Vietnamese, and I would have lost that language if it were not for the Vietnamese church. Our church service was translated into Vietnamese, but our Sunday school was conducted in English, so every Sunday we were able to practice both languages. My knowledge of Vietnamese is still fairly elementary, but the only reason I can still speak it at all is because of our church.

I envied boys like David at first because I desperately wanted to fit in, but as my brothers and sisters and I got older, we felt sorry for boys like him. Thai even came up with a sympathetic name for Vietnamese kids who could no longer speak Vietnamese: lost gooks. They had lost part of their root, and in the process lost a sense of identity and direction that the church helped people like us retain.

For us, the Vietnamese church in Fort Smith was a community where people with similar problems and needs could come together and help one another; it was a place of learning and spiritual growth; and it was where we learned to serve others and to give back. We were a poor refugee family "fresh off the boat" in America, but we felt blessed to be here and believed we had a responsibility to give back, and the more we gave the more we received. That's a mistake often made in America: we spend our lives seeking to be served, instead of seeking to serve others, and the more we receive, the less we seem to have.

I walked a path two inches wide and eighteen years long, and I'm grateful the church and my family were there to help me do it. My father had to walk that same path, only his path was a little longer: his journey lasted twenty-three years, and he had to do it all by himself.

Thirty-Three

THE FACTORY

WITHIN DAYS OF OUR ARRIVAL IN FORT SMITH, MY father was out looking for a job, and he quickly discovered that the only jobs available to an illiterate Asian refugee were jobs involving manual labor. Many of the first-wave refugees, who had arrived in Fort Smith back in 1975, were former military officers or government officials who were skilled and educated; they found it easier than later arrivals to find jobs and adjust to life in America. A third of them had completed high school, and a sixth had even attended college; almost two-thirds of them could already speak English, and that made it much easier to find employment. Unfortunately there were no job openings in America for "military officer" or "government official," so former generals often found themselves working as janitors or waiters. The rare few who actually qualified for white-collar jobs found it impossible to advance beyond an entry-level position because they were automatically assumed to have "poor communication skills" or "lack of leadership potential." It was a phenomenon that came to be known as the "bamboo ceiling."

In Vietnam my father had been the COO of a multimillion-dollar rice-milling, shipping, and commodities trading empire; in America his first job was fabricating fiberglass at the minimum wage of $2.90

an hour, which brought home a paycheck of about $90 per week. He endured that job for three months, working through the winter in an unheated warehouse, making go-cart seats and fiberglass water tanks without heavy clothing to keep him warm. He wore a respirator to protect his lungs, but nothing protected his exposed flesh, and every night he came home tormented by the invisible glass fibers embedded in his skin.

After those three months he took a job working in residential construction, which increased his salary to $4.50 an hour. The term *residential construction* is misleading; in reality my father's job was to do any menial task that did not require the skills and union membership of a carpenter—such as sweeping floors, hauling lumber and pipe, and breaking up concrete with a jackhammer.

In the evenings my father would walk to a nearby adult education center that taught ESL classes. He met lots of other Asians there who were trying to improve their prospects by learning the English language, and they kept telling my father that if he really wanted to get ahead in America, he would need more than just night school courses—he would need to go to a real college and get a real degree. He knew they were right, but that was easier said than done. My father had a wife and eight children to support, and he was too busy getting by to have time to get ahead.

He found his next job through an employment agency—at Ball Plastics, a now-defunct factory that molded plastic panels for refrigerator interiors. The move to Ball Plastics meant another increase in pay—from $4.50 to $6.50 per hour this time. He worked the swing shift from 3:00 to 11:00 p.m.; but when he worked overtime, he often didn't get home until 3:00 a.m.—and he worked overtime whenever it was offered because overtime paid time and a half. His job at Ball Plastics paid more money, but having to work the swing shift meant my father would no longer be able to take ESL classes in the evening. That put a permanent end to his adult education.

The jobs my father chose had nothing to do with his abilities and interests, and they had nothing at all to do with a career path or a sense of personal fulfillment. He worked to provide for his family, and he chose each job by the paycheck it would provide and nothing more. He was always scouting for a better job, and when he heard about a job that paid almost $9.00 an hour, he jumped at it without even asking what the job was. It turned out to be the last job he would ever take. On my father's birthday in 1983, he stepped up to an assembly line at Rheem Air Conditioning, and twenty-three years and two months later, the factory bell rang, and he picked up his lunch pail and went home.

Rheem manufactured residential and commercial heating and air-conditioning units, and it was one of the five biggest employers in Fort Smith. The factory employed more than a thousand workers, and along with the Whirlpool plant on the edge of town, it was considered the best factory job you could get. My father had no seniority when he first started at Rheem, so every morning he just walked into the factory and waited for a supervisor to tell him what he would be doing that day. Sometimes he worked a press, feeding large sheets of metal into a machine that was powerful enough not only to stamp out parts but also to remove fingers. Sometimes he worked on an assembly line, piecing together the various parts that make the condenser coils for air-conditioning units. When there was no other job available, he swept floors or cleaned machines or even worked as a janitor.

The factory was hot, and it didn't help that my father started work in mid-July, when the temperatures in Fort Smith often topped ninety-five degrees with humidity to match. Ironically, Rheem Air Conditioning was not air-conditioned; a factory that manufactured devices to cool other people let its own employees sweat. To get to the assembly line, my father had to walk past a long row of air-conditioned offices inside the building where the managers worked. Each office had a large picture window that looked out over the factory, and as my father walked by, he could see the managers sitting behind their desks in their sweat-free dress shirts and colorful silk ties. He loved the days when his job on the assembly line put him near one of those offices because every time the office door opened, he could feel a brief rush of cool air.

The job was demanding, and the hours were exhausting; but one of the hardest things for my father was the isolation. The factory was cavernous, and it was so loud that conversation was impossible—and even if it had been possible, Rheem did not allow its employees to talk on the job. There was a good reason for that rule: the machines were dangerous, and conversation was distracting; there had been more than one serious job-related injury there. My father once had to be hospitalized when a four-ton forklift backed into him, and on another occasion he almost had his hands amputated by a malfunctioning press.

But that no-talking rule had an unforeseen effect on my father; he spoke only a few words of English, and the place where he spent most of his day denied him the opportunity to practice and learn. He was already isolated by his lack of language skills, and at Rheem it wasn't going to get any better. When he retired twenty-three years later, his English wasn't much better than when he first began.

He was forty-six years old when he started at Rheem, though the factory thought he was only forty-two. That was no accident. While we were still at the refugee camp back in Singapore, my father heard a rumor that older men had a harder time finding jobs in America, so when it came time to fill out his paperwork, he lied about his age. Instead of listing his birth year as 1937, he wrote down 1941, and since he had no birth certificate from Vietnam, there was nothing to contradict him. He was forty-two in Singapore, but with the stroke of a pen, he became a youthful thirty-eight. Fiberglass wasn't the only thing my father fabricated.

But that little fabrication eventually caught up with him at Rheem. He should have been able to retire at age sixty-five, like everyone else, but according to his factory employment record, he was only sixty-one, which forced him to work four years beyond his true retirement age. He wasn't able to retire until he was sixty-nine; my father subtracted four years to get started, but he was forced to add them back on at the end.

Many of the assembly line workers at Rheem were young men just out of high school, and some of them had dropped out before

He took
all the overtime he was offered and worked a double shift whenever

He took
all the over

graduating. My father couldn't relate to those younger workers, and he had a hard time understanding the older ones as well. The factory ran twenty-four hours a day, and my father was willing to work any shift he was given: the morning shift from 7:00 to 3:00, the swing shift from 3:00 to 11:00, or the night shift from 11:00 to 7:00. He took all the overtime he was offered and worked a double shift whenever it was available. He put in every hour he could to make every dollar possible, and he couldn't understand why American workers always seemed to want time off.

My father saved every dime he could. There was a vending machine in the factory that sold Pepsis for fifty cents; but regardless of how hot it was, he never bought one because he thought it was a waste of money. The younger workers seemed to live week-to-week, grabbing their paychecks on Friday and blowing their earnings over the weekend, so every Monday it was as if they were starting over. That made no sense to my father; he was determined to succeed in America, and wasting money didn't seem like the way to do it.

There was something else that added to my father's isolation: the same racist attitudes he encountered everywhere he went. At the factory, though, they were worse because there he wasn't just a foreigner moving into the house next door—he was a foreigner taking a job away from some deserving American. And he wasn't just any foreigner; he was from Vietnam. It had been only eight years since the Vietnam War ended, and more than half of all Americans personally knew someone who had been killed or wounded in the war. I remember opening the trunk of my father's car one day and finding an old, beat-up baseball bat—and he didn't play baseball.

At the end of every shift, he came home smelling like machine oil, smoke, and dust, and on the days he installed insulation, my sisters had to shake the fiberglass out of his clothing. No matter what shift he worked or how late he came home, my mother always waited up for him and had something for him to eat; if it was early enough she cooked him something fresh, and when he was late she warmed up a plate of whatever she had made for our dinner that night. After eating, he often lay down on the sofa for a nap, and if my brothers and sisters and I were still awake when he came home, we were given the job of plucking his gray hairs while he slept. He paid us a penny for every ten hairs pulled, and we collected them on a little towel to keep track of what we earned. Bruce, budding entrepreneur that he was, used to pull black hairs along with the gray ones to increase his profits.

During those days at Rheem, my father used to sometimes wonder why his life had turned out the way it did. The factory served as a constant reminder of everything he had lost. In Vietnam he had been in authority over several hundred employees, and now he was forced to take orders from supervisors half his age. He knew he had the intelligence and experience to work in one of those air-conditioned offices, and he also knew he never would—but he vowed that his children would have that opportunity.

Because my father worked such long hours, I didn't see a lot of him growing up. He wasn't like the other dads I saw; he didn't help me with my homework, he didn't attend my sporting events, and he never took me hunting or fishing. He worked—that was his role, that was his responsibility, and my brothers and sisters and I understood that. I never heard my father complain about the menial jobs he was forced to take to support our family, and it was years later before my mother confided to us that he sometimes came home so depressed that he felt like crying. At the time I was too young to understand the sacrifice he was making, but I understand now, and I'm humbled by the choice he made.

To my father, America was a land of opportunity, but his family was a world of responsibility, and he was forced to choose between them. He gave up his dream of being a doctor for his family, and he gave up his education so his children could have one. Our success meant his failure; giving us a future meant giving up his own. But in a sense, my father never really did give up his dream of being a doctor.

He just passed that dream on to us.

Thirty-Four

THE AMERICAN DREAM

AFTER TWO YEARS AT ALLIED GARDENS, IT BECAME obvious my family could no longer squeeze two adults and eight growing children into an 1,100-square-foot apartment, so my father went searching for an affordable house in an area east of Fort Smith, called Barling. In the summer of 1982, we became genuine American homeowners for the first time.

Barling was the place to go for affordable housing because it was a low-income, high-unemployment area with housing values significantly lower than the state average. It was a working-class town with neighborhoods interspersed with run-down trailer parks, where a home security system meant a rottweiler without a leash. The houses were nothing to look at; most of them needed paint or repair, and some of them had broken-down cars rusting on cinder blocks in weed-infested yards. But the houses were definitely inexpensive, and that was the selling point for a family like mine.

We purchased a three-bedroom house with one and a half baths and a single-car garage, which we walled off to add an additional room. Since Bruce was the oldest boy, he claimed the garage for himself, and since he was also the biggest, he got the privilege of sleeping on a bed all by himself. The other four brothers had to share a bedroom with a single bunk bed; two of us slept together on the top, and the other two on the bottom. There were mattresses on the bunk bed, but sheets were optional, and most of the time we didn't bother. There were no assigned places for sleeping. The first one to get into bed got his choice of locations, and when the last space available required climbing over someone on the top bunk, it was usually easier to just sleep on the floor. The sleeping arrangement was intimate, to say the least; when one of us wet the bed, two of us had to change.

The girls all shared a bedroom, too, but their sleeping arrangements were based on seniority. Number-one-daughter Jenny got a twin bed all to herself while her sisters had to share a bunk bed. Number-two-daughter Yen claimed the convenient bottom bunk, and number-three-daughter Nikki was left with the top.

My parents had a bedroom all to themselves, but with eight children and only one and a half baths, they had to share the only shower with the rest of us, and that was the worst thing about the house. Getting ready for church every Sunday taught us the meaning of eternity because my sisters barricaded themselves in the bathroom for hours, and it drove the brothers crazy. The boys required less privacy; when it was our turn in the bathroom, we left the door unlocked and rotated in and out as needed. While one of us was in the shower, scrubbing, the next in line was taking off his clothes and trying not to stumble over the brother sitting on the toilet while he yelled to the brother in the shower to leave some hot water for him. I never knew what hot water felt like until I went to college.

Living in a house was more expensive than living in an apartment, and we had to look for ways to save money. My father loved to find a bargain; he read the *Southwest Times Record* from masthead to classified ads and clipped every money-saving coupon he could find. His favorite place to shop was the new Walmart because they promised to match anyone's prices—but they sometimes set a per-customer limit on our most-needed items, such as toilet paper. To circumvent that rule, my father used to take us to Walmart with him and hand each of us a coupon with instructions to check out at different registers. Somehow I doubt that anyone was fooled when eight Asian children all bought toilet paper at exactly the same time.

My mother had spent her entire life learning how to make ends meet, and those lessons came in handy in Barling. She loved to barter, and she drove a hard bargain. She was different from my father in that respect; my father loved to find a bargain, but he hated to negotiate because it embarrassed him. My mother was never embarrassed to haggle, and she didn't mind doing it in broken English or just by waving a coupon in someone's face and pointing—and she usually got what she wanted.

She planted flower and vegetable gardens, but instead of having nice brick borders, she used random pieces of scrap wood that my brothers and I scavenged around town. Sometimes she would be working in the backyard and would call to us, "I need another piece of wood! Go find one for me!" and off we would go. She used the leftover wood to build things for the house; once she built a box to put the trash bag in so the dogs would not get into it before the garbage man could pick it up. She nailed the box together with rusty nails and covered the top with a piece of screen wire from an old door. It didn't win any prizes for original design, but it did the job.

She sewed clothing for us out of old curtains, like Maria in *The Sound of Music*. She could convert any piece of clothing into something we needed; she used to get hand-me-down bell-bottoms from Uncle Lam in Virginia and magically turn them into straight-cut jeans. Everything got passed down; we have photos of five different brothers wearing the same shirt.

Eight children required a lot of clothing, and that meant a lot of laundry. We no longer had to go to the Laundromat as we did at Allied Gardens because in Barling we had our very own washer and dryer. My brother Thai and I took turns doing laundry. We each kept track of how many loads we did, and it became a form of exchange for us: "I did three loads of laundry, and you did only two. You owe me a load." We kept careful accounting, and we were expected to pay our debts. I once went to Virginia with my mother to visit her brother and sisters, and when I returned, Thai told me, "You owe me sixty-five loads of laundry."

Eight children required a lot of food, too, and my mother could turn anything into a meal. Squirrels, eels, even the leg of a black bear once—you name it; she could butcher it and cook it. One time we were given an entire deer, and when my brothers and I dragged it up onto the deck for her, she gutted it and skinned it like an experienced hunter. Nikki hated it because the deer reminded her of Bambi, so in an act of brotherly compassion, Bruce and Thai put the deer's head in the freezer for the next time she opened it.

Every day my brothers and sisters and I came home from school, dropped off our books, and ran around the neighborhood until dinnertime. Our favorite thing to play with was our bicycle. It was a thing of beauty: a black BMX dirt bike with mushroom grips and bear-claw pedals. We found it on sale at Walmart for $85, which was an unthinkable amount for us, but my father agreed that if my brothers and I would earn $60, he would pay the rest. It took months for us to save up the money, and when we finally brought it home and assembled it, we couldn't wait to ride it. We lined up and took turns riding once around the block, but we soon got tired of waiting and decided that the four of us could all ride it at the same time. Anh sat on the handlebars, Hon straddled the bar behind him, I took the seat and pedaled, and Thai held on to the seat behind me with his feet on the rear axle posts and the tire spinning between his legs. Space was limited, so we eliminated any unnecessary items like helmets and took off around the neighborhood.

I was probably in the safest position because I had an actual seat and two five-year-old air bags to protect me—but Thai was precariously balanced on those axle posts. One time we got going fast and went over a bump; Thai's feet slipped off, and he came down, straddling that spinning tire. There was nothing he could do but hold on while his thighs gripped the tire like human brake pads and brought us to a gradual stop. Thai saved the day, but his thighs paid the price; to this day he still has scars from that event.

But Thai was always accident-prone, so no one was surprised

when we were riding our bike one day and Thai fell off and hurt himself. Grandmother Truong was visiting from Virginia at the time and saw what happened. Even though Thai got up and dusted himself off, my grandmother was afraid that her grandson might have suffered invisible internal injuries. Fortunately for Thai, Grandmother Truong was a practitioner of Chinese folk medicine and knew exactly what to do: she mixed ginseng in an herbal tea and then added a powerful secret ingredient—the urine of the family's youngest child. In our case that was Hon, who dutifully delivered a dose of secret ingredient, and when Grandmother Truong mixed it into the tea, she made Thai drink it down.

Thai was instantly cured of his nonexistent ailment, which not only convinced my mother that the remedy worked, but that Hon himself had mystical healing powers. To this day, if my family is in a restaurant and someone begins to choke, my mother will turn to Hon and say, "Go over and see what you can do for him." It has to be Hon because only Hon has healing powers, and only he can produce the secret ingredient.

A year after we moved to Barling, my mother received some totally unexpected news: she was pregnant again, despite her "thin blood" that was supposed to make it impossible. And she was not only pregnant; she was pregnant with twins, which seemed like a tender mercy after her tragic miscarriage on the beaches of Malaysia. It would be her second set of twins, and if not for the brutal conditions in Malaysia, it might have been her third.

My mother knew that adding two more children to our family would really stretch the household budget thin, so after my twin brothers Bao (pronounced *Bow*) and Toan (pronounced *Twon*) were born, she decided to earn some extra money by taking a job. She went to work for O.K. Foods, a poultry processing plant in Fort Smith, but she left after three months because they kept the factory so cold that her hands kept going numb.

Next she tried working as a seamstress in a clothing factory, where she sewed the same things over and over again for just a few cents per finished item. But she began to get so tired that she could barely keep her eyes open at the sewing machine, and she couldn't understand what was wrong with her.

She was pregnant again.

My mother was almost forty-six at the time, and she felt a little embarrassed to be bearing another child at that age, but she considered each child to be a gift from God. My father loved the idea because children were a form of wealth to him. There is an ancient Chinese proverb that says, "Who has children cannot long remain poor; who has none cannot long remain rich," and my father believed that. Other Vietnamese men used to tease him about the size of our family; they looked at our tiny house and asked, "How can you all fit in there?" or "How can you even breathe?" But later on those same men admitted to him, "I wish I had as many children as you do."

On Halloween in 1988, my mother gave birth to her eleventh and final child, my brother Du—which, believe it or not, is pronounced *You*. At that point working outside the home was no longer realistic, and she decided it was time to retire from the public workforce to enjoy a leisurely life at home—which meant figuring out how to stretch her husband's salary to feed, clothe, and care for eleven children ranging in age from twenty-one years down to a newborn.

"Who has children cannot long remain poor," the proverb says, but my family managed for quite a while.

Thirty-Five

PEER PRESSURES

BARLING WAS A LOW-INCOME AREA, BUT IT HAPPENED to fall within the school district of an upscale junior high school called Chaffin. Chaffin drew most of its students from the more affluent areas on the south side of Fort Smith; so when I began seventh grade in the fall of 1988, I found myself in a situation I had never experienced before: I was a poor kid surrounded by rich people—at least compared to me.

By the time I started, Jenny, Bruce, Yen, and Nikki had graduated from Chaffin and moved on to high school; only my brother Thai was still there, in ninth grade. At Chaffin there were very few minorities, which made everyone in my family feel glaringly conspicuous. There were only a handful of blacks, and the only fellow Asians we could find were two Vietnamese sisters and two Laotian brothers who all spoke fluent English, which made it easier for them to relate to the American students than to us.

What made us feel most conspicuous was our relative poverty. My brothers and sisters and I were part of a program that provided free lunches to students who otherwise could not afford them. Every Monday morning we had to go into the cafeteria kitchen to get a meal card for the week, and each time we received a free lunch, the card was punched for that day. We were grateful for the food, but it was humiliating to have to walk up to the cashier and pull out our little punch cards when everyone else was paying for their lunches with cash. When my older siblings were at Chaffin, my mother was doing laundry one Saturday and she found meal cards in their pockets that had been punched only once or twice that week. My father scolded them for skipping lunch and foolishly passing up free food, but coming from his background, he had no way to understand the shame they felt.

To the casual observer, we probably stood out most in the way we dressed because in junior high the label on your clothing was enough to determine whether you were in style or not. Our clothing didn't even have labels; my mother bought most of our clothes at flea markets, and she never passed up a bargain. She once found T-shirts for my brothers that were very reasonably priced due to a minor flaw—the enormous number "2" emblazoned across the chest had been accidentally printed backward. She bought shoes for my sisters that cost four dollars a pair, and the other girls used to giggle and say, "Oh, look at your shoes!" I know how my sisters felt because my classmates were all wearing Nike Airs while I was wearing Winner's Choice tennis shoes from Walmart.

My father probably had a coupon.

My mother always bought our clothing two sizes too large so we could grow into them. Bruce had a pair of jeans like that. Every year as he grew taller, my mother let down the hems another inch, and by the time he wore the jeans out, there were three lines on each leg that told the age of his pants like the rings of a tree. But Bruce was clever, and he knew how to improvise. He had a secondhand shirt with a little penguin on the front, and it was the only shirt with a logo that he had ever owned. When the shirt finally wore out, he just cut the penguin off and had my mother sew it onto a different shirt.

I wasn't as creative as Bruce, but I was resourceful. When wealthier kids left unwanted clothing in the locker rooms, the items were put in a lost and found, and if no one claimed them after a certain period of time, anyone was allowed to take them—which I did. I once found a very nice girl's jacket that I took home for Yen, and she wore it all the way through college and into her career.

That was my advantage: I had no shame. It wasn't because I was so confident. I just couldn't have cared less about clothing, and I couldn't understand why anyone else would. Clothing was communal in my family. With eight boys it just was not practical for each brother to own his own clothes. When my mother took laundry out of the dryer, she just dumped it all in baskets according to category: all shirts went in one basket, all shorts in another, and all socks in a third. When my brothers and I got dressed each morning, it was first come, first served; we just grabbed a pair of shorts, found a shirt roughly our size, and picked two socks that sometimes even matched. We never fought over clothing, and none of us could ever claim, "That belongs to me!" Style was irrelevant, and the idea of trying to match colors or patterns never crossed our minds. The only thing that mattered to us was that it fit, and "fit" was only approximate. The first one to dress each morning got to be comfortable that day, and the last one to dress learned the virtue of rising early.

When clothing is handed down from brother to brother, it gets a lot of wear and tear, and my mother patched ours so many times that sometimes it seemed as if the original article of clothing had disintegrated, leaving us wearing a quilt worked of patches. And the patches didn't always match the clothing. For my mother, the only consideration was durability, and if "durable" happened to come in a different color or pattern, that was what we wore.

Sometimes my mother allowed me to buy my own clothing. When I was in seventh grade, she once took me to a clothing store that was going out of business, and I picked out some shorts that were extremely affordable. The next morning at the bus stop, one of my friends asked, "Vinh, why are you wearing boxers?" I had to ask him what boxers were; and even after he told me, I didn't care. They were the most comfortable shorts I had ever worn.

Chaffin was not only our first exposure to comparative wealth; it was our first experience of real hostility due to our ethnic background.

Surprisingly, the greatest animosity didn't come from the wealthier students at Chaffin—it came from the poorer students who lived around us in Barling. There were kids in our neighborhood that cursed at us, made "slanty eyes," and told us to go back where we came from. A couple of kids once even chased us with an axe. Sometimes when we answered the phone, a deep voice would say, "Let me come over there and kick your butts with my patriotic boots," and then hang up. During a Sunday service at our Vietnamese church, some-one spray painted *Go home gooks* on the church van, and there was nothing we could do but wash it off and turn the other cheek.

Then I began to learn a better way to deal with hostility. Thai and I had to walk about a mile and a half to our bus stop each morn-ing, and the shortest path took us through the middle of a trashy trailer park, where unshaven men in grease-stained undershirts used to sit on their front stoops and glare at us as we walked by. One day, out of the corner of my eye, I saw a very large, angry-looking man staring at us; and just as we were about to pass his trailer, he got up from his lawn chair and opened his mouth to shout something—but before he could get a word out, I turned to him, flashed a big smile, and said, "Hi! How are you doing?"

He sat down again without ever saying a word.

I didn't say hi to be friendly to the man. I said it to prevent him from being unfriendly to me. I was launching a preemptive strike, and I was using a weapon I was just beginning to develop—words. Ever since arriving in America, I had felt powerless and out of control because of my inability to speak English. I got in trouble for saying the wrong thing and never knew the right thing to say to get out of it. Most of the people in Fort Smith and Barling were kind and gracious to my family, but hostility could erupt at any moment, and there was no way to predict the time or place. It was like living with a jack-in-the-box; most of the time there was pleasant music, but at any moment the lid could fly open and an ugly clown could pop out. We lived with a constant sense of nervous anticipation, a feeling that something could go wrong at any moment and that we were never quite in control. But I was beginning to understand how to control a situation with words. I was learning that if I said the right thing, in the right way, at the right time, I finally could be in control.

The hostility we encountered from poor students at Chaffin was blunt and direct, but with the wealthier students it took a subtler form; to them we were invisible. We tried to be as friendly as we could to everyone, but every time we smiled or said hello to people as we passed them in the hallway, they just looked the other way. We were just too different, and at that age everyone was too concerned about being cool to associate with the ragtag refugees. We felt isolated and ignored, and it just wasn't fair.

It's not fair might be the most common thought that ever crosses a refugee's mind. The political climate in his country forces him to leave the land of his birth; that's not fair. He doesn't get to choose the city he will move to or sometimes even the nation; that's not fair. He can't get a decent job, regardless of his talents, because he doesn't have a diploma from a school he could never attend; that's not fair. He can't learn the language any faster, he can't change the color of his skin, and he can't help it if his nation was formerly at war with yours. None of it is fair, and in the refugee it creates a longing for justice.

I found justice at Chaffin, but it came in two unexpected ways.

My brother Thai was the closest to me in age, and we were competitive in everything we did. Because he was two years older than me, he was better at everything. He was bigger, stronger, quicker, more popular—he even ate faster than I did, and in my family that was a big advantage. There was only one thing I could beat him at, and I discovered it in first grade. He was in third grade at the time, and one day when he was doing his arithmetic homework, he was reading the problems out loud, and I kept calling out the answers before he could write them down. I was thrilled to discover that I could finally beat my older brother at something, but I was even more thrilled that I had discovered something that actually came easily for me—math.

There is a well-known stereotype that Asians always excel at mathematics, and like most stereotypes, it isn't true. Some Asians excel at math, and some do not. There is nothing in Asian DNA that produces accelerated mathematical ability, but there is something in the refugee experience that draws us to mathematics: our frustration with the English language.

For someone who grows up speaking Vietnamese or Cháo zhōu, learning English involves far more than just memorizing a new vocabulary; it requires a completely different way of thinking. The grammar is different, the syntax is different, and the English language contains thousands of bewildering exceptions and rules that make no logical sense at all. Why is there a *w* in the word *answer?* Why doesn't the word *enough* end with an *f?* Why do the words *flammable* and *inflammable* mean the same thing?

But mathematics is a language of its own. A number is a noun, and an equal sign is a verb, and if you know what those terms mean, you speak the language. The language of mathematics is a foreign language to everyone at first, so someone who speaks English has no advantage over someone who speaks Vietnamese. Even more important, it's a language everyone begins to learn at the same time. When I started first grade, everyone else in my class had five years' more experience with the English language than I did, which put them years ahead of me in every subject that required a knowledge of English. But the day we started to learn arithmetic, we were all beginners, and that meant there was finally a subject I could compete in.

By the time I was in eighth grade, I was a member of our school's math team that won a statewide contest; in ninth grade I won the Arkansas state algebra competition as an individual—but at the same time that I was winning math contests, my verbal test scores ranked me in the 24th percentile. No wonder I found math so appealing.

But what really made mathematics attractive to me was it appealed to my desire for justice. Math had clearly stated rules. If you kept the rules, you were rewarded, and if you broke the rules, you were penalized. There were right answers and wrong answers, and they had nothing to do with the color of your skin or where you happened to be born. To me, math was an island of justice in an unjust world, and it gave me a way to finally stand out.

And then there was football. I signed up for football by accident. I thought I was just signing up for athletics, whatever that was, but when I showed up for the first practice in seventh grade, they started handing out shoulder pads and helmets, and I was scared. I had no idea what was going on. I wanted to run track, not run into someone else. My older brothers never played football, so there was no one to teach me about the game or even what equipment I would need to get started. At the first practice, I saw that everyone else had cleats, but all I had was a pair of Bruce's old Avias that I had touched up with a white shoe marker, and the soles had been worn so bald, they had no traction at all. I didn't own a cup either. I didn't even know what a cup was, and no one bothered to tell me. It was two years before I found out, and I learned the hard way when I tried to hurdle an offensive lineman and he stood up unexpectedly. I went directly to Walmart after the game, and I didn't care whether I had a coupon or not.

There was something about football that I found liberating. Ever since I had come to America, I had been biting my tongue and avoiding confrontation, and when I was finally given the chance to run over someone, I felt as if I were tapping into something I never had been able to use before. My entire life had been about restraint, and football was all about release. I was actually allowed to hit someone as hard as I possibly could, and it was completely legal and ethical—even my church approved.

In the classroom I was all meekness and restraint, but on the football field I was all energy and passion. I was fearless—I honestly believed I was invulnerable and that there wasn't anyone that I couldn't run over. Before long, there wasn't. I got stronger and faster all the time, and by eighth grade I was playing on the ninth-grade team.

As strange as it sounds, I loved football for the same reason I loved mathematics: justice. Football took place on a level playing field. It didn't matter where I was from or that I spoke with an accent, and it didn't matter what part of town I lived in or what my father did for a living. What I put into the game, I got back. If I worked hard, I was rewarded, and if I worked harder than the guy lined up across from me, I walked back to the huddle while he picked himself up off the ground.

My mother and father had doubts about my playing football because they were afraid I might get injured, but my brother Bruce thought it was terrific. He even took me to the mall and bought me a thirty-dollar pair of Nike Sharks, the cheapest pair of cleats in the store. My brother was proud of me, and for the first time in my life, I was proud of myself—and it felt very, very good.

Thirty-Six

THE RESTAURANT

I T TOOK TWENTY-THREE YEARS WORKING OVERTIME AND double shifts at Rheem Air Conditioning for my father to increase his hourly salary a grand total of $7.00. Each year my father worked in the factory, his salary increased by an average of thirty cents per hour.

But he wanted more for his family, and he knew he could never get ahead working for an hourly wage, so he decided to start a business on the side. There were very few business options available to someone like my father; whatever business he attempted couldn't require start-up money or a college degree—it had to be something he could succeed at with nothing but his own blood, toil, sweat, and tears. And so in the summer of 1989, our family opened a restaurant.

My father and mother had different motivations for starting a restaurant. Aside from additional income, my father's chief goal was to keep his children out of trouble. We were all growing up: I was starting eighth grade that year, Nikki and Thai were in high school, Bruce and Yen were already in college, and Jenny was about to get married. My father constantly heard stories about other Vietnamese kids who were growing up and getting into serious trouble, and he was afraid it could still happen to us. He figured there were two good ways he could help keep his children on the straight and narrow: by keeping us all where he could see us and by making sure we were so busy we didn't have time to get in any trouble.

My mother's motivation was more pragmatic: she wanted to make sure her children would never go hungry. That was a motivation that went all the way back to Vietnam for her, when we were exiled to that tiny farm and forced to eke out an existence day to day and meal to meal. She vowed back then that her children would never go hungry, and owning a restaurant seemed the perfect way to ensure we never would. She saw it as a practical use of her time too: cooking for eleven children was almost a full-time job for her, and she knew there was no way she could help her husband start a new business and keep cooking at the same time—unless the new business happened to involve cooking.

Chungking Chinese Restaurant—the name was my father's idea. He thought the name was clever and original, and none of us had the heart to tell him that there was already a company called Chun King that sold half of all prepared Chinese food in the United States. Since my father had once been the COO of an entire business empire, starting a small restaurant was a relatively simple project for him. He estimated that all we would need to get up and running was a building, a staff, and a menu.

Finding the right building wasn't easy. Constructing one from the ground up was out of the question, and converting an empty space would have required purchasing a lot of necessary equipment: ovens, dishwashers, tables and chairs—that would have been expensive too. What he needed to find was an existing restaurant that he could just take over, and he eventually found one. Yuan's Restaurant was a struggling Chinese establishment on Rogers Avenue whose owner was looking to sell. The building had a red roof that looked as if it might have been a Pizza Hut in a previous incarnation, and it had everything we needed: a complete kitchen, eight tables and accompanying chairs, and a serving line for a buffet. The owner even promised to give us all of his recipes to help us get started.

Staffing the restaurant was the easy part—my family was the staff, and free labor was an essential part of the business plan. We couldn't afford to hire workers; if we had to pay them even minimum wage, the restaurant never would have made it off the ground. Chungking Chinese Restaurant was a family business in the truest sense of the term, and everyone in the family would have to participate if it was going to work. Though Bruce and Yen were in college at the time, they were badly needed because they were the only ones in our family who had actual restaurant experience. Bruce had worked as a busboy, dishwasher, and waiter, and once he even worked as a hibachi chef at a Japanese steakhouse, stacking onion-ring volcanoes and flipping a fried egg into his chef's hat while the patrons applauded.

Yen was good with money and held the job of cashier at a restaurant called Jade Garden when she was only fourteen. She had to manually count thousands of dollars in receipts every night, and the balance always had to come out exactly right. Every day she was given a certain amount of change to use that evening, and sometimes the owner would sneak a little out or add a little extra just to see if Yen would be honest enough to report the discrepancy—she always passed the test.

Bruce and Yen agreed to finish college later and come home to work in the restaurant full-time, and at that point we had all the bases covered. Bruce and my mother could cook, Yen could handle the register, Nikki could wait tables, and Thai and I could fill in as kitchen staff, busboys, waiters—whatever was needed. Anh and Hon were not quite twelve at the time, but they could help scrape dishes and load the dishwasher.

Now all we needed was a menu. Unfortunately the owner of Yuan's Restaurant forgot his promise to turn over all of his recipes to us and left town, which meant we would have to start our own menu from scratch. Bruce was the creative one, so he began to visit local Chinese restaurants and sample all their dishes, then go home and duplicate the recipes through a process of trial and error. He invented his own seasoning salt: three parts sugar, two parts salt, and one part secret ingredient—MSG. He concocted a white sauce for seafood and a dark sauce for beef, and he came up with a version of General

Tso's Chicken, which we cleverly renamed General Chung's Chicken to disguise its source. Bruce's best recipe of all—a true Chungking Chinese original—was butter-fried chicken wings. The recipe called for deep-frying chicken wings, dipping them in French butter, then rolling them in our special seasoning salt. Our chicken wings may have clogged a few arteries, but our customers must have thought it was worth it because they were the best-selling item on the menu.

Running a restaurant required longer hours than any of us antici-pated. We opened at nine or ten every morning, which required us to be there by eight to cut vegetables and make other preparations for the day, and we closed around nine or ten at night, though we never closed until the final customer left. Even if a customer walked in just when we were about to flip the switch to turn off the Chungking Chinese sign, we served him and stayed open until he was finished—another satisfied customer and one more dollar in the register. When the last customer finally left, Bruce, Thai, and I used to jog down to a local park and play pickup basketball until the lights went off at eleven, then go back to the restaurant to clean up and haul the trash to the Dumpster.

Bruce, Yen, and my mother worked full-time while the rest of us worked after school during the week and full-time on Saturdays. We were closed on Sundays, though I still had to go in for a couple of hours to drain and dump the old cooking oil and get the soups started for the next day. I had football practice after school every day, so I had to hurry over as soon as I was finished, wash all the lunch dishes, and work until closing—and squeeze in a little homework whenever I could. Bruce and Yen worked fifteen hours a day, six days a week, and Nikki, Thai, and I averaged eighty hours a week during the summer.

And the kitchen was hot. The front of the restaurant was air-conditioned, but the kitchen was not, and when the heat of a blazing stove was added to a sweltering Arkansas summer, the kitchen thermometer topped 110 degrees. One of my glamorous jobs was to prepare all the chicken that would be used in recipes like General Chung's. O.K. Foods made daily deliveries of cases of whole chickens packed in ice, and they left them on the floor by a drain because the kitchen was so hot that the ice quickly melted. By the time I got to the restaurant after football practice, I was racing against the clock to cut up all the chicken before it spoiled, and at $40 a case that was something we could not afford. My job was to remove the skin and then cut the whole chicken into its component parts: white meat and dark meat for the various chicken recipes, fat and skin for the grease, and bones to make soup. My brother Thai and I got so fast at doing it that we could dissect an entire chicken in less than a minute.

Though working at the restaurant took all of our spare time, none of us was paid for working there. As members of the family we were expected to work on behalf of the family, just as my father and his brother had worked for Grandmother Chung back in Vietnam. Every dollar my father had earned went to Grandmother Chung, and she had given him money as he needed it. We had a similar arrangement: every dollar a customer paid and every tip any of us received all went into the cash register, and every Saturday night Yen would open the register and give each of us a small allowance for the week.

When the restaurant first opened, the youngest three children were not old enough to work. Bao and Toan were only four at the time, and baby Du was only ten months old. Since the entire family worked at the restaurant and we couldn't afford to hire a babysitter, we just brought the young ones along with us. There was an enormous refrigerator in the kitchen, and beside it was a wooden pallet stacked with sacks of rice. Bao and Toan sat in the small open space between them and played with pots and pans all day. Du was a bigger problem because he was so small; we had to put him in a plastic tub that was used to bus tables and give him a few plastic spoons to play with. When Du got a little older, we used to put him in a high chair and set him in front of the window that looked out from the kitchen into the restaurant. Du was our doorbell; whenever someone walked into the restaurant, he would shout, "Customer!" and when anyone approached the cash register, he yelled, "Checkout!" When Du was old enough to walk, he thought he owned the restaurant; he used to walk from table to table and ask customers, "Is everything good here? Is everything okay?"

The restaurant was located about five miles from our house in Barling, and with all of us having to commute back and forth each day, my father decided to look for a house closer to the restaurant. Just a few months after the restaurant opened, he found one; in fact, it was exactly one hundred yards away. It was larger than our house in Barling, but we were all larger, too, and we had all been accumulating more possessions. The brothers' room was a disaster area. Two or three layers of clothing were always draped over everything, and shoes and backpacks were left scattered all over the floor.

There were eight boys in our family and five beds in our bedroom—two bunk beds and a queen-sized mattress. At any given time there might be five, six, or even seven brothers sleeping there, and we were all too old and much too large to sleep four to a bunk as we used to do in Barling. This time berths were assigned by a simple pecking order: the older brothers got beds while the younger brothers got booted out and either slept on the sofa or crawled in with one of the sisters.

The kitchen was the nerve center of the house because that was where my mother always was, and my sisters congregated around her. They were always talking, and they spoke in Vietnamese with phrases of Cháo zhōu and English interspersed. They talked fast and loud, and the tonal nature of the Vietnamese language made the kitchen sound like an open-air market.

Once the restaurant opened, my mother would seldom cook at home anymore. Monday through Saturday we ate our meals at the restaurant, but Sundays were different because that was the one day the restaurant was closed and my father didn't have to work. On Sunday my mother would cook an enormous pot of stew along with rice, noodles, vegetables, and some salted pork or beef, and by the time we came home from church, it was ready to eat. Since none of us ate breakfast, we were ravenous, but my father was especially cranky by that time. When he didn't get his food fast enough, he used to curse before gathering us around the table to give thanks.

That seemed a bit inconsistent to us, but none of us thought it would be a good idea to point it out.

We had a big round table, and the girls always sat around it and talked with my mother as they ate while my brothers and I grabbed a plate and headed into the living room, where the television was. We had only one small TV in the house, and everyone understood that it was my father's domain; whenever he sat down, he put on the channel he wanted, and whatever he watched, we watched—and we always looked forward to Sunday afternoons because that was when he watched *Kung Fu Theatre*.

If there was any stew left over after lunch, my mother warmed it up again for dinner, and if there was any left after dinner, she served it the next day. We ate until the food was gone, and none of us ever asked, "Do we have to eat this *again*?" It was food, and we were grateful to have it. In my family it was a sin to waste food. I can still recall the first time I watched Nickelodeon and saw a food fight. I remember thinking, *Do they have so much food in America that they can throw it away?* Where I came from, things were different. In a country where food is scarce, food is sacred. In Vietnam, if you wanted to insult a woman, you called her "skinny girl" because it implied that she didn't have enough money to eat. In America if you call a woman "skinny girl," you may have made a lifelong friend.

Chungking Chinese Restaurant stayed in business for five years. The restaurant was open during my entire high school career. I started eighth grade the month it opened, and I left for college the month it closed. The restaurant turned out to be a break-even financial proposition for us, but it didn't matter to my father because profit was never his primary goal. It definitely fulfilled his goal of keeping us all where he could see us. The restaurant brought the entire family together to work side by side, and that was what my father wanted most. It fulfilled his second goal too: it kept us so busy we didn't have time to get in trouble. For five straight years I went to school, played football, worked in the restaurant, went to church, and slept—and almost nothing else.

I think my father had a third goal in mind when he opened that restaurant, and that was the one that changed my life the most. He wanted us to experience working long hours in a terrible environment, doing a thankless job that paid no money. In other words, he wanted us to know what his life was like—and he wanted us to dislike it so much that we would set our sights on something better.

Thirty-Seven

GHOSTS OF THE PAST

MY MOTHER WAS A WOMAN WHO COULD BUTCHER A deer, carve up a pig, and decapitate a chicken with the flick of a knife—but she was afraid of mice. She was in the kitchen one day when she spotted a mouse scurrying across the floor, and she began to scream. That was a sound my mother rarely made. All the children came running to the kitchen to see what was wrong, and when we saw the mouse, some of us began to scream too. A moment later my father calmly walked into the room, looked at everyone screaming, then raised one bare foot and stomped the mouse flat, which made everyone scream even more.

That was my image of my father growing up: strong as steel and tough as leather—considering the things he had experienced in his life, it was understandable that he would appear that way. But the terrible things he experienced growing up had another effect on him, and it was something we had to deal with every day.

Whenever a human being suffers trauma or experiences extreme stress, there are predictable psychological consequences; this is especially true after the trauma of war. The mental and emotional struggle that soldiers often experience in the aftermath of war has been given different names over the years. Centuries ago it was simply called "nostalgia" or "exhaustion," and during the Civil War, it was given the tender name "soldier's heart." In World War I they called it "shell shock," and in World War II it was known as "battle fatigue." Today we know the phenomenon by its official name: post-traumatic stress disorder, or PTSD.

But in the wake of the Vietnam War, when half a million American soldiers were trying to forget the horrors of war and return to their normal lives, their mental and emotional struggle was called "post-Vietnam syndrome." It was appropriate that the syndrome was labeled "post-Vietnam" and not "post-combat" because soldiers are not the only ones who struggle after a war. My father never fought in a war, but he grew up surrounded by its terrors: Viet Minh uprisings, Cambodian reprisals, Viet Cong kidnappings and assassinations— even a full-scale invasion and the overthrow of his country. He experienced many of the same horrors that American soldiers did, so it's no surprise he suffered some of the same aftereffects.

When my brother Thai was a boy, he was taping up posters in our bedroom one day and wanted to place a poster high on the wall near the ceiling. He couldn't reach that high, and we didn't have a ladder, so he used the bed like a trampoline to leap as high as he could and try to stick the poster to the wall before he came down again. On his final jump he caught his finger on the sharp metal hook that holds the curtain rod, and it ripped his finger open. He tried wrapping it with every Band-Aid in the house, but the cut was too deep to heal without stitches, and it was impossible to hide. Thai finally had to show the cut to my father, and when my father saw the blood, he became almost hysterical. He flew into a panic and demanded to know how something so terrible could possibly have happened. Judging by my father's response, you would have thought Thai's arm had been severed at the shoulder.

My father couldn't stand the sight of blood, which is not a quality commonly associated with someone strong as steel and tough as leather. It wasn't because he was weak; it was because he had been constantly exposed to the sight of blood growing up, including the severed head of a Viet Cong that someone had placed in a paper cone and hung by the bridge in Tham Don near one of the rice mills. Whenever my father saw blood, no matter how small the amount, it brought back the memory of all the terrible things he had ever seen.

Of course, my brothers and sisters and I had no way to understand that. We thought our father just had a bad temper, so we did everything we could to avoid making him angry. When I was growing up, I rarely cried because crying would have signaled something was wrong, and that might have set my father off. I feared getting injured, not because of the pain but because my father might find out and get angry. When he got angry, he exploded, and there was no way to talk him out of it—we just ran for our rooms and locked the doors.

It wasn't just the past that fueled his anger; it was the present too. Each year when he received his thirty-cent raise, he was bitterly reminded of everything he had lost and all the things he would never have again. There was a Vietnamese saying he quoted from time to time: "I have eaten more salt than you have eaten rice." He was a quiet man who didn't share his emotions; he never once said "I love you" to us kids, and he never apologized because he never admitted he was wrong.

Most of the time, his worries and frustration just made him irritable. My mother once cooked a dish for him that he thought was too salty, but since she had been cooking that dish for years, she disagreed—so my father pasted a big label on her salt shaker that read, This Is Salt And It Is Very Salty. At other times he just blew up, and after it happened my mother would always come into our rooms and quietly try to explain why my father got angry. That was my mother's role: she was an interpreter, a translator, a mediator between us and our father.

We learned to go to her first whenever there was a problem, and she would help us fix things before our father found out. She had a different style of discipline than her husband. She never shouted or got angry; she just told us stories that always had a moral or lesson attached. There was the story about the Vietnamese girl who ran away from home, got pregnant, and brought shame to her family; and there was the story about the Vietnamese boy who got involved with drugs, dropped out of school, and never amounted to anything. Some stories were tragic and some were inspiring, and she had a way of telling them in a calm and quiet voice that could reduce us to tears.

My father just got angry. If a bill arrived in the mail that he had already paid, he exploded. If any of us got into trouble, he was furious. When anything broke or whenever there was an unexpected expense, it all came out in anger. Once he cooled down, his anger was not only gone but forgotten. He never carried a grudge, and sometimes he couldn't even remember why he got mad; the event itself was only a trigger. My father was like a geyser that constantly built up pressure until it just had to let off steam. Unfortunately we were often standing near the geyser when it went off.

It was often fear that triggered his anger—fear that something might go wrong. That was understandable, too, considering that unexpected things went terribly wrong throughout his childhood. His house burned down, his father died, and he was left in poverty; he knew that the worst could actually happen, and he was afraid it might happen again. My father's way of dealing with that fear was to avoid all potential danger and minimize every possible risk. My mother has a driver's license, but she has never driven a car because my father is afraid that something might happen to her if she does. She could never drive us to school, and a friend or neighbor always had to drive her to the grocery store. My mother is in her seventies now, and she still doesn't drive.

My father always feared that the worst would happen, and he worried until he knew everything was okay. When any of us traveled, we had to call him as soon as we arrived because he wouldn't be able to sleep until we did. If we drove somewhere and our car broke down, he would say, "Why did you have to go out at all? If you hadn't gone out, your car wouldn't have broken down, and I wouldn't be so angry." That was the way he reasoned. If you take no risks, nothing can go wrong. Stay here, sit still, and be safe.

Hypervigilance, controlling behavior, overwhelming feelings, overreacting, fear of change—they are all common symptoms of post-traumatic stress. My father was a Vietnam veteran; though he never served a day in the military, he was a veteran of the conflict nonetheless. One American GI recalled his experience in Vietnam this way: "Fear of the unknown was my biggest fear—the constant worry about what's around the bend, booby traps, enemy contact or incoming enemy mortar rounds. It seemed to take a lot out of you physically and mentally." Those were my father's fears too: the hidden dangers, the concealed enemies, the unexpected threats that could come from anywhere.

Another Vietnam veteran once wrote, "A tree line two hundred yards away across a flat meadow still triggers my PTSD," and he wrote that forty years after his final combat mission. A simple tree line across a meadow was enough to trigger his overreaction or overwhelming feelings, just as the sight of blood or a potential risk could trigger my father's.

I have no way to know for certain that my father suffered from actual PTSD. It's possible he had only a general anxiety disorder or that he had a temperament like Grandmother Chung's. That's what some of my siblings say: "He just got it from his mother," and it's possible he did. Maybe his anger and fear were genetic, or maybe he became like his mother because they both grew up in the same war-torn nation and shared many of the same traumatic experiences.

My father knew the Chinese proverb, "Life can never give security; it can only promise opportunity," but he wanted both for his children, and he was constantly torn between the two. He wanted all of us to go to college, but he couldn't understand why any of us would want to go any farther than the University of Arkansas, just down the road. He wanted us to have every opportunity that he never had, but he was constantly worried that something would go wrong along the way. It must have been a terrible tension for my father to live with—to wish for something that he feared at the same time. For his children to have opportunity, they had to take risks; but when we took risks, it scared him to death.

There is nothing more difficult to understand than someone else's irrational fear because understanding requires reason, and there is nothing reasonable about the irrational. I was in high school before I realized my father's behavior was not normal and all fathers did not act the way he did. A part of my life's journey has been to understand my father, and I think I finally do—at least in part. I've learned a lot about his experiences growing up in the Mekong Delta, and I think I understand how painful and terrifying they must have been. But I'm not able to feel them the way he did—and until I can do that, I will never fully understand the power they have over him.

What impresses me about my father is that he did not give in to his fear. He did not let his longing for security deny his children opportunity, and when he saw us take those opportunities, it made his struggle seem worthwhile.

When I was a senior in high school, my father walked out to get the newspaper one morning. He had been working in the factory for a decade by then, and the day before had been a brutal one for him; he had even said to God, "I don't know how much longer I can take this." When he opened the paper, he saw a photograph of his own son on the front page, and I was holding a football in one hand and a calculus book in the other. The caption told him that his son had been voted Arkansas male scholar athlete of the year—and my father wept.

Thirty-Eight

FLYING BLIND

THERE WERE TWO HIGH SCHOOLS IN FORT SMITH, Northside and Southside, which were named after the two main regions of the city. Both schools had about the same number of students, but Northside had eight times more African Americans, four times more Hispanics, and three times more Asians than Southside. All eleven Chung children attended Northside High School, and needless to say, we felt much more at home there than we did at our junior high.

In my first year at Northside, I made the varsity football team. I continued to love everything about football: the game itself and the liberating feeling it gave me. I especially enjoyed the respect that my physical size and strength earned me from my classmates. I kept a growth chart, hoping I had inherited my father's stature. My goal was to grow two inches and gain twenty pounds every year until I reached six foot two and weighed 220 pounds, and for a few years I was actually on track to do it. But it didn't help to have a five-foot-two mother, and I eventually topped out around five foot eleven and two hundred pounds. That wasn't very big for a guard and defensive end, especially when you consider that a high school lineman in Arkansas these days often weighs three hundred pounds. I wasn't the strongest or the fastest in my school, but I was faster than the big kids and bigger than the fast kids, and what I lacked in size and speed, I made up for in aggressiveness.

An Asian who played football—that was a category-breaker for a lot of people. When the football coach first saw me, he wanted me to be a kicker because as everyone knows, all foreigners play soccer and, therefore, can kick. My coach soon discovered I could not kick at all, but I was very good at running into things, which was something I had a lot of experience doing due to the fact that I was legally blind.

In the United States a person is considered legally blind when his best-corrected vision is 20/200 or worse. The prescription 20/200 means that what other people could see from two hundred feet away, I couldn't see unless it was practically in front of my nose. "Best-corrected" means "with your glasses on"—but when I played football, I couldn't wear my glasses because they always got dirty and fogged up under my helmet, and my family couldn't afford contact lenses. Without glasses my vision was 20/200, which meant that on a football field I was as blind as a bat.

Kickoffs instantly vanished, especially at night—and I was on the kickoff team. Sometimes I played defensive end, and on more than one occasion I accidentally tackled the running back carrying the ball—which was the right thing to do, only I thought the other running back had the ball, and I was actually aiming for him. My coach would always shout, "Great tackle, Vinh!" and I would look over at the sidelines and wonder which blur was the coach.

I didn't even get glasses until I was in sixth grade. Until then the chalkboard was just a green fog, but I assumed it looked the same way to everyone else. At my first eye exam the optometrist said to me, "Son, you've been missing out on a lot in life," and he was right. When I came home with my new glasses, I discovered for the first time that roses have petals and leaves. It was a great relief to finally get glasses, but they didn't help my social life; I could afford only the cheapest frames, and the glasses I was forced to wear had "Nerd" stamped all over them in several different languages.

But my glasses didn't really hurt my social life because I didn't have one—there just wasn't time. I never had time for a girlfriend. None of my older siblings had boyfriends or girlfriends until they were about to get married. My parents never said I couldn't have a girlfriend; the idea just seemed impossible. To me, having a girlfriend was as unthinkable as owning a horse: What would I do with one? Where would I put it? How much time would I have to spend taking care of it? There were girls who used to wait for me outside the locker room after football games, but I had no idea why, and I didn't ask. I heard rumors that there were girls who had a crush on me, but I had no clue what to do about it, so I did nothing.

My plan after graduating was to become a doctor, though to be honest I had very little idea at the time what a doctor really did or what it would take to become one. No one in my family had ever been a doctor, so no one was able to warn me that it would require four years of undergraduate studies, four years of medical school, then three to seven years of residency. I was shocked when I found out that to become a doctor, I would have to go to school until I was thirty. *Thirty*—surely there was a better way to become a success.

My father didn't think so. When he was a boy, he dreamed of becoming a doctor, too, though like me, he really didn't know what being a doctor entailed. In a way it didn't matter to him because what he really wanted was to be a success, and in Vietnam a doctor was considered to be the epitome of success. So it's understandable that when my father urged his children to be successful, what he really had in mind was that we would all become doctors.

If you ask my father today what he really wanted for his children, he will say, "I just wanted each of them to be as successful as possible"; but if you ask my brothers and sisters what our father wanted for us, they will tell you, "He wanted each of us to become a doctor." In a way, both are true.

Jenny was the first to go to college, which was an accomplishment in itself. If my family had remained in Vietnam, my sisters might not have been encouraged to attend college at all. But in America my father wanted all of his children to have a college education and a chance at a high-paying job, which was a very enlightened attitude for a traditional Chinese man such as my father. Jenny had no money to pay for college, and my father couldn't help much, earning $22,000 a year. But she applied for every grant, loan, and scholarship she could find and was able to enroll at the University of Arkansas in the fall of 1986 to begin her premed studies.

But Jenny put in only one year at Arkansas before moving to Virginia to live with Grandmother Truong, and a year later she was married to a man from my mother's hometown of Bac Lieu—a match that was *assisted* by Grandmother Truong.

Bruce was next in line, and my father's expectations for Bruce were especially high because he was the oldest son. Bruce had always been clever and inventive, but he was only one grade behind Jenny, and he faced many of the same academic challenges that she did. In high school Bruce was a C student, but that did not diminish my father's hope that he would become a doctor. If he just applied himself more, my father told him, he could still make it happen.

But applying himself was the problem for Bruce. He grew up with a close circle of Vietnamese friends, and they all went off to the University of Arkansas together. There were two things they shared in common: since they all came to America at about the same age, they all had struggled through school, and since school was difficult for them, they all liked to party more than study. Bruce's grades suffered as a result, and he began to struggle with the demanding premed curriculum. He managed to make it through biology and chemistry, but when it came to organic chemistry, physics, and biochemistry, he hit a wall. He just could not do it, and that was when he knew he would never be a doctor.

At the end of Bruce's second year, my father called Bruce home. He was furious with Bruce. He thought his firstborn son had wasted an opportunity that he himself had never had, an opportunity that my father made possible for Bruce through years of backbreaking labor and sacrifice. Bruce told our father that he had tried his best, but the goal of becoming a doctor was just beyond his ability; my father, however, couldn't hear it—he was just too overwhelmed by disappointment, grief, and a tragic feeling of loss.

That might sound like one of my father's overreactions, but it was the reaction of a refugee. When an average American boy goes off to college and parties a little too much his first semester, it might merit a lecture and a stern warning from his parents—but in our family there was no margin for error. The path we walked was narrow, and when Bruce stepped off that path ever so slightly, my father was devastated.

Bruce didn't fail college—he only failed to become a doctor, as do thousands of other college students every year who start premed programs and decide later to change majors. But my father's deepest hopes and dreams were invested in his oldest son, and I think when Bruce dropped out of college, my father felt his own dreams dashed to pieces. He sent Bruce to work at O.K. Foods, which was the worst job any of us could imagine, and Bruce obediently worked there until Chungking Chinese Restaurant opened at the end of the summer.

Yen was next. She was a good student in high school, and she enrolled at the University of Arkansas in the fall of 1988. Her first year went well, but when she heard my father's idea of opening a family restaurant, she caught the vision. Yen had experience working in restaurants, and she believed that with her help the restaurant just might become a way for everyone in our family to succeed. She made the decision to postpone her education after her freshman year, and for the next five years she lived at home and worked in the restaurant.

Nikki never did like school. She was younger when she arrived in America, so she was able to pick up English much more easily than Jenny, Bruce, or Yen. But Nikki didn't like to read, and she didn't like to study—it just didn't interest her. When she graduated from high school, she didn't bother to apply to any colleges; she just went to work in the restaurant with the rest of us.

One day Nikki walked into the restaurant with a suitcase. When she set it on the table and opened it, there was a mannequin head inside wearing a wig, and she announced to all of us that she had decided to go to beauty school. We were all shocked at first, but my mother just asked her if she was sure that was really what she wanted to do, and when Nikki said yes, my mother was fine with it.

To everyone's surprise, my father was fine with it too. I'm not sure he ever expected Nikki to become a doctor, and it wasn't because she lacked intelligence. I think my father knew she just wasn't interested.

Then came Thai. Thai was an excellent student and graduated fourth in his high school class of 318. Because of his academic success, he qualified for an Arkansas Top Ten Graduates scholarship, and along with his other grants and loans, it covered his tuition, his books, and even his room and board. Thai even had a little money left over, so he sent it home to my mother and father. When Jenny was in college, she did the same thing: she worked at the university library, and at the end of every week she mailed her paycheck home—every penny. Even as college students, everyone contributed to the family.

But Thai continued to be accident-prone, and during his junior year of college, he was involved in a serious car accident that knocked him unconscious and put him in the hospital. He suffered no permanent injuries, but his grades suffered for the rest of the year. He still graduated with honors, but admission to medical school was extremely competitive, and his MCAT scores were not quite high enough to get in. He applied three times and was even wait-listed, but after his third rejection he decided not to try again.

When my father found out, he was crushed—and for the fifth time, because not one of his five older children had succeeded in becoming a doctor. It was hard for Thai to think that he had let my father down because he had come the closest of all of them. I think Thai best illustrates the high expectation of success and zero tolerance for failure that existed in my family. Thai was a boy who arrived in America unable to speak a single word of English, yet he was able to finish fourth in his high school class and graduate with honors from a four-year university. How is it possible that a performance like that could be considered failure? Like his brother Bruce, Thai didn't fail—he only failed to become a doctor.

I come from a family of failures. While working in Virginia and raising a family, Jenny managed to go back to college and finish an associate degree in business. While working full-time at the restaurant, all Bruce did was take courses in his spare time until he had an undergraduate degree in cytotechnology and a master's degree in science management. Yen spent years juggling work and part-time classes but stopped with only a four-year degree in nuclear medicine technology. Poor Nikki worked at the restaurant until it closed, then worked part-time and put herself through college to only get a bachelor's degree in elementary education. And Thai was a failure too; he graduated with honors in biology and was willing to settle for a master's in information systems.

My five older siblings have five undergraduate degrees and two master's degrees among them. That's the kind of failure that most parents dream of for their children. If you ask my father today if he is disappointed in any of his children in any way, he will tell you, "Absolutely not!" and he means it. He is extremely proud of everything his children have accomplished, from Jenny right on down to Du. All he ever wanted was the very best for each of us, but when we were growing up, his passion for us to succeed was compounded by his fear that we might fail, and that placed a burden on us that was sometimes difficult to bear.

When Thai decided not to apply for medical school again, my father turned to me. I was next in line to become a doctor, and I was still on track to fulfill his wishes. I had the grades, I had the determination, and I had a plan for my future: I would enroll at the University of Arkansas just as my brothers and sisters had, I would do whatever people do to become a doctor, and then I would return to Fort Smith to live out my life as a very big fish in a very small pond. It sounded good to me, and I couldn't imagine how a plan like that could possibly be improved.

I had a plan, but I had no vision. I didn't even know what vision was—but I was about to meet a girl who had enough vision for both of us.

Our Redeemer Lutheran Church, Fort Smith, Arkansas, sponsors my family to the United States and provides a house for us to live in for six months.

We are greeted at the Fort Smith airport by a kind, welcoming party from Our Redeemer Lutheran Church.

Our house has no furniture, but we are happy to be safe and together.

My dad saves enough money for us to become genuine American homeowners. This is our first house in Barling.

Our yellow Pontiac: ten of us squeeze into this car.

Grandmother Truong surrounded by her grandchildren; I'm on the far left, standing.

The former home of Chungking Chinese Restaurant . . . now a doughnut shop. We had the best butter-fried chicken wings on the planet.

My mother, the chef at Chungking restaurant.

When I'm not in school or playing football, I'm at Chungking restaurant. This is where I learn the useful skills of skinning and deboning an entire chicken in less than sixty seconds.

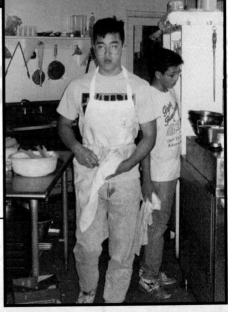

Leisle and I meet at Arkansas Governor's School. As usual, my clothes don't match, but Leisle doesn't seem to mind.

My senior year of high school football: a proud member of the Northside Grizzlies. Football is my first love.

I pose with Leisle for high school prom. Her fourteen-year-old brother has to accompany us as a chaperone to my prom in Fort Smith.

I arrive at
Harvard with all
my possessions
in an army
duffel bag.

My graduation from Harvard: L to R: Bruce, Thuvan (Bruce's wife), me, Leisle, Thai, Jenny, Hung (Jenny's husband), and Nikki. Down front are Rebecca and Tiffany (Jenny's daughters).

At my graduation
from Harvard,
I stand with my
roommate of four
years, Dan Schneider,
who loaned me his
computer throughout
college.

I'm getting married! L to R: Dan Cohan (college roommate), me, Thai, and Dan Schneider (college roommate).

My parents and heroes, Hoa and Thanh Chung.

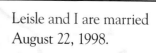

I weep when she walks down the aisle.

Leisle and I are married August 22, 1998.

I stand on the "family farm," where my family lived after the fall of South Vietnam to the communists.

I meet family members who never made it out, including those who were on the three boats that drifted back. I stand between my two half brothers, sons of my father's mistress. My uncle, the man to the left with the glasses, is my father's older brother, who organized the boat escape.

I return to Bac Lieu: behind me are shacks where poor families live.

My father holds my Harvard Medical School diploma and wears my cap and gown. He earned it.

Christmas 2012: The Chung Family with our parents, 11 children, 11 spouses, 20-plus grandchildren, and growing.

Leisle and I now live in Colorado Springs with our three beautiful children and with another one on the way.

Thirty-Nine

AIMING FOR THE STARS

LEISLE CHUNG WAS BORN ON A SMALL FARM IN Seongnam, South Korea, in 1975. The farm belonged to her grandfather. Her father, Han, had been born and raised there along with his older brother, Kae Hoon, and five other siblings. Farming is a hard way of life even in good times, but in 1975, the people of South Korea were still struggling to recover from the devastation of the Korean War. Entire cities had been burned to the ground during that conflict, and almost three times more civilians died than soldiers. Leisle's grandparents had been left dirt-poor, and Leisle's father used to go to school with nothing to eat all day. Children from more fortunate families brought rice to eat, and if their family was especially prosperous, they even had an egg, while Leisle's father could only sip his water and watch them eat.

It cost money to go to school in Korea, just as it did in Vietnam, and when Han reached high school age, his father called him in one day and told him, "I can't afford to send you to school anymore. You need to come home and work the farm so we can send your older brother to school." As in most traditional Asian families, the priority went to the oldest son; everything the family did would be dedicated to making sure the oldest son became educated and successful, and then that son was expected to help the rest of the family.

Han's older brother was very intelligent and did well in school. He was even accepted to Seoul National University, the most prestigious college in all of Korea. But to continue funding Kae Hoon's education, the family had to sell off parcels of the farm until there was barely enough land left to work. For Han it was like standing on an ice floe that was melting all around him and wishing he knew how to swim.

What made it even more difficult for Han was that he was very intelligent too. He dreamed of all the places he wanted to go and the things he hoped to accomplish, but he was a common laborer trapped on a small farm with no education, money, or opportunity; and as he watched his older brother succeed, he saw his own future slipping away. But Han was a good son who remained loyal to the family and sacrificed his own future to help ensure his brother's success, and after graduating from Seoul National University, Han's brother pursued that success by moving to the United States.

One day Han met a beautiful young woman named Sunny, and before long they fell in love and married. Following Asian tradition, Sunny moved in with her husband's family, and it was painful and embarrassing for Han to see his young bride forced to share in his family's poverty. Leisle was born the following year, and it was even more painful for Han when he saw that his wife had to walk to the river each day to wash the baby's diapers just as poor Korean women had done for thousands of years.

Han decided he was tired of waiting for his chance at success. Sunny agreed to remain in Korea with baby Leisle while her husband went ahead to the United States, and when he had found a decent job and had saved enough money, he would send for his wife and daughter to join him.

Han's previous work experience had been mostly in farming, so when he came to America, he first moved to Iowa to try working as a farmhand; but the long Iowa winter was more brutal than anything he had ever experienced in South Korea, and he decided not to stay. Just nine months after he arrived in the United States, Han was living in Denver with a steady job and a place to live, and he immediately sent for his wife and daughter. Little Leisle was almost a year and a half old by that time and didn't even recognize her father at first; she was old enough to talk by then and she kept calling her father "Mister."

Once the family was reunited, they began to move from place to place in search of higher-paying jobs and better opportunities. Atlanta was their next stop, followed by Russellville, Arkansas, and they finally settled in the small town of Lincoln, Arkansas, about forty miles north of Fort Smith and only a few miles from the Oklahoma border. Lincoln was a tiny rural town of just fourteen hundred people, and the average income at the time was close to the poverty line. The ethnic makeup of the town could be described in one word: *white*. There were almost no blacks, the only Hispanics were the migrant Mexican workers who passed through town, and it was highly doubtful that anyone in Lincoln had ever met an Asian. That might not sound like a land of golden opportunity for a Korean family, but the town had one thing going for it: Lincoln had the cheapest land in all of Arkansas. Han and Sunny would be able to afford fifty acres of land, so they decided to settle, and Lincoln became their home.

In some ways the story of Leisle's family sounds a lot like my own: poor Asian family leaves their homeland and travels to America in search of opportunity. But there is one major difference in our stories, and its significance cannot be overstated: Leisle's parents were immigrants while mine were refugees. Han and Sunny left Korea because they chose to; we left Vietnam because we had no choice. They chose America; America chose us. They hoped for a better life; we just hoped someone would take us in. Those seemingly minor details account for an enormous difference in the mind-set of an immigrant and a refugee: an immigrant is motivated by the desire for success while a refugee is often driven by the fear of failure.

In Korea there had been no outlet for Han's ambition, but in America he saw endless possibilities. He arrived with just two hundred dollars in his pocket, but he took every odd job he could find, even working as a janitor in a French restaurant, until he had saved enough money to buy a farm. When he first arrived, he didn't know a word of English, so he taught himself by attending church services and going to public parks, where he could strike up conversations and learn. He was a voracious reader, and he was constantly studying and taking correspondence courses to expand his horizons. He was always experimenting with side businesses just to see what might catch on. He raised deer and planted an herbal garden; he started an Asian pear farm to see if he could sell pear cider and vinegar; he eventually developed a successful business, selling herbal remedies and alternative medicines. When a business failed, as most of them did, he was disappointed but never allowed himself to get discouraged because he believed that in a land of possibilities there was no such thing as a roadblock—only detours. Han and Sunny believed they could accomplish anything they set their minds to in America, and to me the most important thing they ever accomplished was passing that attitude on to their daughter.

Leisle grew up surrounded by her father's books, and in the margins she found notations scribbled in Korean and words and phrases circled and underlined to be looked up later. Her father didn't read books; he devoured them, and Leisle learned to do the same. There was a small public library in Lincoln, and anyone checking out a book there was likely to find the name *Leisle Chung* written on the back because she read every age-appropriate book on the library's shelves.

Han and Sunny instilled in their daughter the belief that she could do anything. Han told Leisle that Koreans were naturally intelligent, and Sunny told her daughter that Koreans were simply superior people—but at the same time they taught her Christian humility, which allowed their daughter to be confident without becoming arrogant. It's an attitude that ought to be instilled in every child: "I am a naturally intelligent person. I was born to be a superior student. Anything is possible for me if I work hard enough."

But Han and Sunny gave their daughter more than confidence; they also gave her discipline. School and study came before everything else, and nothing less than an A was acceptable. When Leisle was only in eighth grade, she took a yearlong high school course in geometry, and she finished one semester with a B—quite an achievement for a girl two years younger than everyone else in her class. But her parents said, "You obviously don't understand the subject matter. You have to take the class again." And she did. In ninth grade her parents made her repeat the entire year of geometry to prove that she was capable of getting an A. She wasn't proving it to her parents; they already knew. She was proving it to herself.

Han and Sunny also gave their daughter vision; they constantly challenged her to aim for the stars regardless of the outcome. In middle school Leisle ran for student council secretary and won. When she told her mother the good news, her mother asked, "Why didn't you run for president?"

"A popular boy was running for president," she said. "I wouldn't have won."

Sunny shook her head. "I would rather you go for the best and lose than try for second best and win."

It's no surprise that in high school, Leisle was the president of every club she was in. Going for the best was her only option; it was the only thing her parents allowed her to do—and Leisle soon discovered that when she went for the best, she usually succeeded.

I marvel sometimes at the power of the attitude that Leisle's parents instilled in her. I came to America as a refugee from a despised country, so I constantly felt that I was weak, inferior, and second-class. Leisle's parents taught her to be proud of her Korean heritage, so she constantly felt that she was strong, superior, and always top of the class.

Han and Sunny were wise enough to recognize that they were only two voices in a town of fourteen hundred, and they knew it would be difficult to keep their daughter shooting for the stars if no one around her was doing the same. They wanted to expose their daughter to a community that valued achievement as much as they did. There was a Korean church in Springdale about forty-five minutes away, and they met on Saturdays because that was the only time the church building was available. There Leisle found an entire culture of adults who shared not only her parents' Christian faith but their attitude toward achievement. She couldn't help noticing that when their children went away to college, they always seemed to go to schools such as Duke, Stanford, and Georgetown. Three of Leisle's cousins went to Harvard; one of them went on to Harvard Law School, one to Harvard Medical School, and one to Harvard Business School. Leisle grew up thinking that's just what Asians did.

Han and Sunny had very modern ambitions for their daughter, but at the same time they were a traditional Korean couple and followed traditional roles. Leisle has a brother named Isaac who is three years younger than her. Sunny once walked into the kitchen and found her son washing dishes, and she told him to stop. "When you're married, break a few dishes," she advised him. "Your wife won't ask you to do dishes anymore." Han insisted that his daughter learn how to cook, or else she would never find a man who would marry her. Who would want to marry a president who can't cook?

If there was anything lacking in Leisle's education, it was social. To keep her focused on her studies, dating was out of the question for her in high school, and since she had an eight o'clock curfew, her dates wouldn't have lasted very long anyway. Leisle's parents had reason to be protective of their daughter; her high school had the highest pregnancy rate in the state of Arkansas, and it was the first high school in the state to offer contraceptive advice in the school health clinic.

By the time Leisle graduated from high school, she was valedictorian and student council president. She applied to Yale early because that's what Koreans did, and she was accepted in December of her senior year. When Leisle's parents heard their daughter had been accepted to Yale, her mother collapsed on the sofa and wept while her father scooped up Leisle in his arms and swung her around until she was dizzy.

In some ways Leisle and I were similar, but in other ways we could not have been more different. We were both high achievers, but we did it in different ways and for different reasons. Leisle was confident, but I had something to prove. She was disciplined while I stayed busy. She was focused like a laser beam, but I was like a fire hose with no one holding on to the end. She knew where she was going, and she worked hard to get there; I worked hard, too, but with no particular destination in mind. Leisle's motto was, "Aim for the stars and see what you can hit." My motto was, "If you hit what's right in front of you, you don't have to aim."

But despite all our differences, there was one quality we had in common that would ultimately bring us together: she knew nothing about boys, and I knew nothing about girls.

Forty

BOY MEETS GIRL

HERE IS A WISE OLD CHINESE PROVERB THAT SAYS, "Even when a girl is as shy as a mouse, you still have to beware of the tiger within." My mother taught me the truth of that proverb, so I should have known better when I met Leisle Chung.

In the spring of 1993, I was completing my junior year of high school and thinking about the upcoming summer. While my classmates were looking forward to pleasant summer jobs working retail in air-conditioned malls or ogling attractive girls from a lifeguard stand, I was facing another brutal summer in hell's kitchen at Chungking Chinese Restaurant.

Just before school ended, I was told I had been recommended for a summer program called Arkansas Governor's School. After an entire year of classes and homework, the idea of another school-related event didn't interest me at all, but when I read the brochure carefully, I realized that it was exactly the kind of academically enriching program I was looking for: it lasted most of the summer, it took place out of town, and it was free. Harry Truman was famous for saying, "If you can't stand the heat, get out of the kitchen," and I decided to take his advice. I filled out the application, wrote the required essay, and was accepted.

When my brother Thai heard about it, he was furious because he was going to be home from college for the summer and would have to cover for me in the restaurant. "You lazy bum," he grumbled. "You're just trying to get out of work."

I was indignant: "Give me a break! I'm going for an academic program here."

At Lincoln High School, forty miles to the north, Leisle Chung had also been recommended for Governor's School and decided to attend for reasons nothing at all like my own: it was a highly regarded program that would look good on the résumé she planned to include with her applications to Ivy League colleges.

Governor's School was held at a small liberal arts college called Hendrix College in Conway, Arkansas, just outside Little Rock. It began in early June, which was perfect timing for me because it was just about the time the temperature in Arkansas started to peak. On the first day of the program there was an orientation, and when I looked for my name on a list of attendees, I spotted a name just before mine that said "L. Chung." At first I thought it might be a mistake, but then I met this L—an attractive, articulate five-foot-tall Korean girl named Leisle.

It might seem like an odd coincidence that we happened to have the same last name, but Zhang happens to be the most common surname on earth, and it's often transliterated *Chang* or *Chung*. There are an estimated one hundred million of us out there, so running into another Chung was statistically no more unlikely than one Smith or Jones bumping into another.

We all were assigned mailboxes for the summer, and because there were 440 students attending, we each had to share a mailbox with another student. Apparently they were assigned alphabetically because my box-mate turned out to be none other than Leisle Chung.

It's hard to imagine what I must have looked like to Leisle when we first met. My brothers all shared clothing, so when I packed for Governor's School, I had to pick from what no one else was wearing that day. My pants were usually too big; whenever I stood up straight,

I had to hitch them up, and some of them had a big patch on the crotch that didn't match the other material. I had a cowlick that stood up defiantly, regardless of what I did to try to plaster it down, and Leisle told me later that the Nerd on my glasses was clearly readable in Korean.

What I had going in my favor was that I was tall, I was in good shape, and I was one of the first Asian boys Leisle had ever seen. Sometimes it helps to be first in line.

Leisle liked me right away. I like to think it was because I was tall and good-looking, but the truth is she liked the fact that I was sociable and outgoing and seemed to smile all the time. She didn't realize that my pleasant demeanor was part of my coping mechanism to avoid rejection and confrontation; I had learned long ago that people tend to be nice to nice people, so I was as nice as they came. We met at our mailbox every day, and after every brief conversation we liked each other a little more.

Leisle got letters and care packages from home almost every day, but she noticed that I rarely got any. When I finally did, she asked, "Is that from your girlfriend?"

Sheepishly I replied, "No."

"Doesn't your girlfriend write to you?"

"I don't really have a girlfriend," I mumbled.

Clever girl—she didn't need Facebook to figure out my relationship status.

The Governor's School program exceeded my expectations—there were only a few classes each day, and the rest of the time was free. There was a boys' dorm and a girls' dorm, and after hours the students liked to hang out in the lobbies and fraternize. Leisle was in the lobby, playing cards one day when I returned from a workout. I ran and lifted weights every day to stay in shape because it was the summer before my senior year and two-a-day football practices were going to begin in August.

I walked into the lobby with no shirt on and sat down right next to Leisle. For some reason she got unusually quiet; in fact, she wouldn't even make eye contact with me—her face just got red and she kept shuffling cards. I had no clue what was going on, and she had to explain it to me later—much later.

I knew nothing about girls at all. I can honestly say that at that point in my life, I had never had a single meaningful conversation with a member of the opposite sex, including my mother and sisters. I talked to my sisters only when I needed help with homework or chores, and the most profound thing my mother ever told me was that swallowing a live gecko will cure asthma. My mother was a very loving woman, but she didn't express it in words—my family just wasn't like that. My mother and father never hugged me or told me they loved me. They loved me by providing for me and keeping me safe, and I always knew that I was loved; what I didn't know was how to talk to girls.

The only time I ever spoke to girls in school was to say, "Hi" or "Excuse me." Part of the reason for my reticence was ethnic, part was my own insecurity, and part was because I just had no idea what to say to a girl. When I started to excel at football and mathematics at Northside, I became well-known but didn't know anyone well. My only relationships were on the football team, and we mostly communicated by butting heads and swatting butts. All the other football players had girlfriends, and they seemed to talk to them about deep things all the time, but I never had that experience myself.

Leisle was way ahead of me. She never had a real boyfriend, but her family was much more expressive than mine. They hugged each other and said "I love you" all the time—they even kissed, and not like the Vietnamese do. In traditional Vietnamese families, they don't kiss; they sniff. They don't pucker up—they press their lips together, lean forward, and sniff. No wonder my parents never had the sex talk with me.

Leisle understood emotions far better than I did, and she was comfortable talking about her feelings, but since she had never been allowed to have a boyfriend, there were a lot of topics she had never discussed with a boy. When she met me, she was ready to talk, and I was surprised to discover that I was ready too.

There was a jazz concert during the first week of Governor's School, and we both attended because there was nothing else to do. Neither of us really liked jazz, so after a few minutes we decided to go somewhere and talk. We ended up talking for hours; it was the longest conversation I had ever had in my life. I didn't think it was possible to talk that long, and the idea that I could talk that long with a girl was mind-altering.

And Leisle was not only a girl; she was an Asian girl. Though her family's specific experience was different from mine, our cultures had much in common, and we could actually understand each other. When she told me that she could never look her father in the eye when she disagreed with him because it would have been disrespectful, I understood—it was the same way in my family, and no one outside my family had ever been able to understand that.

For me, it was more like an explosion than a conversation. There were hundreds of topics that I had never been able to discuss with anyone, and when I connected with Leisle, they all came pouring out. Social issues, political issues, theological issues—I wanted to talk about all of them, and I was so excited that I was almost shouting. At first I would pick a topic and take a controversial position just to see what Leisle would do, and her responses were always insightful and challenging. Whenever I pushed, she pushed back—and she could push hard. I didn't find out until later that Leisle was a two-time Arkansas debate champion.

I was amazed. I kept telling Leisle, "I didn't know girls were that smart," which I'm sure impressed her. I thought only scientists and mathematicians were really smart, and I figured men were always superior in those fields. It was a remarkably ignorant position, and I should have known better since my own experience as a refugee had taught me that discrimination stems from ignorance—but I was so ignorant about girls that I was blind to my own form of prejudice.

I felt like a biologist who had just discovered a new species; I probably told her that and impressed her again. From that day on we spent every spare minute at Governor's School talking. We talked for hours every day, seven days a week, and we talked so late into the evening that we had to run back to our dorms to make curfew. Our relationship grew closer every day, and every day the topics became more personal.

One day, out of the blue, she asked me, "When was your first kiss?"

I started blushing. "I can't believe you asked me that!" I blurted out. "How could you ask me that?" It was obvious to her that I had never been kissed before, but being a boy, it still took me a couple of days to admit it.

Though Leisle never had a boyfriend, she had been kissed before. When she was in junior high, she realized one day that she was the only one of her friends who never had been kissed, and she didn't like being behind. She knew there was a boy in her class who had liked her for a long time, so she walked up to him one day and told him that she liked him too. After two days the boy got up enough nerve to kiss her, and then she broke up with him—problem solved.

Before Governor's School was over, I solved that problem too—I kissed Leisle.

I was in the habit of keeping a journal at the time, and in my entry that evening I wrote:

> I did it. For the first time, I KISSED.
>
> It wasn't as bad as I had expected. I enjoyed it. The sensation was far more appealing than the thought.

For me, that was practically poetry.

Then one day our conversation turned to plans for the future. Leisle asked me what I planned to do after graduation.

I shrugged. "Go to college. Become a doctor."

"What colleges are you applying to?"

Colleges? Why would anyone apply to more than one college? "U of A," I said. "That's where all my brothers and sisters have gone."

"Have you thought about the Ivy League?"

Ivy League—I had never heard of it before, but it didn't sound particularly appealing. Northside High was the Grizzlies, and Arkansas was the Razorbacks—who in the world picked *Ivy* for a mascot?

I turned the conversation back to her. "Is that where you're going?"

"I plan to go to Yale," she said. "I want to major in history or political science; then I plan to go to Yale Law School and eventually become a Supreme Court justice."

My mouth dropped open. I thought I was ambitious, but this girl was aiming over my head. I had a few plans, but she had an overarching vision. She knew what she wanted to do and had a path in mind to get there, and for me, it was just the opposite: I had a path in mind but only a vague idea of where I wanted to end up.

But it wasn't the clarity of her vision that impressed me most; it was the sheer size of it. Leisle thought big—bigger than I ever thought I was allowed to think. She was planning to do things that I assumed were impossible for someone like me. Could a little Korean girl from a farm in Seongnam actually become an American Supreme Court justice? Was that even possible? What astonished me was that she actually thought it was.

Leisle's vision and confidence were infectious, and after six weeks of exposure to it, I was beginning to catch the disease. I kept thinking about how similar we were and how much we thought alike. And then the thought occurred to me: if she believed things like that were possible, maybe I should try believing it too.

When Governor's School was about to end, Leisle asked me the hardest question of all: "What are we, Vinh? Are we boyfriend and girlfriend? What are we really?"

I really didn't know. I knew the feelings I had for her, but I was unable to name them—they just felt consuming and confusing. How could I be Leisle's boyfriend if she wasn't allowed to date, and how could she be my girlfriend if I didn't have time for one? We lived an hour apart; we would never see each other, and when we graduated from high school in a year, we would be headed in different directions—me to the college down the road and her to Alpha Centauri. The only thing I knew for certain was that I did not want to let her get away—but I had no idea how to answer her question.

"You're more than a friend," I said. "But you're not really a girlfriend." Then it came to me: "You're my special good friend."

We all have flashes of brilliance in our lives, but that wasn't one of mine. I was so confused about the nature of our relationship that I invented a whole new category for it: special good friend. When I look back on that conversation, I'm surprised Leisle didn't just roll her eyes and walk away because it must have sounded to her like a complete lack of commitment on my part—which it was. I didn't know how to commit, and this was all so new to me that I wasn't even sure what I wanted.

Fortunately Leisle understood I was sailing in uncharted waters, and for that matter, so was she. It was the first real relationship either of us had ever had, and we were just going to have to fumble our way along and figure things out as we went.

And so we parted as "special good friends." Arkansas Governor's School turned out to be the most important program I never attended. My course of study was outside the classroom, and I had discovered I had a lot to learn.

But I had never enjoyed homework so much.

Forty-One

SPECIAL GOOD FRIEND

WHEN LEISLE AND I RETURNED HOME FROM Governor's School, we were immediately reimmersed in our busy lives. We were both about to begin our senior years of high school, me at Northside High in Fort Smith and her at Lincoln High, and we each had plenty to occupy our attention. Leisle had studies, student council, and debate, while I had studies, football, and dissecting chickens. But we had started something at Governor's School that did not go away when we got home, and neither of us was quite sure what to do about it.

When Leisle's parents came to pick her up from Governor's School, she introduced me to them but only as one of several friends she had met there. We had to be careful because in her parents' eyes I already had three strikes against me: I was a boy, I wasn't Korean, and I was a potential distraction for Leisle. We both knew her parents were not ready to hear that their Yale-bound daughter had picked up a "special good friend" at summer camp, so I just said a quick hello and tried to make a good first impression in case my name ever came up again.

We knew we wouldn't be able to visit each other, though Leisle lived only a short distance away. I couldn't drive to see Leisle because

I was supposed to be concentrating on becoming a doctor. The way my parents looked at it, I would have plenty of time for girlfriends after medical school—a brief delay of nine years.

Leisle wouldn't be allowed to visit me because in her parents' eyes it would have made her look cheap. She was a respectable young woman with her virtue to consider, and only a loose woman would go chasing after a man. Just as important, their daughter had not been accepted to Yale yet, and her senior year of high school was not the time to take her eyes off the prize.

When I left Governor's School, I knew I would miss Leisle, but I never expected to miss her as much as I did. We started corresponding as soon as we got home, though we had to hide our correspondence from our families. That wasn't always easy when we stayed up all hours of the night, composing the next day's magnum opus:

Dear Leisle,

My brother Thai left the room because he couldn't sleep with the lights turned on. See the problem with sharing a room? I'm surprised he didn't threaten to beat me up for staying up writing to you . . . It's 3:47 a.m., and I'm done responding to your letter. I better sleep now. Do you know that I haven't taken a shower yet? Yeah, I have mud and dirt all over my arms and face and my bed right now.

We wrote to each other several times a week, and some of our letters were thirty pages long. I wrote to Leisle everywhere: at home, at school, even on the bus on the way to football games—and writing love letters was not the ideal way to mentally prepare for a game.

The art of writing special-good-friend letters was new to me, and at first I was a little awkward at finding the right words to express my heart. Sometimes I sounded more like a mathematician than a poet:

Leisle, I really would like to see you. Yeah, I really miss you. I miss everything about you. At least I'll be talking to you this Sunday. Yeah, I really, really, really[4] (to the 4th power) enjoy being with you.

And sometimes my words didn't come across the way I intended:

Leisle, I believe you are more "masculine" than most, if not all, of the girls I know. Weird! I like a "masculine" girl who likes politics, scores higher than I did on the ACT, argues with me constantly and has the last name "Chung." . . . Leisle, if I were to have dreamed about a girl like you a year ago, it would have been a nightmare.

But Leisle was always patient with me and was much better at expressing herself:

Dear Vinh,
If a year ago, I had a dream about a guy like you, I would have been in anticipation all year to meet you.

Through my long-distance relationship with Leisle, a whole new side of me was emerging, and I struggled to understand what was happening to me. Sometimes I was afraid Leisle was changing me into someone I didn't even recognize:

Dear Leisle,
I need to stay away from you. You're taking away my sleep. You're entering my thoughts during the day. You're "harassing" me! Oh, but I asked for it, didn't I? I, well not my logical side, my emotional side wants to think about you. It wants to have you around all the time. My logical side says, "No, Vinh! She's making you sensitive, too emotional."
Leisle, I think my emotional side has won.

We kept encouraging and challenging each other through our letters. We both had SATs coming up, so we checked out test-prep books from our libraries and tried to include as many SAT words as possible in our letters to each other. I once wrote to her, "Because of my state of ambivalence (SAT word), I sometimes don't know what I really feel."

And Leisle kept challenging me to be more ambitious, which was beginning to annoy me because I had already told her my goals: to apply to the University of Arkansas and also Hendrix College, where Governor's School had been held. Hendrix offered a prestigious financial award called the Hays Scholarship, and U of A had its own version called the Sturgis. I planned to apply for both of them, and whichever scholarship I was awarded would be the college I would attend. Both were good schools, and either scholarship would have completely covered the cost of college and allowed me to graduate debt-free. What was wrong with a plan like that?

But Leisle always thought bigger:

Dear Vinh,

You want to live your life safely, retire in ten years and relax. No way. Really? Wouldn't you get bored? What about a Nobel Prize or something like that?

I wasn't opposed to winning a Nobel Prize, as long as I could pick one up on the drive back to Fort Smith. But Leisle kept encouraging me to apply to schools like Stanford, Georgetown, and Yale. She kept challenging me to go for more, to think beyond the school of convenience just down the road, and the more I caught her vision, the more conflicted I felt:

Dear Leisle,

Before AGS, I was quite content and happy because I basically accomplished everything I wanted. Only I didn't want very much so I really didn't accomplish much. After meeting you, I was shaken. I realized that I haven't pushed myself hard enough. You shared with me your goals and I . . . I had basically NO future goals. I wasn't sure which college I'd go to, what type of person I'd marry . . . etc.

So you talk me into "aiming high" like apply to Stanford/Yale. All of a sudden, I say "Yes! I'm gonna try to be all I can be." So now, I'm afraid I can't make it. As a result, I argue against strong ambition because it has caused me to fear / to be challenged / to be discontent / to be insecure.

I felt tortured. Before I met Leisle, I was complacent but happy, and now, thanks to her, I was ambitious but miserable—not exactly my idea of a good trade. I found Leisle's ambition infectious, but I was already suffering from a long-term disease of my own: the fear of failure. The higher the ladder, the greater the fall. Did I really want to set myself up for that? I was on my way to being a big fish in a little pond, but in the ocean I could get eaten. What was I supposed to do?

But as always, Leisle was the voice of encouragement and reason:

Dear Vinh,

It is good to reach for things, even if they are impossible because the higher you reach, the higher you'll go.

Don't let your fear of failure hold you back but let it be the reason that you would try so hard . . . so that you never have to face that failure. So basically, I'm glad you have decided to reach high, even if it brings disappointment.

I knew she was right. Neither choice seemed good at first: ambition with the possibility of failure or mediocrity with the certainty of success. But there really was no choice; once Leisle raised my sights, I couldn't lower them again. My old goals now seemed flimsy and pathetic, and I knew I would have to choose bigger ones even if it meant I might fail.

For the entire fall we kept our relationship a secret, though our parents were gradually catching on that there was something going on between us. But around Christmas things changed for us; Leisle was accepted to Yale that December, and at that point, as far as her parents were concerned, Leisle could do no wrong—she was even allowed to come visit me in Fort Smith.

Leisle was nervous about making a good first impression on my parents, and I was worried that my family would look impoverished to her. Leisle wanted to know if she should bow to my parents since that's what Koreans would do. I told her that the Vietnamese might nod, but they don't bow; she should just be very polite and shake their hands.

The first meeting went well. My father was already favorably disposed toward Leisle because he had seen some of the envelopes her letters came in, and he thought her handwriting showed strength of character. When he first met her, he was surprised that Leisle was so small, but he was impressed by her firm handshake; he was even more impressed that Leisle was going to Yale.

My mother liked Leisle, too, but later on she voiced some of her concerns: "Her hands are so little; they're like baby hands. How is she going to cook for you? Is she going to cook Korean food? How will you eat that?" By the time Leisle left, my mother liked her a lot; she even told me that she hoped I would find a nice Chinese girl just like her.

For Christmas Leisle gave me a gift I will never forget. It was a small leather portfolio with a pad of paper and a pen inside. She said I should use it when I went on interviews for colleges or scholarships. Inside the portfolio there was a packet of twenty-nine–cent stamps—that was the real gift. She knew I was poor, and she knew it was costing me a lot to mail her all those letters, and she wanted a way to help me without making me feel ashamed.

In the spring of our senior year, the theme of our letters changed. In the fall I had been inspired by Leisle's vision to apply to four colleges that I never would have considered before I met her: Stanford, Georgetown, Harvard, and Yale. Now it was spring, when acceptances and rejections were beginning to arrive, and we had a new topic of discussion: Which college should I choose if I'm accepted?

I was accepted to both U of A and Hendrix, and I was awarded both the Sturgis and Hays scholarships—my ultimate goal fulfilled. But by the end of the spring, I was also accepted to Stanford, Georgetown, Harvard, and Yale. Before long I had narrowed the choice down to Harvard or Yale, and at that point our topic of discussion changed again. The question was no longer "Which college should I choose?" but "Should I choose the same college as Leisle?" In one of her letters Leisle asked me if I would choose a different college just to avoid her, and I immediately gave her a firm answer:

Dear Leisle,

You asked, "Would you go to a different college just to avoid me?" The answer would be yes, probably . . . I guess . . . not sure. Maybe . . . I guess . . . but not no. It is possible.

Later on in the letter I added, "Do you know what the heck I'm talking/writing about?" But then I gave the subject a bit more thought and wrote back to her again:

Dear Leisle,

You know what? I think it would be BETTER for me if I were to go to school with you. YES!!! If I were to go to school with you, I would not have to spend time writing. I would not have to think of you so often. You'd just be right there. I can talk to you anytime. BUT . . . this leads to another problem. What if you're always around? What if I spend the whole day talking to you instead of studying? It was all right at AGS because no grades are given. If I spend as much time with you as I did at AGS, I'd flunk every class. Spend too much time writing to you or thinking about you VERSUS too much time with you.

Both are bad. Which is worse? I believe both are or can be equally bad. However, I do enjoy the second one more. Yeah, I'd rather be with you than write to you or think about you. If, in either case, I'm being deterred from school, I might as well be deterred in a more enjoyable way? What is your opinion?

Leisle wrote back:

Dear Vinh,

Okay, I'll start by saying that this is absolutely ridiculous! I could see someone going to the same college because he/she is serious with someone but not going to a different college to avoid becoming serious. What is it you're trying to avoid?

If it's for your sake, I will ignore you for four years if that's what you want. I won't even "exist." If it's for my sake, don't worry about stuff like this with me. In college, especially the first two years, I have more important concerns than becoming serious about anyone.

I care about you too much to let you base such a crucial decision on something like this. Base it on atmosphere, scholarships, academics, or even cafeteria food, but not on avoiding me.

So Leisle set my mind at ease. If I went to Yale, she promised to ignore me for four years, and if I went to Harvard she had more important things to worry about than me, especially in the first two years. Two years of indifference or four; Harvard was starting to sound good to me.

Leisle graduated valedictorian at Lincoln High and in her senior year won the Arkansas state debate championship a second time, with her freshman brother as her partner. I graduated valedictorian from Northside, and we were both on our way to college, though Leisle and I didn't know what that would mean for our relationship or where our paths would take us in the future.

But in the summer, as we were both preparing to leave for college, she wrote me this:

Dear Vinh,

Once upon a time, there lived a cute little prince named Vinh in the bustling metropolis of Fort Smith. He had a beautiful smile that could melt anyone's heart and an adorable southern Asian accent . . .

In another land, in a palace nestled in the Ozark Mountains, Princess Leisle played silly games with her younger brother. Although she had pet bears and deer to keep her company, the lovely, compassionate, kind, sweet, intelligent, talented Princess Leisle felt lonely and in need of a special, good friend.

Prince Vinh grew up to become a very handsome young man. During the fall, he knocked people on their butts for a ball that wasn't even round, and all year, he labored in kitchens and delivered royal feasts in his trusty car. Hardly a job befitting the handsome prince, but Vinh was a charming prince with a noble heart.

One summer, Vinh decided to get away for six weeks to study natural science at a program called Arkansas Governor's School. Meanwhile, Princess Leisle decided to attend the same school to study social science (the good science).

There, the prince and princess met. They shared the same last name, a mailbox, a dislike of jazz music, and a liking for star-gazing from the top of a library. So, in a week, Vinh became the special good friend that Leisle had wanted . . .

All too soon, AGS came to a close. Prince Vinh returned to the bustling metropolis of Fort Smith and Princess Leisle returned to her palace in the Ozarks . . . So, although apart, the prince and princess remained special good friends and tried to visit ever so often . . .

However, in order to become individuals befitting to inherit their crowns, both Leisle and Vinh chose to part once more and battle dragons, cross rivers, and ride giant silver birds to distant lands for four years.

Prince Vinh chose to face his challenge in a land that harbors Harvard, while Princess Leisle chose to confront her dragons in a land that havens Yale.

So, once again, the prince and princess bid each other farewell and parted for distant lands . . .

To be continued . . .

Forty-Two

HARVARD

I T WASN'T EASY FOR ME TO DECIDE BETWEEN HARVARD and Yale. Since so much of my future depended on my choice, I wanted to take a careful, rational, and objective approach to the decision-making process—so I decided to flip a coin twenty-five times and go with the winner. But when Yale turned out to be the winner, I sensed a gut-level feeling of regret that the coin toss did not go to Harvard, and that was how I knew that Harvard was the place I really wanted to go. So much for rational and objective.

There was another criterion that I carefully considered that swung the decision to Harvard: Harvard had a lousier football team. Selecting Harvard over Yale based on their football teams might sound like choosing a BMW over a Mercedes because the BMW had a full tank of gas, but it was more than that. In my senior year of high school, I had been named to the All-Conference and Arkansas All-State football teams at offensive guard, and I entertained the possibility of playing college football. At five foot eleven and two hundred pounds, I never would have made the team at a Southeastern Conference school like Arkansas, but Harvard and Yale were much smaller colleges, and I thought I might have a chance of making the team at one of them. Harvard had the weaker team at the time, so off to Harvard I went.

When Leisle and I enrolled at Yale and Harvard, the annual cost of both schools was around $35,000 per year. When Leisle first opened her acceptance letter from Yale, she looked at her father and asked, "How will we ever pay for this?" Her elated father said, "Don't worry. We'll sell everything we own if we have to." That was a generous offer, but even if her parents had sold everything they owned at the time, it wouldn't have been nearly enough to put Leisle through Yale.

When I saw the cost of tuition, room and board, and fees, I suffered a serious case of sticker shock myself. The market value of the house my family was currently living in would have barely covered the cost of my freshman year. The cost of attending Harvard gave me second thoughts about turning down Hendrix and Arkansas because I had been offered a full ride to both of those schools, plus spending money on the side. But both Leisle and I spent our senior years applying for every scholarship and grant we could find, and by fall we were packing for our first semesters at Harvard and Yale.

I couldn't afford suitcases, so I packed everything I owned into two cardboard boxes and a backpack. My mother brought me a few extra clothes to fold in, which meant that Anh and Hon would have less to wear to high school that fall, and she handed me some pencils and a plastic cup and said, "Here. You should use these." The only thing my parents could afford to contribute to my college education was a one-way bus ticket from Fort Smith to Alexandria, Virginia, where Jenny and her husband were to meet me and drive me the rest of the way to Boston. The one-way bus ticket was symbolic of what my parents had been saying to me all my life: "All we can do is get you there; after that it's up to you."

The bus trip from Fort Smith to Jenny's home in Alexandria took thirty-one hours. Jenny's husband, Hung, took me to an army surplus store and bought me two canvas duffel bags to upgrade my cardboard boxes, and Uncle Lam bought me my first watch and an alarm clock. When Jenny's husband dropped me off at Harvard, he asked, "Is there anything else you need?" The *Harvard Independent* had a list of suggested items for incoming students that included a desk lamp, wastebasket, bed linens, fan, laundry money, computer, calling card, bicycle, camera, umbrella, duck boots, mittens, guide-books of Boston, and formalwear.

I shook my head. "I guess this is it."

In my first days at Harvard, I was overwhelmed. The student body included movie stars, sons and daughters of famous politicians, stu-dents whose dormitories were named after their grandfathers, and even a princess from a Middle Eastern country—and there I was with my two army surplus duffel bags. In Fort Smith I had been a big fish, but Harvard was like Sea World. All my classmates seemed to be bril-liant; some of them had won national competitions in math, science, or geography, and some had already published papers. I had won state-wide math contests back in Arkansas, but when I took my first math class at Harvard, I thought, *This isn't math—this is something else.*

Leisle was struggling to adjust at Yale too. The first time her par-ents drove her to New Haven, they took the wrong exit and had to drive through the worst part of town. When it came time to say good-bye, Sunny broke into tears, and in Leisle's first care package from home, she found a can of Mace. Leisle was so lonely at first that she was calling home almost every day, and her mother finally had to say to her, "Leisle, I love you. Do not call home this often."

In my first week at Harvard, there was an open tryout for the football team, so I walked on and made the team as a linebacker—but within a week I quit. High school football had been more than just a sport for me; it was a world of justice and fairness and honor. My high school coach talked about sportsmanship and character constantly, and if a player ever cussed, my coach would run him until he gave back his lunch. At Harvard the coaches cussed a blue streak, and no one on the team seemed to be having any fun. To me, the sport had been hijacked; it was still the same game, but the heart had been ripped out of it, and football quickly lost its appeal.

My scholarships and loans completely covered my tuition and housing, but I had no money for books and no spending money either. I would have to get a job to earn that money, but the only job-related skills I had involved preparing soup broth. There was a job working at the college library that would have paid me $7.00 an hour, which sounded good because that job would have allowed me to study while I was working—but when I heard about a job that paid $8.25 an hour, I grabbed it without even asking what it was. My father would have been proud.

The job was cleaning toilets. The official name was Dorm Crew, which was a student-run organization that essentially paid poorer students to clean richer students' bathrooms. I worked four hours per day, five days a week, and during each four-hour shift, I was expected to clean eight bathrooms. I did the math: that was thirty minutes per toilet.

Every day I went to the superintendent's office to get a master key to all the dorm rooms, then went to the janitor's closet to collect a bucket, a mop, a can of Comet, a spray bottle of pink liquid cleaner, and rubber gloves—and then I spent the next four hours knocking on dorm rooms and shouting, "Dorm Crew!" If anyone was home, they were supposed to let me in; after thirty seconds of silence, I let myself in. Sometimes I opened the door a little too quickly and got a tutorial in human biology. Those were actually good situations for me because the embarrassed couple usually ordered me out—and that meant one less bathroom to clean.

One thing the restaurant taught me was how to work quickly, and I turned bathroom cleaning into a science. Step one: turn on the shower and use it to wet everything down. Step two: cover everything in sight with Comet. Step three: spray down the toilet and sink. Step four: scrub the bathtub, toilet, and sink. Step five: rinse everything and mop my way out backward. Women had the cleanest bathrooms, but they had the dirtiest ones too; athletes were terrible because they left wet gear everywhere; seniors were worse than freshmen because freshman dorms were not allowed to have parties; and the bathroom of a senior woman athlete was the perfect storm.

It was supposed to take me four hours to clean eight bathrooms, but I became so efficient at it that I could finish all eight in an hour and a half. I did the math again: that was only 11.25 minutes per toilet. I calculated that if I was being paid $8.25 per hour to clean eight toilets but finished the job in an hour and a half, I was actually earning $22 per hour. I suddenly felt wealthy; when I worked at the restaurant, I used to receive an allowance of $30 per *week*, and now I was making $22 per *hour*—that was more money than I had ever seen. I had been at Harvard for only a few weeks, and already an Ivy League education was paying off.

At first it didn't bother me to have to clean my classmates' bathrooms, but after a while I began to notice that only poor kids like me worked for Dorm Crew. I had to qualify to attend an elite university like Harvard just like everyone else did, but the other students were out studying or having fun while I had to clean their toilets. Some of the students understood how I felt; when I knocked on their doors, they would say, "Our bathroom is fine—you don't need to clean it." That was very gracious. But there were other students who just didn't understand. Once I cleaned the bathroom of a woman I knew personally, and after inspecting my work, she said to me, "Vinh, couldn't we do a little better job here?"

Once I was facing a very tough final in organic chemistry, and I needed every minute I could get to study for it. When I knocked on one door, shouted "Dorm Crew!" and no one answered, I opened the door and saw organic chemistry textbooks and class notes spread all over the floor. Whoever the student was, he was preparing for the same test I was, but while he was studying, I was cleaning his toilet. That was hard for me because I knew the two of us might end up competing for the same spot at a medical school, and he had an unfair advantage.

On Friday nights I met with a Christian fellowship called InterVarsity while Leisle was involved with a group at Yale called Cru. We both considered it an important part of our busy schedules. Harvard and Yale were incredibly competitive environments, and it was easy for high achievers to become obsessed with grades and lose sight of the larger picture. Like our churches at home, our student fellowships gave us a sense of community and helped us grow spiritually—and also reminded us not to base our self-worth on the outcome of the next exam.

Since I was so efficient at cleaning bathrooms, I decided to pick up a second job to earn even more money, so I started delivering newspapers. The *Harvard Independent* was delivered to every student's door, and I was assigned a delivery route that was supposed to take me four hours to complete—but I got it down to forty-five minutes. I was able to speed it up so much because I ran up and down the dormitory stairs while I was delivering papers. I figured I could get a workout at the same time I was earning money. Then it occurred to me that I could double my salary by delivering a second local newspaper using the same route. After a while I became a familiar sight around the dorms, though no one could figure out exactly what my job was. I was either the paperboy who cleaned toilets or the janitor who delivered newspapers.

I saved money every way I could, and thanks to my mother's training, I was always looking for a bargain. I got a free Sprint T-shirt when I bought a long distance phone card so I could call Leisle, and I applied for a credit card because it came with a free Visa T-shirt. I managed to save a lot of money, but I didn't win any prizes for style; every shirt I owned had some company's logo on it, and at times I looked like a walking billboard.

By the end of my first semester, I had saved enough money to buy myself a plane ticket to fly home for Christmas—no more thirty-one-hour bus rides for me. After buying my ticket, I had a thousand dollars left over, so I mailed the money home to my parents, and when my mother received it, she immediately called me and demanded to know where I had gotten so much money. She wanted to know if I had joined a Vietnamese gang at Harvard or if I had broken into someone's car and stolen a stereo. I tried to explain to her that there were very few Vietnamese gangs in Cambridge and that I wasn't in the habit of breaking into cars. But my mother had always warned us growing up, "Don't pick fights, don't join a gang, and don't break into cars and steal stereos." She figured that just because I was at Harvard didn't mean I couldn't get into trouble.

I had the good fortune to be assigned a terrific roommate, a young man named Dan from Chicago who came to Harvard to study physics and applied mathematics. Dan owned one of the latest laptop computers, an Apple PowerBook with a black-and-white screen, and he allowed me to use it whenever I wanted. What I especially appreciated was the gracious way he did it; he never reminded me that the computer was his property or ordered me off of it so he could use it himself. Dan understood that, for me, owning a computer would have been like owning a yacht, and he wanted to be generous without making me feel ashamed. That was a very special gift, and it was one of the reasons we remained roommates all four years and became lifelong friends. I made a promise to Dan that when his own children go to college one day, I will buy them any computer they want—as long as they share it the way their father did.

It took a long time before it finally sank in that I was actually at Harvard. It seemed too good to be true, and something inside me secretly feared that maybe it wasn't true—maybe it was all a mistake. The entire time I was at Harvard I felt that at any moment someone might tap me on the shoulder and say, "Mr. Chung, you don't belong here. There's been a mistake. You have to go home." I was haunted by that feeling for four years—right up until the moment I finally held a Harvard diploma in my hand. I thought that feeling might have been the refugee part of me, the part that never felt that it deserved anything and never quite felt at home. But as I got to know other students at Harvard, I came to realize that just about everyone there felt the same way.

I actually had one advantage over most of the students at Harvard: I had been working long hours all my life, and I had learned how to juggle multiple tasks at the same time. There were students at Harvard who did nothing but study, and some of them still dropped out because of the pressure. When I was growing up, I never had time to feel pressure—I was too busy doing the next thing. I had spent my entire childhood scrambling, stumbling, recovering, improvising, and learning how to do things after I did them. That wasn't always easy, but it turned out to be very good preparation not only for Harvard but for life as a whole.

I knew how to juggle multiple jobs, demanding classes, physical exercise, and spiritual development—what I didn't know was how Leisle fit in. But I couldn't stop thinking about her, and it didn't take long for me to realize that there was something missing in my curriculum.

Forty-Three

LOVE STORY

W HEN LEISLE AND I FIRST LEFT FOR COLLEGE, WE agreed that we would communicate as little as possible. The reason wasn't a fear of commitment; it was a fear of distraction. We both had definite goals in mind—medical school for me and the Supreme Court for her—but neither one of us knew how difficult college would be, and we didn't want to distract each other from our studies. We nobly agreed that while we were away at college, we would both be free to date other people; but since Leisle was the first girl I had ever really talked to, and since I was Leisle's first Asian friend, dating someone else wasn't likely for either of us. Still, the agreement was important in principle, and we both went off to college free and clear.

We mailed a few letters back and forth at first, but they were nothing like the thirty-page tomes we used to compose in high school. Then one day we were introduced to a remarkable new technology that made waiting by a mailbox obsolete: electronic mail. E-mail allowed us to jot quick notes back and forth and receive an almost instantaneous reply. It was a fast and efficient way to spend twice as much time writing to each other as we had been doing by snail mail, and when we discovered instant messaging, it was almost like talking to each other face-to-face.

Almost.

At Thanksgiving, Yale had a weeklong break and most of the students left campus. Leisle didn't want to be the only one remaining in her dorm, and a week was not enough time for a visit home to Lincoln, so she decided to come up to Cambridge to attend the annual Harvard-Yale football game, which Leisle insisted on calling the Yale-Harvard game. The game was being played in Cambridge that year, and when I heard that Leisle was planning to come, I invited her to stay longer and make it a personal visit.

I heard it was a terrific game, but I had to take Leisle's word for it since I had taken a part-time job in the college library, earning $7.00 an hour, and I had to work during the game. The annual Harvard-Yale game is the only game anyone in Cambridge really cares about, so the library was like a tomb during my entire shift—but I made $28, and I could never afford to pass up money.

Leisle's visit was a turning point for us because that was when we decided to upgrade our relationship status from "special good friend" to official boyfriend and girlfriend. After that visit we were officially dating, though we agreed not to announce our new status to our parents just yet; we figured there was no sense in starting a panic before it became necessary.

Soon after that visit I took the relationship up yet another level by telling Leisle that she was not only my *girl*friend, but my *best* friend. I'm not sure Leisle could appreciate the distinction, but it was a big step for me because I had never told anyone he or she was my best friend before. From special good friend to girlfriend to best friend in a single semester—our relationship was taking off like a skyrocket. By the end of my freshman year, I finally did it: I told Leisle I loved her, and I was greatly relieved when she told me that she loved me too.

That was the first time in my entire life that I had ever said the words *I love you* to anyone.

But we still had three years of college ahead of us, and that was only to get our undergraduate degrees. I had dropped the L-bomb during our freshman year, and I didn't know where to go from there. What else was there to say to a woman? What was I supposed to do next? I had no idea because no one had ever told me. I never talked about things like that with my father or older brothers, I never had a mentor, and I never went to the movies to watch romantic comedies—I had barely said hello to a girl before I met Leisle. No one had ever taught me the rules of relationships or the etiquette of dating, and I was clueless about what was appropriate to say or not say—which is probably the reason I asked Leisle to marry me without intending to.

It happened during the summer after our sophomore year, when I went on a six-week mission project with InterVarsity to Xinjiang, China. Xinjiang is one of the remotest regions in China, so instead of writing letters to Leisle that I wouldn't be able to mail, I decided to take a tape recorder along to record my thoughts and experiences and give them to her when I got back.

A very strange thing happened to me while I was in China: I missed Leisle. Every day I saw breathtaking panoramas and met fascinating people, but I kept thinking, *This is great, but I wish I had Leisle here with me to see it.* That feeling surprised me; it was something I had never experienced, and it made no sense to me. Why would I need to have someone with me to enjoy an event? But for some reason the experience seemed incomplete without her, and I wanted her to be a part of it. I really missed Leisle, and that sense of longing reassured me that I must really be in love.

I couldn't wait to tell her what I was feeling, and there was no way I could call or write, so instead, I poured out my heart to the tape recorder so she could listen to it later. When I returned to Arkansas, I gave Leisle the tape, and I was eager for her to listen to it because it told about everything I had seen and done in China and everything I was feeling while I was there. Somewhere in the middle of the tape, she heard me say, ". . . Oh Leisle, I miss you so much, and I really love you, and I want to marry you and spend the rest of my life with you . . ."

I was not proposing. I had no intention of proposing. I was not ready for marriage at that time, and in my opinion, neither was Leisle. I was only telling her how I felt: I *felt* like I wanted to marry her, and I *felt* like I wanted to spend the rest of my life with her—that was all. How could anyone interpret the words *I want to marry you* as a proposal?

Leisle managed to explain the problem to me without using the word *fool*, which I very much appreciated. Something positive even happened as a result of my ignorance: after that event we both knew we were headed in the same direction.

My lack of education wasn't limited to relationships. I was behind in all my social skills, which was made painfully clear to me when I decided to take Leisle to a classy restaurant for her twenty-first birthday. I heard about a restaurant on the top floor of the Prudential Tower, Top of the Hub, that overlooked the city of Boston. That sounded fancy enough to me, so that's where we went.

I knew I was in trouble when I saw that the waiters were all dressed up. I was always intimidated by people who wore suits and ties because to me they symbolized authority and brought back feelings of powerlessness. Sometimes they even made me stutter, and it's hard to impress your special good fiancée when you're trying to order duck *à l'orange* with a stutter.

I looked around the restaurant and was disappointed to find no buffet. Asians tend to love buffets because we get a lot of food for our money and we don't have to be embarrassed trying to order from an English menu. But apparently it wasn't Asian Night at Top of the Hub, so I opened the menu and took a look at the prices.

My first thought was, *Wow—that's a lot of toilets.* I was working with Dorm Crew at the time and was in the habit of calculating the cost of everything in terms of toilets. I earned $4.12 for every toilet I cleaned, so I always calculated how many toilets I would have to clean to pay for any particular item. I looked at the menu and realized that I was going to be cleaning bathrooms for a long, long time.

Since it was Leisle's twenty-first birthday, I decided to order wine, so I selected a three-toilet vintage with an impressive-sounding name. When the sommelier brought the wine, he removed the cork and handed it to me, and since I had no idea what to do with it, I dropped it in my pocket. He poured just a little wine into my glass and then looked at me and waited. I kept watching my glass, waiting for something more to happen, but when I glanced up at the somme-lier, I could tell by the expression on his face that he was expecting me to do something—so I turned to Leisle and asked, "Do you want some too?"

But the evening was more than a series of social faux pas; I threw in a few relationship faux pas too. Earlier that evening I had given Leisle twenty-one roses for her birthday, and on each rose I attached a strip of paper where I had written one of the reasons that I loved her. On one of them I wrote, "I want to spend the rest of my life with you," and on another one I put, "You'll be a good mother and wife one day."

I was slow, but I was learning.

During our junior year our visits to each other became regular. The moment classes let out on Friday, I caught the Red Line on the MBTA subway from Cambridge to South Station in Boston, grabbed a Greyhound bus to New Haven Union Station, and then took a shuttle to the Yale campus. The bus trip from Boston to New Haven took exactly four hours and fifteen minutes, with a changeover in Hartford, and we kept shaving minutes off the schedule to get as much time together as possible.

Our parents were beginning to catch on that our relationship was growing, so we decided it was finally time for them to meet. Leisle's parents invited mine to visit them in Lincoln, which was hard for my father because he didn't like to drive out of town. It was a stressful meeting for both sets of parents because it was not only a meeting of potential in-laws; it was a clash of two cultures. Leisle's mother was worried about what to serve for dinner; what in the world should a Korean cook for a Chinese couple from Vietnam?

The meeting began with an exchange of gifts. Over the years my parents have given the Chungs mangos, durian, coconut cake, egg rolls, wine, and various vegetables, while Leisle's parents have reciprocated with gifts of herbs, dried mushrooms, figs, pears, baked goods, and Korean food. After the gift exchange our mothers headed directly for the kitchen, and Leisle and I went with them to help with translation. Leisle's mother didn't speak a word of English, so all communication between them had to pass through us; I translated my mother's Vietnamese into English; then Leisle translated the English into her mother's Korean. Wars have probably been started that way, but despite a little initial awkwardness, the conversation went well.

Our two fathers sat down in the living room together. Leisle and I wondered if they would end up just staring at each other because the only language they had in common was broken English. But in some strange way their common experience of suffering and sacrifice transcended the language barrier, and before long they were pouring out their life histories to each other, and my father was in tears. The refugee and the immigrant became devoted friends that night, and to this day if Leisle happens to mention my father's quick temper, her father will come to his defense: "When you come out of a war, Leisle, you find that there is a lot of inner anger that is difficult to deal with."

By our senior year we were thinking about marriage though we still were not officially engaged. We were both home for Christmas break when I called Leisle and asked, "Can my parents come over to your parents' house to talk about us getting married right after we graduate?" It seemed to me like the practical thing to do because neither one of us was going to be home for spring break; if we didn't get our parents together to talk about wedding plans now, we would have had to wait until summer, and by then it would have been too late to have a summer wedding. I'm sure Leisle would have been thinking exactly the same way if I had actually asked her to marry me.

When I told my mother I wanted to get married, she responded with, "What are you, crazy?" She immediately told my sister Jenny, who called and asked, "Vinh, what's going on? Is something wrong with Leisle?"—implying that Leisle must be pregnant, or I wouldn't be in such a rush to get married. I assured her that Leisle was just fine.

By approaching marriage the way I did, I was actually violating the social customs of the Chinese, Korean, and American cultures all at the same time, which was not easy to do. My family was upset because I had three older siblings who were not married yet, and I was cutting in line. Even worse, I had had the audacity to pick my own bride before checking with the women in my family to get their recommendations. And what about the engagement ceremony? In Korea the bride- and groom-to-be were supposed to exchange gifts, but in Vietnam only the woman received gifts. There was supposed to be a ceremonial tea party and platters of food, and my mother was supposed to accompany me when I went to buy the ring, and then there was supposed to be a formal ceremony to present it. Everyone was expecting something different, so in some way everyone felt cheated, disrespected, or ignored.

I think our parents' greatest fear was that our marriage might derail our plans for the future. I was the fifth child in my family to attempt to become a doctor, and I was still on track to do it. "Why risk everything now?" they wondered. My parents would not give us their blessing until Leisle promised them that she would make sure I completed medical school. Once she assured them that she would, everything seemed to fall in place, and the cultural differences were eventually worked out.

Despite the competing demands of my premed curriculum and my desire to be with Leisle every spare moment, I somehow managed to graduate magna cum laude with a major in biological sciences, and that turned out to be enough to merit a seat at Harvard Medical School. Leisle and I were married on August 22, 1998. When I slipped the ring on her finger, I asked, "Do you know how many toilets I had to clean for that?" She made me promise never to tell her.

I never cried when I was growing up—not in kindergarten, when I fell back against an electric iron and split my head open, and not in high school, when we lost to Southside in the final minute of the game. Sometimes I wished I could cry, and sometimes I thought I was supposed to, but for some reason I just didn't know how. But when I saw Leisle walking down the aisle in her wedding dress, I started to cry, and it was more than just a few tears—I was weeping. I didn't know where it came from, and I didn't know why it was happening. I thought crying was something you did only when someone died or if someone hit you hard enough, but there I was, crying my eyes out. When my sister saw me, she started to cry, too; then Leisle started to cry, and soon just about everyone in the room was crying—except for my brothers, who wouldn't learn how until they saw their own brides walking down the aisle.

In 1998, I received two diplomas for the completion of two different courses of study. One was imprinted with the words *Harvard University, at Cambridge in the Commonwealth of Massachusetts* while the other read, *Marriage License, State of Arkansas, County of Washington.* I was proud of both of them because the first one meant that, at last, I was a college graduate, and the second one meant that though I had never been engaged, I had somehow managed to get married.

Forty-Four

CAP AND GOWN

D URING MY ENTIRE HIGH SCHOOL FOOTBALL CAREER, my father attended only one of my games, and I didn't know he was there. It was the biggest game of my senior year, against our perennial rivals, Southside High. The bleachers were packed, and the band was playing as loud as they could to be heard over the crowd—the players could barely hear each other in the huddle. We lost that game in the final sixty seconds, and as I trudged back to the locker room with my head hanging low, I heard my father's voice calling my name. I looked up at the bleachers, but my vision was so poor I couldn't see him—he just kept calling my name from the crowd.

That was probably the first football game my father had ever seen, and I doubt he knew what was going on. But he came, and he cheered for me though I never saw him.

I think that football game was a symbol of my entire childhood. Some of my teammates that I bummed rides with spent entire games sitting on the bench, yet their fathers never missed a game. But I knew my family was different. I didn't expect my father to attend football games, PTA meetings, or awards ceremonies because I knew he was always working, and I knew he was working for our family. My father made it possible for me to accomplish a lot of things, but he usually wasn't there to see it happen—not because he didn't want to be there but because he couldn't.

I graduated from high school as valedictorian, but my parents were not there to see it. My mother's mother, Grandmother Truong, died from a massive stroke just prior to my graduation, and my parents had to miss my graduation ceremony to attend her funeral in Washington, DC. Grandmother Truong was seventy-two when she passed away, and my mother inherited some of her genes. During my sophomore year at Harvard, she suffered the first of a series of ministrokes that temporarily took away her ability to speak. She recovered, but each stroke seemed to take a little more out of her and leave her with less energy. When I first left for college, my mother was the five-foot-two spitfire I had always known, balancing work in the restaurant, cooking for the family, and caring for five-year-old Du. But during my college years, I didn't see her for months at a time, and each time I came home for Christmas break, she seemed to be moving a little slower.

My mother was ill again when I graduated from Harvard, and since my father needed to be with her, my parents missed that event too. Graduating from Harvard wasn't a big deal to me, in a way, because I knew I was bound for medical school, and my undergraduate degree was just a stop along the way. But my graduation from Harvard was a very big deal to my father. When I was first deciding what college to attend, I wrote this in a letter to Leisle:

Dear Leisle,

My dad wants me to go to Harvard. Cool, huh? I almost didn't apply to Harvard. I'm so glad I did. My dad heard that I got interviewed for Harvard and looked up "Harvard" in the encyclopedia and in his Chinese dictionary. He was really impressed. He told me that he heard of Harvard when he was about nine years old in Vietnam! Yes, he's really impressed. He read about it in the encyclopedia. Now, he knows more about its history than I do.

When my father was a boy back in Vietnam, he saw a group of Chinese men reading newspapers one day, and one of the papers was called Měi Guó. Měi is the Mandarin word for "beautiful," and guó means "country"—when you put the two words together they mean "America." My father remembers reading that newspaper and seeing the name Hā fó dà xué, which in Mandarin means "Harvard University." For some reason that name stuck in his mind, and when I mentioned Harvard almost fifty years later, it triggered a very old memory. For my father, my graduation from Harvard was more than the completion of a four-year degree; it was the fulfillment of a fifty-year-old prophecy.

After my first year of medical school, I received terrible news: my mother had suffered a major hemorrhagic stroke while she was visiting Jenny in Virginia. She had just finished delivering a testimony at a Vietnamese church, and the moment she sat down, she collapsed and had to be rushed to a nearby hospital. Neurosurgery was necessary to stop the bleeding, and afterward she lapsed into a coma that lasted two days before she finally began to regain consciousness. Her recovery from that stroke was painfully slow; she spent almost a month in the hospital, followed by an extended stay with Jenny until she was strong enough to return to Arkansas.

Jenny called me and told me the terrible news, and when I heard, I was afraid I might never have the chance to speak to my mother again. But my classes had ended, and I was free for the summer, so I could stay with her for two or three weeks while she began the long process of rehab. My family took turns spending the night with her in the hospital, and as I watched her lying motionless on the bed while each of us rotated in and out of the room, it made me realize again that this precious little woman had always been the sun that our planets revolved around.

My father realized it too. He was beside himself at the thought that he might lose his wife, and he kept berating himself for every selfish or thoughtless thing he had ever done to her, despite the fact that all those things had been "dropped in the ocean" long ago. I think that after years of struggling together, he could not imagine his life without her. In Vietnamese there is an expression, *nhà tôi* (pronounced *nya thoy*), which literally means "my house," but it can also mean "my spouse." There is a profound truth behind that double entendre that my father understood: after years of living together, his wife had become more than a marriage partner—she was his home.

Though my mother recovered remarkably well, when it came time for me to graduate from Harvard Medical School, she was still too weak to travel. The twenty-five-hour drive from Fort Smith to Cambridge was out of the question, and for some reason flying drained her of energy and left her feeling confused for days, so my father was the only one able to attend the ceremony.

Two years prior to my medical school graduation, Leisle decided to pursue an MBA at Harvard Business School, and we both completed our degrees and received our diplomas on the same day. On our graduation day more than fifteen thousand students gathered in Harvard Yard for an opening ceremony, but Leisle and I both had to miss it. It was a wet, rainy morning. Leisle was three months pregnant, and her parents insisted that a pregnant woman should not sit in the rain. As always, Leisle honored her parents' wishes, and since she didn't attend the ceremony, I didn't either.

By afternoon the weather had cleared for our individual school graduations. The business school and medical school ceremonies were scheduled just minutes apart, so we had to split up to cover both of them. Leisle and her parents headed over to the business school to pick up her diploma, and as soon as her ceremony ended, they rushed over to the medical school to try to catch the end of mine.

My graduation ceremony was uneventful. Medical students tend to be a bit more subdued than the average undergraduate, so when the diplomas were handed out, no one performed an embarrassing display of enthusiasm or disrobed and streaked across campus. The ceremony was held under a tent, and the graduates sat quietly in long rows and waited for their names to be called. The highlight for me was hearing my professional title used for the first time—no longer just Vinh Chung but *Dr.* Vinh Chung. After receiving our diplomas and handshakes, we all returned to our seats and pretended to pay attention to a congratulatory speech delivered by someone we didn't recognize. At the end of the ceremony, we were officially pronounced doctors, and Leisle and her parents joined the other grateful families in an enthusiastic standing ovation.

When the ceremony was over, an outdoor reception for the graduates and their families was held on the medical school quad, a beautiful grassy area surrounded by three magnificent buildings with marble facades and Roman columns. We decided to take a photograph on the steps of one of those buildings, and as I stood there in my doctor's cap and gown, proudly displaying my medical school diploma for Leisle's camera, I noticed my father standing in the background and watching with satisfaction while his son had his picture taken.

I had to work long and hard to get to that day, but my journey had been nowhere near as long and hard as my father's. As a boy I had to struggle every day against the awkwardness and confusion of an unfamiliar culture and the isolation and feeling of inferiority caused by a language I couldn't speak—but I never had to fear the Imperial Army of Japan or live under the rule of the colonialist French or dodge the machetes of the Cambodians and Viet Minh or hope that a Viet Cong assassin did not have a rifle trained on my back.

I had to struggle with hunger because I hurried off to school without eating breakfast, but I never had to wonder where my next meal was coming from—not even once.

I had to suffer the heat and humidity of a restaurant kitchen owned by my own family, but I never had to work the dirt of a ten-acre farm, where I had been banished by my own government.

I had to spend long, boring hours studying to get into the college of my choice, but I didn't have to spend long, boring years working in a factory because I had no choice.

As I looked at my father, my mind went back to that high school football game against Southside, when he was sitting in the stands. He came to the game though I never saw him; I learned later that he had been there watching and cheering for me all the time. That was what he had been doing for me all my life: sitting in the stands because he couldn't play the game himself, cheering me on while no one cheered for him, then heading back to work after everyone else went home.

I wore a doctor's cap and gown and paraded across a stage to receive a gold-embossed diploma while my father's only reward was a sense of personal satisfaction. He was the one who had made it all possible for me. I was the one who should be cheering for him.

I called my father over.

I pulled off my gown and put it over him, set my cap on his head, and handed him my Harvard Medical School diploma.

He looked around nervously. "Are you sure it's okay? Will we get in trouble?"

"Sure, it's okay," I told him. "I rented this gown, and we don't have to return it for a few more hours."

My father looked down at himself and grinned. The look of sheer delight on his face was something I had never seen before, and I knew that I wasn't just seeing my father in a costume. I was seeing the man he would have become if only his life had gone differently. It was my graduation gown, but it fit him too.

I put my arm around him and said to Leisle, "Now take the picture."

Leisle's mother later made the comment, "It was a long journey and well deserved."

And she was right.

Forty-Five

GIVING BACK

A STORY IS TOLD ABOUT A MAN WHO WAS TRAPPED IN a terrible flood. He clung to a pole while the flood waters rose all around him, and he looked up into the heavens and prayed, "God, I trust You! I know You can save me!"

While the man was praying, a boat rowed up behind him and a rescue worker called up to him, "Sir, get in the boat!"

"No!" the man called back. "I'm trusting God to save me!"

The rescue worker had no choice but to row away, but when the water had risen almost to the man's chin, the rescue worker tried again.

"Please, get in the boat!" he shouted. "You'll drown!"

"Go away!" the man shouted back. "I'm trusting God to save me!"

Then the water rose over the man's head, and he drowned.

In heaven, the man said to God, "I trusted You! Why didn't You save me?"

God replied, "Who do you think sent the boat?"

Who do you think sent the boat? is a question I have asked myself many times over the years. There were four derelict fishing boats that the Malaysian navy towed out to sea and abandoned, but my family's boat was the only one rescued; the other three eventually drifted back to Vietnam. Two of them made landfall somewhere along the Ca Mau peninsula not far from our original point of departure. The third boat, which carried Grandmother Chung and my uncle's family, missed the coast of Vietnam completely and drifted almost 375 miles northeast before it finally came to rest on a small, rocky island called Phu Quy.

My family was near death after six days at sea. Grandmother Chung and her family had to endure more than three weeks of hunger and thirst, and a little boy on their boat died along the way and had to be buried at sea. After landing at Phu Quy, the passengers were turned over to the Vietnamese authorities, who briefly imprisoned them before releasing them to return to homes that were no longer theirs.

In 1993, my father returned to Vietnam for the first time since our midnight departure from Ca Mau fourteen years earlier. Grandmother Chung, my uncle, and many of the other passengers on that third boat had resettled in the Mekong Delta. Grandmother Chung was eighty-five by the time of their visit, and though her body had aged, her temper had not cooled a bit. The first time she saw my father, she hit him and shouted, "Where have you been so long? Why didn't you think of me?"

Several years later my parents both returned to visit Bac Lieu, my mother's hometown and the place where my father had lived until he was eight years old. They were greeted as returning heroes in Bac Lieu; many of the older residents remembered the second-most beautiful woman in Bac Lieu, and some of my father's former rice mill employees came to pay their respects. A ninety-two-year-old man even rode his bicycle from miles away just to have a chance to see him again.

My parents never said a lot about those trips. I think the reason was it was sad for them, but I never realized how sad until Leisle and I had the chance to visit Bac Lieu ourselves in the spring of 2002. Grandmother Chung had passed away by then, which was sad in itself because she was a larger-than-life character to me, and I really wanted Leisle to have the chance to meet her—despite the Chinese proverb that warns, "Two tigers cannot share one forest."

I met many of my cousins and other relatives on that trip, and I was shocked by the conditions some of them were living in. Some of their houses were little more than shacks; they were dark and oppressive, with bare lightbulbs that dangled from electrical cords and walls plastered over with newspapers. There were no beds to sleep on, and the toilet was a makeshift device attached to a garden hose. One of my relatives was living in a hut in his older brother's backyard, and it had no running water; I felt so bad for him that I went to the nearest ATM, withdrew all the cash it would give me, and handed him the equivalent of half his yearly income.

When the Vietnamese government relinquished some of the businesses and property it had "borrowed" from its citizens after the war, my uncle had been able to recover one of the family's rice mills. When I went to see the rice mill, it was a ghost town; it still had the original fifty-year-old milling machinery, but it was in such rusted disrepair that it hadn't been operating for years. The rice mill was no longer a business; it was just a memento of my family's former prosperity. For some reason my uncle was still holding on to it; his oldest son even slept there with a few dogs to guard the property, though I could see nothing there worth stealing.

My uncle took us to visit a family shrine, which was a shabby little building in the woods with no electricity or running water—yet my uncle's oldest daughter stayed there to guard it. She lived by herself and cooked her meals over a little fire with bamboo shoots she dug up in the woods. When my uncle introduced us, she walked over, looked up at me, and started to cry.

"Why is she crying?" Leisle whispered. "I thought she didn't know you."

"I think she's sad," I said.

"Why?"

"Because of where I am and where she is."

For me, visiting Vietnam was like walking into a parallel universe—the life that would have been mine if the current had been a bit stronger or if the wind had shifted direction. As I stood there in my parallel universe, looking at my alternate life, I found myself feeling guilty and ashamed—guilty because I had received a blessing they had not, and ashamed because I had not done more to help them.

Why me? Why my family and not theirs? Our boats were all set adrift at exactly the same location; why did the same wind take our boat in one direction and theirs in another? We were blessed—there's no other way to say it—but why weren't they? Were we more worthy in some way? Were we more deserving of rescue? I don't see how; my family's entire contribution to our rescue was to lie there waiting to die.

The only answer to the question "Why?" is, "God only knows", so rather than philosophize about a question I cannot answer, I prefer to ask two other questions that are much more practical: "Who do you think sent the boat?" and "What does He expect me to do now?"

My Christian faith has always played a central role in my life, and it supplies answers to those two questions: "Who do you think sent the boat?" Answer: God sent the boat. "What does He expect me to do now?" Answer: Now that I am safely ashore, He expects me to send the boat back for someone else.

I was twenty-six years old when I returned to Vietnam. I still had two years to go at Harvard Medical School, followed by a one-year internship in a predominantly Vietnamese section of Boston, a three-year dermatology residency at Emory University, and a highly specialized yearlong fellowship in Mohs Micrographic Surgery. I spent fifteen years of my life in college and medical school, and I was thirty-three before I ever saw my first patient independently. I worked long and hard to get where I am today, but the humbling truth is that all my hard work has been possible only because of a blessing I received that I did nothing to deserve. I believe that blessing is something I am expected to pass on to other people in any way I can. I think that's what we all are expected to do.

Jesus once said, "When someone has been given much, much will be required in return; and when someone has been entrusted with much, even more will be required" (Luke 12:48 NLT). I used to wonder who Jesus had in mind when He spoke of those who have been given much because I sure didn't think it was my family. We arrived in America with nothing but the secondhand clothes on our backs. And who exactly has been entrusted with much? Not us—everything my family owned was taken away from us before we left Vietnam. The way I saw it, my family had been entrusted with nothing and had been given nothing, and I just hoped those rich and powerful people would read Jesus' words and take them to heart.

But when I went back to Vietnam and stood there in my parallel universe, looking at my alternate life, I finally understood: He meant me. At that moment I was overwhelmed by the realization of just how much I had been given and all that had been entrusted to me. I was the one who made it out; I was the one plucked dying from the South China Sea; I was the one granted asylum in a country where education was available to everyone and prosperity was possible for anyone willing to work hard enough. If not for those rare and precious gifts, I might have spent my life wandering down some dirt road, tapping the haunches of a water buffalo with a bamboo rod.

I believe individual people can make a remarkable difference. What was a man like Stan Mooneyham doing in the South China Sea? He literally had no business being there because World Vision was a land-based organization. Stan Mooneyham wasn't really sure what he was doing, but he did it anyway, and I think that's what I respect most about what he did. He was an ordinary man who allowed his heart to be broken by the sight of suffering and did what he thought God wanted him to do. If not for him and his colleagues at World Vision, my life would have ended anonymously at the age of three in the South China Sea. My gratitude for what World Vision did for my family and my respect for the compassionate work they continue to do all over the world is the reason I now serve on their board of directors.

I often have been asked the question, "When did you become an American?" The answer to that question depends on another one: What makes someone an American? From a legal perspective the answer is simple: I went through the naturalization process and became a US citizen when I turned twenty. But I've come to believe that being an American involves much more than birthplace, legal status, or ancestry; it involves a set of shared values and beliefs about opportunity, prosperity, and fairness. Generations of refugees and immigrants who came to this country understood and shared those values and beliefs, and by doing so some of them became more American than many who were born here.

My parents wanted me to grow up American but never lose my root. In some ways I've been able to do that, but in other ways I have not. I can still speak Vietnamese, which is a great source of pride for my parents since most Vietnamese refugees have lost their native tongue by my age. But I chose my own bride, and when I married her, we didn't move in with my parents as we would have in Vietnam. It's the same with Leisle: she still speaks Korean and honors her parents' wishes whenever possible, but she also had the audacity to marry a Chinese man, and she doesn't do all the cooking—and not just because of her tiny hands. Leisle and I like to think that even though we have abandoned some Asian customs and traditions, we have retained our tap root—the deepest part of our Asian heritage that we consider part of our identities.

We have three children of our own now, and we want them to keep that tap root, too, but they're growing up in a different world than we did. I write this book from the comfort of my Colorado Springs home. When I look out my window to the west, I can see Pike's Peak, the Air Force Academy, and a breathtaking panorama of the Rocky Mountains. When I look out another window, I can see the beautiful new elementary school my children attend. The school is close enough for them to walk to every day, and there are no chained-up pit bulls or dilapidated trailer parks anywhere along the way. We tell our children we love them, we hug them, and we kiss them American-style. We have taken each of them to an eye doctor to make sure they can see the blackboard. They each have their own clothing, their own toys, and their own bicycles—and they even speak English, just like everyone else in their class.

But that was not the world I grew up in, and those were not the forces that shaped my life and character, and it causes me to wonder: How can I give my children all the things I never had without allowing them to become complacent? How do I teach them that America is a land of opportunity but was never meant to be a place of entitlement? How do I allow them comfort and ease but instill in them the value of hard work? How do I allow them to grow up American but still pass on that tap root my parents left to me?

I am a refugee, and I always will be. But in a way, all of us are refugees. We all are born in a time and place we didn't choose, born without language, property, or money, dependent entirely on the decisions of others for our very survival. We all are strangers in a strange land, left to fend for ourselves in a world we barely comprehend, and as we find our way in this world, we need to help others do the same. We all have been blessed—every one of us—and we all are expected to give back.

My mother and father still live in Fort Smith, Arkansas. They remained in that three-bedroom house across from the former Chungking Chinese Restaurant until 2011, when Leisle and I bought them a new one—a three-thousand-square-foot house in the very same neighborhood as the affluent junior high where I used to bring home discarded clothing from the lost and found. If you ask my father what he thinks of his new house, he will tell you, "It's a waste of space." I think he likes it anyway.

My mother recovered remarkably well from her stroke, and she is almost as feisty as she used to be. Not long ago I asked my father, "How do you think Mom has changed as she's gotten older?" and he said, "She talks back more than when she was young." When I asked my mother the same question, she said, "When I was young, I was stupid." My mother and father still don't tell each other, "I love you," but it's not unusual to find them walking around the lake behind their house, holding hands.

Their greatest source of satisfaction is their children and their accomplishments, the most important of which are their families. Jenny and her husband have two grown daughters and still live in northern Virginia, where Jenny is studying to become a respiratory therapist. Yen and her husband live in Houston with their two children; she works as an ultrasonographer. Nikki and her husband live in Edgewood, Maryland, where she taught school for several years before choosing to focus her time and attention on her three kids. Thai and his wife have a son; Thai works as a senior systems engineer for Comcast in Reston, Virginia. My twin brothers Anh and Hon are both optometrists; they both live in Arkansas, and both are married. Anh has two children, and Hon has three. Bao was recently married and is a family physician in California, and his twin brother, Toan, and his wife live in Texas, where he works as a dentist. Du, the youngest of my brothers and sisters, recently became engaged; he's a dentist too.

And my brother Bruce has a master's degree in science management and is team leader of cytology at a hospital in Albany, Georgia. When my family gets together every Christmas, my father still tells him, "You know, you could still become a doctor."

Leisle gave up her dream of becoming a Supreme Court justice. When I began medical school, she took a job with a consulting firm to help pay the bills and decided she liked the business world, so she picked up an MBA at Harvard and now runs the business side of our medical practice in Colorado Springs. I'm grateful for the sacrifice she made on my behalf, but the legal world will be worse off without her.

We are a family of refugees. Our country of origin didn't want us, and we traveled eleven thousand miles hoping to find one that did. Everything we once owned, everything we once were—it was all dropped in the ocean, and it rests with a derelict fishing boat at the bottom of the South China Sea. But we were rescued from that ocean, and though we lost a fortune, we found a greater treasure.

We are Americans now, and we're finally home.

For you, O God, have tested us;
    you have tried us as silver is tried.
You brought us into the net;
    you laid a crushing burden on our backs;
you let men ride over our heads;
    we went through fire and through water;
yet you have brought us out to a place of abundance.
—PSALM 66:10–12 ESV

ACKNOWLEDGMENTS

Where the Wind Leads IS TRULY A STORY TOO BIG for one person to tell. When you read my words, you are hearing the voices of my entire family, and I wish to thank each of them for contributing the memories and stories they alone could tell. This memoir reflects how I have interpreted the collective memory and how I experienced this story. If there are other views, I leave that story for someone else to share.

I thank my parents, Thanh and Hoa Chung. They are my heroes. It is their difficult decisions that have allowed a story to be told at all. I also am grateful to each of my siblings: Jenny, Bruce, Yen, Thai, Nikki, Anh, Hon, Bao, Toan, and Du.

I would like to pay a special tribute to my literary agent and friend, Lee Hough of Alive Communications. Lee's passion for my family's story was largely responsible for the creation of this book, but unfortunately he passed away before he had the chance to see it published. Lee's influence lives on through this book and many others he helped create. He will be sorely missed.

I want to thank the countless people who went out of their way to show kindness to a Chinese boy from a refugee family: the understanding parents who drove me to football practices and math competitions; Mr. James, the compassionate bus driver who was a guardian angel to me and my siblings; my inspiring Sunday school teachers at Grand Avenue Baptist Church; my calculus teacher, Ms. Haupert; my high school guidance counselor, Ms. Partin; all of my teachers, coaches, and mentors who invested so much in me; and Ms. Gale Beckman, the guidance secretary at Northside High, who typed my application to Harvard and actually believed someone would read it. Thanks to all of you and many others who helped make possible not only this book but also the life I live today.

I am also indebted to the following individuals for their assistance in creating this book: Dr. Ken Waters, professor of journalism at Pepperdine University, who was a member of *Seasweep*'s crew and was responsible for many of the photographs of my family's rescue; Ted Agon, also a member of *Seasweep*'s crew, for his detailed memory of the rescue from *Seasweep*'s point of view; Dr. Stanley Mooneyham, former president of World Vision, whose own book, *Sea of Heartbreak*, provided much of the historical background concerning Operation Seasweep; Rich Stearns, president of World Vision US, who encouraged me to tell my story and to write this book and who carries on Stan Mooneyham's legacy with his commitment and sacrifice to serve the poor; Jim Files, former pastor at Grand Avenue Baptist Church, and Dr. Fred Hagemeier, former pastor at Our Redeemer Lutheran Church, for their recollections of my family's arrival in Fort Smith; Samuel B. Thomsen, former political reporting officer for the US embassy in Saigon, for his memories of the events leading up to the fall of Saigon; my publisher at W Publishing Group, Matt Baugher, and editor, Debbie Wickwire, for their constant encouragement and helpful suggestions on the manuscript; and the rest of the W Publishing staff for their hard work and dedication to the craft of writing.

I also want to express heartfelt thanks to Tim Downs. This book is possible only with his talent. He spent over a year to synthesize dozens of hours of transcript from my family members, kept all the names and dates straight, teased out the nuances of three different languages, and crafted our story spanning over three generations into this book. Tim, thanks for this treasure.

I want to express my deep appreciation and love to my children, Caleb, Luke, Clara, and Timothy. I hope this book will help you understand your roots and that God has a purpose for your life. Finally, I want to thank my best friend and wife, Leisle, for working with me on this project. Just like everything else over our fifteen years of marriage, life is sweeter because she has walked beside me.

ABOUT THE AUTHOR

VINH CHUNG GRADUATED MAGNA CUM LAUDE FROM Harvard University with a BA in biology and attended Harvard Medical School for his MD. Dr. Chung also studied at the University of Sydney as a Fulbright Scholar and completed a master of pharmaceutical sciences. He holds a master of theology in history and theology of Christian doctrine from the University of Edinburgh, Scotland.

Dr. Chung did his medical internship at Caritas Carney Hospital in Dorchester, Massachusetts, located in an inner-city, immigrant community, where he volunteered extensively. He completed his dermatology residency at Emory University, where he served as chief resident and completed a fellowship in Mohs Micrographic Surgery.

Dr. Chung currently serves on the board of directors for World Vision US. He and his wife, Leisle, have three children and are expecting a fourth. They run a successful private medical practice in Colorado Springs.